Canada during the American Revolutionary War

Lieutenant
Friedrich Julius von Papet's

Journal
of the Sea Voyage to North America
and the Campaign Conducted There

15 May 1776 to 10 October 1783

Translated
by
Bruce E. Burgoyne

HERITAGE BOOKS
2012

HERITAGE BOOKS
AN IMPRINT OF HERITAGE BOOKS, INC.

Books, CDs, and more—Worldwide

For our listing of thousands of titles see our website
at
www.HeritageBooks.com

Published 2012 by
HERITAGE BOOKS, INC.
Publishing Division
100 Railroad Ave. #104
Westminster, Maryland 21157

Copyright © 1998 Bruce E. Burgoyne

All rights reserved. No part of this book may be reproduced or transmitted in any form or by any means, electronic or mechanical, including photocopying, recording or by any information storage and retrieval system without written permission from the author, except for the inclusion of brief quotations in a review.

International Standard Book Numbers
Paperbound: 978-0-7884-0857-1
Clothbound: 978-0-7884-9391-1

Table of Contents

Preface v

Introduction vii

Journal of the Sea Voyage to North America and also of the Campaign 1
    Conducted There 15 May 1776 to 5 October 1779

Journal of the Sea Voyage to North America and also of the Campaign 131
    Conducted There 5 October 1779 to 10 October 1783

Notes 210

Index 217

About the Author 223

The Journal of Lieutenant Friedrich Julius von Papet

Preface

One of the most significant and important effects of the English employment of Hessians during the American Revolutionary War was the retention of English control of Canada. General John Burgoyne had taken most of the military strength from Canada for his command when he marched against the American colonists in 1777. However, even after France entered the war, the residents of that former French colony were not strong enough to openly resist the military control exercised by a small English and Hessian command. As a result, England retained Canada under the terms of the Treaty of Paris in 1783.

The present translation was made from the journal of Friedrich Julius von Papet, a young Brunswick officer, who remained behind in Canada when General John Burgoyne began his march against the American colonists in 1777. Although only eighteen years old, von Papet was assigned the important position of brigade major, and because he kept a diary throughout his English service, we had a picture of the military, social, and cultural life in Canada at that time. Surprisingly, even during an obvious period of illness, he apparently had someone else record the daily events.

Therefore, in making my translation, I found part of the diary had been written in a different hand. With the kind assistance of Henry Retzer and his wife, Elfriede, most of the very difficult to transcribe second hand-writing was deciphered. Unfortunately there are still words which could not be transcribed, resulting in a few parts of the translation being at best, only a guess as to the actual meaning. Therefore, and as always, I must caution anyone using the translation for serious research to return to the German manuscript to verify my translation.

Other known Brunswick diaries were written by a Captain Cleve, Chaplain Carl Melsheimer, and both the elder and younger du Roi brothers. The "Diary of Voyage from Stade in Hanover to Quebec in America of the Second Division of Ducal Brunswick Mercenaries", *The Quarterly Journal of the New York State Historical Association*, Vol. VIII, Nr. 4, October 1927, translated by Clara Egli, appears to be part of the diary written by Anton Adolph Heinrich du Roi (the

The Journal of Lieutenant Friedrich Julius von Papet younger du Roi), and confirms a number of entries in the von Papet journal.

Editorial Procedures

For the spelling of proper names I have used spellings, not only used by von Papet, but in some cases as used by William L. Stone in his translation of *Memoirs, Letters, and Journals of Major General Riedesel* (Albany, 1868). Most of the first name identification of Brunswick officers has been taken from the same source. Nevertheless, there are other possible spellings which might have been used. (If I am not mistaken there are about eight various spellings of the simple name Rall, the Hessian colonel attacked at Trenton by General George Washington.) Most identifying information on English officers was provided by Robert Cowan of Lake Kiowa, Texas.

I have used a letter e after the vowels a, o, and u to indicate an umlaut in the spelling of German words and names. Also, in an effort to make the diary more readable, I have standardized the recording of dates, and reduced lengthy sentences and paragraphs to shorter more easily understood ones. Parentheses within the translation are as used by von Papet and information which I have supplied is in brackets.

Acknowledgments

Donald Londahl-Smidt and Robert Cowan have made many valuable suggestions and corrections to create a more scholarly and accurate translation, and Henry Retzer and his wife have helped with deciphering some of the difficult portions of the nearly illegible hand writing of the most difficult to read portions of the journal. The editors at Heritage Books, Inc. of Bowie, Maryland, have provided additional editorial assistance. As ever, my wife Marie has not only encouraged my efforts, but read and reread the manuscript in an effort to reduce the number of my mistakes. Nevertheless, I am still the sole responsible individual for those errors that may remain.

Bruce E. Burgoyne
Dover, DE - 1997

The Journal of Lieutenant Friedrich Julius von Papet

Introduction

Organization of the Brunswick Contingent

In late 1775 and early 1776 Colonel William Faucitt negotiated treaties with the small German states of Brunswick, Hesse-Cassel, Hesse-Hanau, and Waldeck by which military units were placed in English service to assist England in efforts to suppress the revolt in the American colonies. Later he negotiated treaties with Ansbach-Bayreuth and Anhalt-Zerbst, acquiring additional foreign troops, all of whom were generally known as "Hessians" The troops from Hesse-Cassel and Waldeck were eventually sent to General William Howe's command in the New York area, and the Brunswick and Hesse-Hanau units were sent to Canada. The Brunswick troops, numbering 4,300 men sailed in two divisions.

The 1st Division sailed on the Elbe on 22 March 1776, and contained the staff of 22 men, the Prince Frederick Infantry Regiment, the Riedesel Infantry Regiment, a Grenadier Battalion, and a Light Infantry Battalion, a total of 2,282 men. Infantry regiments consisted of a staff of 25 men and five companies of 131 men each. The Grenadier Battalion had a staff of eight and four companies of 139 men each. The Dragoon Regiment had a 24 man staff and four companies of 78 men each, and the Light Infantry Regiment had a staff of eleven men, a chasseur or arquebusier company, and four ordinary infantry companies of 131 men each.[1] Company designations for the units of the 1st Division have not been determined by this translator.

The ship assignments were as follows:[2]

Prince Ludwig Dragoon Regiment

Pallis (Captain Bell) with General Friedrich Adolph von Riedesel, Captain Heinrich Christian Fricke, Captain Heinrich Gerlach, Lieutenants Friedrich Christian Cleve, Johann Conrad Goedecke, keeper of the military chest, Langemeyer (other information lacking), the English officer Captain Edward Foy, and men of the squadron of Major General von Riedesel.

Minerva, with Lieutenant Colonel Friedrich Baum, Captain Carl Friedrich Reinking, Cornets August Ludwig Graefe and Johann

The Journal of Lieutenant Friedrich Julius von Papet
Balthasar Stutzer, Chaplain Carl Melsheimer, Auditor Thomas, and Surgeon Vorbrodt and men of the Leib and Baum Squadrons.

Union with Major Johann Christoph von Maibom, Captain Carl von Schlagenteufel, Sr., Lieutenants Otto Arnold Sommerlatte, Friedrich Wilhelm Dietrich Bothmar, August Friedrich Heinrich Bornemann, Ensign Johann Friedrich Schoenewald and men of the Leib and Major von Maibom Squadrons.

The Grenadier Battalion
James and John (Captain Wadson) with Lieutenant Colonel Heinrich Christian Breymann, Captain August Wilhelm von Hambach, Lieutenants Heinrich Wilhelm Uhlig, Theodor Friedrich Gebhard, Otto Heinrich Rudolphi, Ludwig Casimir Mutzel, Gottfried Julius Winterschmidt, and Regimental Surgeon Henkel and men of the Grenadier Battalion and Prince Frederick Regiment.

Laurie with Captain Ernst August von Baertling, Sr., Lieutenants August Wilhelm Helmcke, Gebhard Thedel von Wallmoden, and Johann Andreas Mayer and men of the Company of Captain von Baertling of the Rhetz Regiment.

Royal Briton with Captain Albrecht Daniel von Loehneisen, Lieutenants Christian Wilhelm Trott, Johann Caspar Balcke, and Heinrich Wilhelm Gottfried von Cramm and men of the companies of Captain von Loehneisen and Captain Morgenstern of the von Riedesel Regiment.

Apollo with Captain Gottlieb Dietrich von Schick, Lieutenants Johann Jacob von Meyern and Carl Franz d'Annieres, Jr., and men of Captain Schick's Company of the Specht Regiment.

Prince Frederick Infantry Regiment
Prince of Wales with Lieutenant Colonel Carl Christian Julius Praetorius, Captains Carl August Heinrich von Tunderfeldt and Georg Ernst von Zielberg, Lieutenants Johann Friedrich Hartz, August Wilhelm du Roi, Sr., Edmund Victor von Koenig, Ensign Johann Christian Sternberg, Auditor Paul Gottfried Franz Wolpers, Regimental Surgeon Johann August Bernt and men of the companies of Lieutenant Colonel Praetorius and Captain von Tunderfeldt.

Providence (Captain George Prissick) with Major Friedrich Wilhelm von Hille, Captain Jacob Christian Sander, Lieutenants

The Journal of Lieutenant Friedrich Julius von Papet

Johann Friedrich Wolgast, Johann Friedrich Heinrich Burghoff, Ensign Friedrich Kolte (or Kotte), Lieutenant Ernst Christian Schroeder and men of Major von Hille and Captain von Tunderfeldt Companies.

Lord Sandwich (Captain Devonsham) with Captain Friedrich Albrecht Rosenberg, Lieutenants Friedrich Wilhelm Volkmar, Ensigns Carl Wilhelm Reinerding and Carl Friedrich Christian von Adelsheim, Surgeon Friedrich August Fuegerer and men of Major General Stammer and Captain von Tunderfeldt Companies.

Peggy (Captain Wilson) with Captain Adolf Lorenz Dietrichs (or Diterichs), Lieutenants Friedrich von der Knesebeck, Gottlieb Christian von Reitzenstein, Ensign Sigfried Heinrich Langerjahn (or Langerjaan) and men of the companies of Captain Dietrichs, Captain von Tunderfeldt, and Captain Carl Friedrich Morgenstern.

Riedesel Infantry Regiment

Harmonie with Lieutenant Colonel Ernst Ludwig Wilhelm von Speth, Captains Morgenstern and Carl Friedrich von Baertling, Jr., Lieutenants Johann Carl Morgenstern, Ludwig Traugott von Burgsdorf, Ludwig Gottlieb von Meyern, Ensign Carl Christoph von Maibom and men of the companies of Lieutenant Colonel von Speth and Captain Morgenstern.

Nancy (Captain Wilson) with Major Otto Carl Anton von Mengen, Captain Ernst Heinrich Wilhelm von Girsewald, Lieutenant Wilhelm Hoyer, Ensign Raimund Gottlieb Haeberlin, Surgeon Johann August Mylius and men of the companies of Major von Mengen and Captain von Morgenstern.

Polly with Captain Gottlieb Benjamin Harbord, Lieutenants Friedrich Carl Reinking, and Christian Theodor von Pincier, Ensign Ludwig Unverzagt, Auditor Carl Friedrich Wilhelm Zink and men of the companies of Major General von Riedesel and Captain Morgenstern.

Elisabeth (Captain Hold) with Captain Julius Ludwig August Poellnitz, Lieutenant Heinrich Julius Freyenhagen, Ensigns Ernst Christian Heinrich Brandes and Carl Conrad Andrae, Regimental Surgeon Pralle and men of the companies of Captain von Poellnitz and Captain Morgenstern.

The Journal of Lieutenant Friedrich Julius von Papet

Martha (Captain Hold) with Lieutenants August Theodor Gottfried Wolgast, Jr., Christian Friedrich Wiesener, August Wilhelm Breva and Carl Friedrich von Reckrodt and 32 horses.

On 7 April 1776, five transports with the Hesse-Hanau Infantry Regiment on board, and a number of transports for English units joined the fleet, so that it numbered 30 vessels when it set sail for America. Most of this fleet arrived at Quebec on 1 June.

The 2nd Division, consisting of the Specht Infantry Regiment, the Rhetz Infantry Regiment, and the Barner Light Infantry Battalion, 2,018 men, set sail on the Elbe on 31 May. The units of the 2nd Division were organized with the following companies:[3]

Specht Infantry Regiment

Company Specht, Company Major Ehrenkrook, Company Captain Plessen, Company Captain Luetzow, and Company Captain Dahlsterna

Rhetz Infantry Regiment

Company Major General Rhetz, Company Lieutenant Colonel Ehrenkrook, Company Major Luecke, Company Captain Schlagenteufel, and Company Captain Ahlers.

Barner Light Infantry Battalion

Company of Arquebusiers, Company of the Major, Company Captain Thomae, Company Captain Geyso, and Company Captain Dommes.

Most of the ships of this division arrived at Quebec on 18 September 1776. The ship assignments were as follows.[4]

Rhetz Infantry Regiment

Jung Bonifacius (Dutch - Captain Wilson) with Lieutenant Colonel Johan Gustav von Ehrenkrook, Captain Wilhelm Ludwig von Fredersdorf, Lieutenants Friedrich Leopold Engelhard Meyer, Johann Ludwig von Unger, Sr., Surgeon Toegel, Auditor Schmidt, Regimental Surgeon Christian Timitheus Schraeder, and 192 men of the Leib company and the Company of Lieutenant Colonel von Ehrenkrook.

Frohe Johanne (Dutch - Captain Noss) with Major Balthasar Bogislaus von Luecke, Captains Conrad Anton Ahlers (or Alers), Georg Philipp Ahrend (or Arend), and Heinrich Urban Cleve, Lieutenants Friedrich Julius von Papet, Jr., Hans Philipp Heinrich von

The Journal of Lieutenant Friedrich Julius von Papet

Dobeneck, Christian Heinrich Modrach, Friedrich Wilhelm Feichel, Johann Heinrich Goedecke, and 318 men of the Leib Company and the Companies of Major von Luecke and Captain Ahlers.

Jungfer Anne Catherine (Hamburg) with Captain Ludwig von Schlagenteufel, Sr., Lieutenants Thedel Wilhelm Bielstein, Carl Friedrich Conradi, Carl Ludwig Peters (or Petersen), Ensigns Bernhard Ehrich (or Erich), Friedrich Bandel, Johann Friedrich Bode, and 125 men of Captain von Schlagenteufel's Company.

Specht Infantry Regiment

Lively (English - Captain Hall) with Colonel Johann Friedrich Specht, Captains Heinrich Jaeger (or Yaeger) and Laurentius O'Connell, Lieutenants Johann Heinrich Meyer and Anton Adolph Heinrich du Roi, Jr., Regimental Surgeon Johann Carl Bause, the English Lieutenant (Samuel) Willoe, and 108 men of the company of Colonel Specht.

Vriesland (or *Friesland*) (Dutch) with Captains August Conrad von Luetzow and Bernhard Richard von Dahlsterna, Lieutenants August Wilhelm von Papet, Sr., Friedrich Ernst Oldenkopf, Heinrich Daniel d'Annieres, Sr., Friedrich Bodo von Unger, Jr., Ensigns Johann Heinrich Carl von Bernewitz and Grimpe, with 354 men of the companies of Colonel Specht, Captains Luetzow and von Dahlsterna.

De gude Sacke (Dutch) with Major Carl Friedrich von Ehrenkrook, Captain Georg von Schlagenteufel, Jr., Lieutenants Daniel Arnold Hertel, Christian Friedrich von Milkau, Heinrich Anton David Dove, Johann Friedrich Julius Kettner (or Kellner), Ensigns Friedrich von Redecken and Samuel Jacob Anton von Ulmenstein, Surgeon Kohle, Auditor Baehre and 180 men of the companies of Major von Ehrenkrook and Captain von Plessen.

Barner Light Infantry Battalion

Margaretha Alida (Dutch) with Major Ferdinand Albrecht von Barner, Captains Maximilian Christoph Ludwig Schottelius and Gottlieb Joachim von Gleissenberg, Lieutenants Johann Andreas Bode, Johann Friedrich Pflueger, Caspar Friedrich Rohr, Regimental Surgeon Kuntze and 308 men of the Jaeger Company and the company of Major von Barner.

The Journal of Lieutenant Friedrich Julius von Papet

Hellegunda Christiana (Dutch) with Captain Georg Ludwig Thomae, Lieutenants Johann Gottfried Kolte (or Kotte), Andreas Meyer, Carl Anton Ludwig Muehlenfeld, Ensigns Wilhelm Lucas Rhenius and de Biers and 167 men of the company of Captain Thomae.

Ost-Rust (Dutch) with Captain von Geyso (or Geusau), Lieutenants Johann Caspar Hannemann, Philipp Sigismund Cruse, Georg Friedrich Gebhard Fricke, Ensign Johann Julius Anton Specht, Captain Leopold Franz Friedrich Balthasar von Plessen, Ensign Johann Edmund Fromme and 108 men of the company of Captain Geusau.

Three Friends (or *True Friends*) (English) with Captain August Friedrich Dommes, Lieutenants Albrecht Christian Raabe, and Johann Gottlieb Gladen, Ensign Georg Leopold Hagemann, Lieutenants Georg Bodemeyer (or Rodemeyer) and Curt von Hessler and 102 men of the companies of Captain Dommes and Captain von Ahlers.

Contents of the Journal

The journal, which covers the entire period of the 2nd Division's participation in the Revolution, provides a daily record of von Papet's activity, from marching to the embarkation port to the return march to Brunswick.

As with similar accounts, the sea voyages to and from Europe, are noted in considerable detail, and as a very young man in a very demanding position, von Papet records the inner reactions among his superiors with a noteworthy caution and understanding not to let his position cause him harm.

In addition to the many reports, true and false, circulating at his headquarters, he was able to note the social and cultural life in the strange, new setting in Canada. As there is a scarcity of information concerning military affairs in Canada during the American Revolution, Von Papet's journal provides a much needed insight into why Canada never became the fourteenth colony.

About the Author

Julius Friedrich von Papet was a lieutenant in the Rhetz Infantry Regiment. He had been born on 5 August 1757 and sailed to America

The Journal of Lieutenant Friedrich Julius von Papet

on board the ship *Frohe Johanne*. When General John Burgoyne was forming his army in 1777 for an advance against Albany, he took all of the German troops in Canada except for a detachment of 600 men, plus officers and non-commissioned officers. Von Papet was one of those officers designated to remain in Canada. It appears from his diary that he was assigned as the regimental quartermaster initially, and then on 20 November 1777, although only nineteen years of age, he was designated the brigade major for Brigadier Ehrenkrook. After Colonel von Specht was named a brigadier in place of Ehrenkrook, von Papet continued as brigade major for Specht. According to William L. Stone, *Memoirs and Letters and Journals of Major General Riedesel*, (Albany, 1868), von Papet, then a captain, died at Maastricht in the Netherlands on 5 April 1793.[5]

JOURNAL

of the sea voyage to North America
and also of the campaign conducted there
15 May 1776 to 5 October 1779

and it is a true account of his own experiences
as set forth by

Friedrich Julius von Papet, Jr.
1st Lieutenant in Major General von Rhetz
Regiment
and
since 20 November 1777
Brigade Major with the German troops in Canada

1st Part

The Journal of Lieutenant Friedrich Julius von Papet

Journal for the Year 1776
Leaving Germany

15 May - We marched out of Wolfenbuettel at six o'clock in the morning,[6] by way of Mascherode and Riddagshausen Cloister. In this region there were many observers from Braunschweig, who accompanied us for an hour from Riddagshausen with their tears and best wishes. Today the regiment took quarters in the three villages of Elsenrode, Kolberta, and Illenbuettel. In Elsenrode the treasurer, von Buelow, welcomed us most politely. The companies which had to march two miles to the two latter places had to arrange for quarters, and white bread and brandy were issued to them. All the officers were then invited to a luncheon at Herr von Buelow's. As the most distant place was five miles away, the march was very tiring.

16 May - The regiment assembled at Fallersleben. We marched through this place with music playing and at Stetfeld we crossed the Aller river. Two hours prior thereto a great heath began and on this day the march was not only long, but also tiring. The place where the staff halted was called Kaesebeck and I marched with the company to Geissing.

17 May - The march continued to Lueder, which was only one hour [two and one-half English miles] from the previous place. We halted for a day of rest. It was a very wretched place. Groats is the most pleasant food. This village belongs to the District of Bodenteich, in which Herr Rautenberg (a brother of the deceased Braunschweig Pastor Rautenberg) is the administrator. I myself saw a person here who formerly served as a chambermaid in Braunschweig and about whom a person can make the observation that fate often plays strange tricks on mankind.

19 May - We marched out at five o'clock. The regiment assembled at Bodenteich and at that place we marched past Colonel [Johann Friedrich] Specht with music playing. The staff halted at Molzen and our company at Oetzen. Uelzen lay to our left. The quarters were somewhat better here than the previous ones. We arrived here at two-thirty.

20 May - It was five o'clock when we marched away. The regiment assembled at Zasdorf, crossed the Aur River and each

The Journal of Lieutenant Friedrich Julius von Papet

company then took its own route to its quarters. The staff went to Beisenbuettel, a post station, for its destination. Our company had to recross the Aur and took night quarters in Hohenbostel.

21 May - The regiment assembled at Hohenbostel. It marched from there to Lueneberg and we arrived at ten o'clock. We marched through that place with dressed ranks at eleven-thirty and on to Bardowich, where our company had night and rest quarters. Our host asked only eight groschen for board for me and the captain.

23 May - The march proceeded to Luhdorf on the Lu River, where our company entered night quarters at ten o'clock, for one night and where it had one death. He was buried at two o'clock in the morning.

24 May - The regiment assembled at Klafter Leeve, near the Ireene Inn and the staff halted at Meckelfeld and the company at Fleste.

25 May - From there, after the regiment had reassembled at Mocksdorf, the march continued to Horneburg. In this small place the entire regiment halted and entered quarters five miles from the previous place. Near the height of Buxtehude, it was possible to see Hamburg behind us, a part of the Elbe River and six ships thereon. From that distance the ships' masts appeared as towers in a city. According to our initial orders, tomorrow was to be a day of rest, but we were in such a hurry that Colonel [William] Faucitt scheduled the mustering already on the next day. Our commander went to Stade with the commissioners in order to protest. Immediately thereafter we received orders to remain here on the 26th and 27th.

26 May - I visited my brother in Buxtehude.[7] He had the merchant Tessier as his host, a very polite gentleman, who himself treated us to all the best.

28 May - We and the Specht Regiment marched to Stade.

29 May - Our regiment and the Specht Regiment were mustered and the regiments then took an oath [to the King of England]. Colonel Faucitt passed through all the ranks and checked each individual very thoroughly. Our regiment pleased him considerably. Immediately after taking the oath, the lieutenant colonel, the staff, and the companies of Captain Schlagenteufel and a part of the company of Captain Ahlers went aboard the two ships, *Duke William* and *Anne Catherine*.[8] During the oath we had the honor to have the ladies of Braunschweig, who were with us, present.[9]

The Journal of Lieutenant Friedrich Julius von Papet

30 May - The Lieb Company of Major von Luecke and the rest of Captain Ahlers Company received orders to be prepared to embark at eleven o'clock. At eleven-thirty this occurred and at three-forty-five we went aboard our ship *Frohe Johanne*. Were the baser feelings on the water not stronger, and had it been permitted by time, it would have been very easy to avoid. Our ship is a Hollander, armed with eight cannons and is still quite new. Although I had never seen one, this is still a very large object to look at. An hour later my pleasant host from Stade visited me. The cabin, which we have, is quite roomy but rather crowded for nine people because of the beds. We are not yet in agreement concerning the places for sleeping. There are only two beds. Because one is used by the major and the other by Captains Ahlers and Ahrend, I and Captain Cleve have found a place on the floor. The others, including the chaplain and the auditor, whose ship sailed and have been accepted by me as guests, sleep in hammocks. We have agreed that each day one of us is to keep watch on the belongings and property. This evening our sea captain told us that if the wind remains the same, we will sail at one o'clock tomorrow. The captain is a Hollander, who commands the ship for pay. He seems to be a very good and competent man with whom we all have reason to be satisfied. An English naval lieutenant is also assigned, who will guide us to America and primarily has charge of the rations.

31 May - The anchor was raised at nine-forty-five and at ten-thirty we set sail. The feelings then could barely be controlled. At twelve-forty-five we passed Glueckstadt, which as a newly fortified place, gave a rather exceptional appearance. The ship sailed with a southeast [wind], so fast that it seemed as if we flew. At four o'clock a storm struck, which partially passed us by. At five-thirty, where the Elbe River entered, the anchor was dropped. We were still three hours from Cuxhaven and many ships which were to sail in company with us were already to be seen lying at anchor. The ship sailed two miles in an hour.

June - This morning most individuals were dissatisfied with their sleeping accommodations, and it is no wonder, because there were only three beds. Three slept on the floor and three in hammocks, from which one nearly fell out. The anchor was raised at six o'clock. At eight-forty-five we saw many sea-dogs, a kind of small seal, in the region near Cuxhaven. At eleven-thirty the ships anchored at

The Journal of Lieutenant Friedrich Julius von Papet

Cuxhaven. We joined the ship *Duke William*, on which was our lieutenant colonel.[10] He had the misfortune that because of two small boats, about which I know nothing, he had to reembark toward evening on the ship *Bonifacius*. Today we had an extraordinary amount of visitors, my brother among them. I was deeply affected by the many well-wishes. This evening the commodore came aboard our ship with the order to prepare our ship so as to be able to set sail at the first cannon shot tomorrow morning. We were still about eight miles from the open sea.

2 June - The anchor was raised at ten o'clock and in a few minutes we had passed Cuxhaven. At twelve-thirty we passed the fortifications. At one-thirty our pilot left us, the only person from whom only the best could be expected. At four o'clock in the afternoon we saw the island of Helgoland. It was seen as numerous islands hanging one beside the other in the sea. The ship sailed six miles, [36 English miles], in four hours.[11] Toward eight o'clock I felt a giddiness. I saw the pumps; I took hold of them and the motion made the giddiness pass. At eight-forty-five I watched the sunset and this magnificent display of nature induced us to enjoy a glass of red wine with the crew on the deck by the ship's helm.

3 June - We continued to sail with the best of winds and our eight ships remained close to one another in a tight formation. At seven o'clock we saw the coast of East Friesland. Our ship remained closest to the commodore at all times. The sea was somewhat rougher than yesterday. Some of our group have begun to show signs of seasickness. I now feel like a man who has been drinking the day before. The movement of the sea, even when it is still, is always stronger than the Elbe. At nine-thirty we saw the island of Ameland and it was possible to see the city castle thereon, very clearly. At five-forty-five Major von Barner's ship came so close that we could speak quite easily with it. At about that time we held a prayer hour because prayer hours were held every morning at seven o'clock and evenings at six o'clock. The ship sailed today just as it did yesterday, six miles in four hours. Our ship's captain assured us however, that if he were permitted to set all the sails, he would certainly be able to reach the harbor at Portsmouth tomorrow.

4 June - A very pleasant day. Our ships were all together, except for one which is from Hamburg and at present at least four miles

The Journal of Lieutenant Friedrich Julius von Papet

behind us. We are now in a region where a pilot is most necessary because at this place a large Holland ship with money was reported to have foundered. At four o'clock a pilot came aboard. A depth of sixteen fathoms was found; when the lead was cast, because of the bottom soil, white sand was detected and in the cavity a Holland deut [a small coin] with the seal of Zeeland, dated 1747. If I had not been present to cast the lead and pull it out again, this incident would have seemed very improbable to me. The ship's captain remarked that the coin was a rarity. At one o'clock we encountered contrary wind and just from the direction of our sailing. The ships had to sail against the wind and all of them spread out widely. These winds forced us to tack for some time, so it may take a long time before we can reach Portsmouth. Our troops are becoming seasick more frequently. I stay most of the time by the forward mast and feel well when there. The rocking of the ship is much more noticeable in the cabin than at this place. At six-thirty the ships turned and our ship's captain was designated the second commander by the commodore, with the order to sail back with his ship and to give the sharpest commands to the ship dropping behind to sail more swiftly. Not three-fourths of an hour later, he brought it back, but only with so much turning that most of the sailors of our crew, including my best friend, A., began to get sick. The overtaking of this ship appeared so dangerous that our hair stood on end. The Hamburger sailed from the side and our ship sailed with the bowsprit so directly toward the other that it appeared as if he would ram us. The Hamburger passed close to our bowsprit and our captain delivered his orders. Toward eight o'clock we went to bed and despite the considerable motion of the ship and the moaning of our sick, I slept rather well.

5 June - The wind remains contrary. I have noticed that there is a great difference sailing with or against the wind. Both of the latter cause a person to feel the strong gusts of wind and at the same time it is so cold that a person really freezes. Our ships are together again, but well-spread out. This afternoon at one o'clock the wind was still contrary. The motions of the ship are so strong that our servants had much difficulty carrying the food. We had to hold onto our plates, also. Everyone, including me, complained of some giddiness until three and my only objection was that it was nearly impossible to stand up. Now I recall how in my youth I often swung in the swing, because that is exactly how, and no differently, I feel at sea when the ship rises and falls. I try, as much as possible, to imagine I am still on the swing. I eat nothing except that for which I have the greatest appetite and this has helped to protect me from the customary attacks. At seven o'clock our commodore fired a cannon shot, which meant that the slower ships should raise more sails in order to catch up. Because of the giddiness none of us could remain active. Most of us went to bed at seven o'clock.

6 June - Today the wind is still as contrary as it was yesterday, but with the difference that the sea is calm and that most of our crew is again feeling better. The best that I can say as a summary is that we all get along with one another in harmony and consider ourselves as one family. The weather is not the best. Because of the rain it is necessary always to remain in the cabin. The admiral of our fleet has not been seen today.[12] Today our captain is the leader of the twelve ships present. At ten-thirty it was still raining, but the sea was again very rough, so that the sailors had to lie down again. At one o'clock the wind changed and our journey improved. It did not last long until dark clouds appeared in the distance and we could see a storm was to be expected. At three o'clock the wind again became contrary as before and our captain took in all the sails. Now the shower is over and God be praised, we were able to tolerate it. Because of the severe motion on deck, in the morning as well as the evening, no prayer hours were held; the troops in their bunks could only sing a few songs. This night has been one of very great disturbance. The rolling of the ship was exceptionally severe. Added to that the ship turned and for one who has never been to sea, nothing is more frightening than when the captain gives orders (through a speaking trumpet) for the sailors to continue shouting and working. It rained hard and we suffered the discomfort in our cabin because it rained in. The ship's carpenter was told about this and he made repairs during the night by stopping up the holes.

7 June - Because of tiredness and because I had not one hour of sleep during the night, I was very wretched today. The wind is still against us and if it does not change, we can float around on this ocean for another fourteen days, or, with a favorable wind, we could be in Portsmouth in two days. At the same time it is very cold. A warm room would be pleasant. Our four sick individuals are no better.

The Journal of Lieutenant Friedrich Julius von Papet

Today my friend Abraham again had a violent vomiting attack. Thank the Lord that I still feel quite good despite the movement of the ship. I have become accustomed to it and learned how to keep my balance well. At twelve-thirty we turned right toward the coast of England, as previously we had had the direction toward the coast of Holland. The sea now became rough. I took this to mean a storm, but our sailors took this movement as immaterial. At two-forty-five, from the mast, we could see a Dutch fleet of eighteen ships, which, in the opinion of our ship's captain, were returning from the East Indies and now because they were saluted with cannon fire, were sailing toward their own province. By seven o'clock the sea was quite still again. After the prayer hour Captain A. caught a fish, which the sailors call a seacock, on a hook. It had a great many similarities with our Kuchtbaarsen and weighed a good half pound less. Roasted it tasted quite similar to our eels. During the night, although it was somewhat stormier, the movement of the ship was more tolerable so that it was more normal and better for sleeping.

8 June - Of our ships, we saw only a single one, and that was the one on which Major von Barner was. The others had all scattered due to the constantly contrary wind. The weather is truly incomparable and we did not make any headway.

9 June - Now we began to become impatient. The wind is still against us constantly and we do not move from the spot. To this is added that we are now in a region where there are frequent sandbars, and if our captain had not been cautious we would have run onto one of the outermost. In this region there is so little of interest that I wish from the bottom of my heart to see something beside sky and water. At six-thirty we passed Ostend.

10 June - The wind still continues the same as yesterday. At five o'clock in the afternoon it changed to our great pleasure and our journey became more agreeable. At six-forty-five we caught sight of the foreland of England. We sailed until ten o'clock, still with the most favorable wind. However, it was also very foggy. We were all so delighted that we celebrated our long, boring journey with a glass of punch. At ten-thirty we went to bed. But who can describe the fright which we experienced when we received a powerful jolt as our ship's bow ran against a sandbar. The shout of our captain who cried out, "Jesus!" and seemed to lose all resoluteness; the bustle and work of

The Journal of Lieutenant Friedrich Julius von Papet

our sailors, and the two cannon shots that were fired as an emergency signal. On the darkest night on the ship, the left side stuck fast in the sand, which was fully shown at ebbtide. All that created many frightening pictures for me, but which I can not describe. And we officers had our hands full keeping the soldiers calmed down. It was not a minute until two English pilots were on the spot, who with the help of the large anchor, which was dropped, gave us hope that we could float free at five o'clock in the morning with the floodtide. Two dropped anchors were used. The largest one from our ship, with God's help, did its job and about six o'clock we were freed from this dangerous place. It was three hours from Dover, at a place, where previously 200 travelers had settled on an island with a city called Good Wind. The impact which the rudder made, despite the ship being stuck, was so violent that the mainmast was raised an inch out of its resting place. If the ship were not new, it would have been unable to withstand the impact, which it had received so forcibly, because it never even developed a leak. The fright of our danger was intensified a few hours later for Major von Barner's ship. That ship was stuck fast also, as ours had been. His troops had to fire by platoons and additionally it had required another twelve cannon shots. The danger to that ship was also greater because it is older. With the loss of 200 barrels, some water, and a portion of their provisions, which they threw overboard, they were finally able to float free. According to the information we received, all the officers except the major had been seasick for three days. The ship had developed a minor leak and that coupled with the above incident during which they had lost their provisions, made it necessary for them to run in to Dover.

    The pilots who had gotten our ship free also recommended that our captain enter the Dover. However, because the captain knew that his ship was solid and good, and also clearly understood that they only sought to have him get them into the harbor quicker because they wanted to say they had taken his ship into the harbor under their guidance, he declined this because of his orders to enter Portsmouth, and was supported in that position by our commander Major von Luecke. When the pilots saw that nothing changed us, they demanded only 300 guineas for their efforts. They had to be satisfied with writing to the captain's agent in London, from whom they received a proportion of their pay, to be divided among them.

The Journal of Lieutenant Friedrich Julius von Papet

11 June - Now, praise God, we are again under sail and seek to again recover from the fright and fatigue we have endured. I can not pass over in silence the bearing of our troops and the resoluteness and cheerfulness with which they have worked, but they also had all of us to lead them on, and we have all helped. About four o'clock in the afternoon the air cleared and it was possible to see the coast of England and France, as well as Dover and Calais, very clearly.

12 June - This morning at eight-thirty Folkstone came into view. It was a very clear day, but the wind was light and we made no progress. Toward evening it became completely calm so that when the flood tide came in, which was against us, we had to anchor. An hour later we again set sail.

13 June - This morning we were off the point of land at Beachy Head. At nine o'clock the wind again became so contrary that at evening we found ourselves at the same place where we had been the day before, and it was the same on the fourteenth.

15 June - We passed the point of land where it was very stormy during the night. As we learned that there are many shoals and sandbars near Portsmouth, we were not in the best of moods.

16 June - By much back and forth tacking we finally arrived at the approach to the harbor at Portsmouth. At eight o'clock our ship fired a cannon to summon a pilot and in less than a quarter hour one came on board. Our ship's captain was so pleased with that, that he told us that he would not be so pleased if he were to receive 100 pounds sterling. It must be clearly understood that as soon as a pilot takes over the maneuvering of a ship, he not only takes over command from the captain, but is also responsible for any damages. However, they are also very well paid. At nine o'clock we arrived at the roadstead of Portsmouth. It provided an unusually pleasant view to see nearly fifty ships lying at anchor there. In the afternoon, together with Major von Luecke, I visited the ship *Bonifacius*, on board which was our lieutenant colonel, and then the ship *Vriesland*, on which was Colonel Specht and my brother.[13] Almost all of the officers had been sick, except for the colonel. My brother had only had one attack of it. Now everyone has recovered. It was the first time I had seen any but our transport ship and I must confess, even in hindsight, that the construction, the furnishings, and even the cleanliness of ours was far superior. In all the cabins it was necessary to step in. In addition to that ours is much brighter and airier. Toward evening troops were unloaded from some of the ships and put aboard another. It was called the *Laible* and our commodore has since gone aboard it.[14] Most of the ships of our division had already been at the roadstead for fourteen days, except for the *Anna Catherine*, on which was Major von Barner and our Captain von Schlagenteufel.

17 June - Today I decided to go into Portsmouth with Captain Ahlers. In order to get some idea of English seapower it is only necessary to visit Portsmouth. Still I can do nothing else but relate the tales of my comrades. Our affairs allowed us to see nothing but the surface of the city. Everything here is exceedingly expensive and what the English demand, they do not yield on. Their noon meals seldom please a German. I ate in one of the best restaurants. The soup was heavily peppered and the appetizer, which was cauliflower and green peas, had only been cooked in water. A butter sauce was served with it. The meal cost two and one-half shillings. The streets did not take on life until eleven o'clock. However, I saw nothing exceptionally noteworthy. The structures are old with most of the houses made of stone, but very small and the streets raised in the middle, well-paved and exceedingly rounded. About noon Major von Barner also came to Portsmouth and entered numerous complaints that his ship should be brought to the royal dock and thoroughly inspected, and that he and his troops should be assigned aboard two different ships. After taking care of my affairs I finally met with my brother again on our ship.

18 June - I remained aboard my ship and entertained myself with the view of so many war and transport ships.

19 June - Some of our officers went sight-seeing in Portsmouth. Their accounts agreed with the tales of what was already known and had been read about English power and the well-supplied harbor. During the night, from twelve to two o'clock, there was a fire on board the ship *Vriesland*. Fortunately it was above deck, where there was cooking for the troops, and little wind. The danger was truly great, but God had looked out for them. My brother, as he was on this ship, related enough about his fright and work.

20 June - The Hessians and Waldeckers arrived here in the harbor. The ships were together and anchored just outside the harbor.

21 June - I went to Portsmouth with Major von Luecke and my brother. I saw the ship wharf, the rope-walk, the anchor, a warship with its rigging still on the spars, and I must admit that surpassed anything I had previously seen.

22 June - I visited my brother aboard his ship *Vriesland* and saw the place where the fire had occurred a few days ago. At the place where the cooking took place, the English, a few days previous had made a cover to keep the rain off and make cooking easier. This caught fire. The best resolution which those on board could find was to throw the burning boards into the sea, which was done at once. During the evening the sea became very rough and I must admit that I had difficulty deciding whether to trust the same little boat which had brought me across. My brother convinced me, although I argued against it, to return to my ship as the waves had made us wet several times.

23 and 24 June - Strong winds and the sea was very restless.

25 June - We raised the anchor at eleven o'clock, went under sail at eleven-thirty, and at one-thirty dropped anchor off the point of Wight Isle. This region is called the St. Helen's Roadstead. During the afternoon Major von Luecke decided to travel to the Isle of Wight which lay one mile from us, with our ship's captain to obtain some victuals for the trip. However, they found it just as excessively expensive as in Portsmouth, even though they now found themselves in the most blessed land in the world where prosperity is to be found in the smallest farmer's house.

The Journal of Lieutenant Friedrich Julius von Papet
Crossing the Atlantic

26 June - Two cannon shots were fired at six-thirty in the evening as the signal to depart and at seven o'clock we set sail with a southeast wind. There were nineteen transport ships and two frigates, one of 26 cannons, the other of twenty, escorting us.

27 June - We learned that we had passed the Isle of Wight during the night and had sailed ten miles. Toward evening the wind was somewhat worse and the first frigate which was escorting us, called the *Amazon* [actually with 32-cannon] and on which Captain Maxim. Jacobs was the commander, turned about and told every ship's commander to raise more sails in order to profit as much as possible from the present wind. The second frigate was called *Garland* [24-guns] and had Captain Beyersen as its commander.[15]

28 June - The past night was very restless. The wind was northeast, good for our journey, but so strong that some waves beat over the deck. Some ships, which we met during the night, caused me a great fright. They approached so close that our captain noticeably raised his voice to warn them away. I arose and could not sleep until I was told the cause of this disturbance by the sailors. The deck was full of our troops because of the violent movement of the ship, which caused many of them to again vomit. Toward nine o'clock in the morning the admiral raised a blue flag on the mainbrace, turned the sails, and lay to. This had the meaning that all ships were to assemble near him. About ten o'clock most were nearby. It was a beautiful view to see them come sailing from left and right. A ship named *Helgegonde* [Christiana] remained lying at some distance to the side, apparently in the belief that it was near enough to the admiral. He at once fired a cannon toward it, so that the ball hit in the water very close to the ship, which immediately began to move and passed the admiral's ship. Our captain explained this event to us most clearly, because he said that all the shots which were fired at the ships had to be paid for and that the money paid was revenue for the admiralty. A shot without a ball cost a half guinea and one with a ball, a full guinea, because each had his instructions. Today our sailors caught twelve mackerel on a line with two hooks. It is a very delicious fish, when cooked as well as when fried. It is noteworthy that it is caught with nothing better than its own flesh. A piece of skin, about a finger long,

The Journal of Lieutenant Friedrich Julius von Papet

is cut out of its side. They are best caught at sunrise and sunset. Today I had the pleasure of speaking to my brother through a speaking trumpet and to learn of his well-being.

29 June - As uncomfortable as it was during the past night, so calm was it today. During the morning we were again closest to the admiral and our squadron was all together over a wide area. This morning we passed the outer limits of England, called Cape Lizard. Toward six o'clock the wind became contrary and we turned about, sailing back and forth and tacking.

30 June - This morning the wind was again more favorable for our voyage. A ship, to which Major von Barner was transferred during our stay in Portsmouth, had held up the other ships' progress because it sailed poorly. The admiral, who noticed this, fastened a rope on its bowsprit this morning and fastened the other end of the rope on the afterpost of his ship and in this manner pulled it along.

1 July - A cannon shot was fired at one o'clock during the night to signal a turn because the wind had become contrary. We then sailed toward the northeast. It rained very hard during the night and toward morning was so foggy that it was difficult to see the ships. At ten o'clock it cleared and our ship passed the *Vriesland*, where I then had the pleasure to once again see and speak with my brother. At four-thirty the admiral again raised the assemble flag and all the ships were ordered to steer toward him.

2 July - Because of the continuously northwest wind we made little headway on our journey. Toward evening it became very stormy so that due to the violent movement of the ship, I was unable to get any sleep. I arose at eleven o'clock in the night and went on deck to get some fresh air. From there I went forward to the bowsprit to observe the force with which the waves beat against the ship. Therefore I was first in the depths and then raised on the heights. It surpassed anything that I had ever imagined and even so, was not a full storm. The spray from the waves, which was thrown up, was worth watching for a while, as if whole clumps of fire were to be seen therein and exceptionally fearsome. I did not remain there long, but because it started to rain again, I once again tried to go to sleep. I had hardly laid down when a new fatality struck. The admiral, who was still towing the ship *Mathaeus Alida*, [later Papet changes the name to *Margaretha Alida*] apparently considered it necessary, because of the

The Journal of Lieutenant Friedrich Julius von Papet

strong wind, to take in his sails. This could only happen if he crossed the sails and only moved slowly at that place. Our ship was under full sails on a course directly at *Matheaus Alida* and the watch forward at the bowsprit did not notice the other ship standing still until it was almost too late. To the left, the side from which the wind came would make only a small difference, not enough to sail between the ships. To the right was another English transport ship. In this danger, the captain called for all the sails, in so far as possible, to be held against the wind and then turned further with the steering rudder. Now, despite the moment this occurred, there was also a complication. The fellow standing there called to the others, "Help! Help!" Our mate, who is an old seaman, was seriously affected during this danger and spoke according to his profession. Therefore it was not long until, with God's help, we were clear.

3 July - This morning was especially gloomy. The wind was strong and we had half a storm. The admiral gave the most distant ships a cannon shot so that they would know his location. About nine o'clock a heavy rain fell and it rained the whole day. The rolling of the ship was much more noticeable than in the North Sea. We must be aware of our balance in everything we do. Until now I have been in the belief that it was an exaggeration when individuals spoke of the sea creating mountains and valleys. However, I have found it to be much worse that it had been told. Therefore it is difficult for me to find relief when it calms down and is just the opposite. I simply can not tolerate the up and down motion of the ship when in my bunk. I find that the fresh air on deck is more bearable. Therefore I must forego sleep and my eyes are very painful. The rain continued this morning until

4 July - at one-thirty. I lay down again at two. Until then the movement of the ship was mostly from front to back, up and down. Suddenly it rolled side to side. The strangeness of this movement affected not only us, but also our belongings, in and outside the cabin. Glasses, bottles, clocks, pipes, -- everything began to move and a canteen of French cognac flowed under Captain Ahler's bunk. This new arrangement of things was bitter-sweet. One thing fell over another and things changed so much that it caused us to laugh. When I queried the mate (because the captain had been sick for 24 hours), about the motion he said the wind had changed and he hoped we

The Journal of Lieutenant Friedrich Julius von Papet

would soon get a better wind. He was right. About nine o'clock the sky cleared and the squadron was again together. During the evening, at seven-thirty, an English ship sailed through our squadron. It came from England, heading for Africa, in order to buy slaves.

5 July - The evening was really quite peaceful but at seven o'clock in the morning we had an almost all out storm. Every last sail was taken in. The ocean was very turbulent because the waves beat against one another from all sides. It rained heavily and the showers passed by the grace of God. The wind blew the entire day from eight-thirty on, from the southwest. Then, after much alternating back and forth, it settled in the northeast. From all appearances of the sky, we could not expect the most comfortable night. Today the movement of the ship was so strong that a glass of wine could not be put to the mouth and a cup fell off the table. The wind howled during the night and it was much louder aboard a three-masted ship than near a church in the middle of the city.

6 July - Today I was not one of the strongest. This was not surprising as I had had very little sleep for three nights. To this must be added that I have had very little appetite compared with when on the North Sea. The wind settled in the north-northeast and it remained there the entire day. The admiral had sought to have the ship *Margaretha Alida* sail alone today by releasing it. Nevertheless it fell so far behind that the whole fleet was held up. Toward evening the admiral found it necessary once again to fasten a rope to it and to continue to tow it along. This took place in view of the whole fleet. This evening I also had the pleasure and reassurance to see and speak with my brother. Aboard his ship everyone, except himself and two officers, was sick and he told me that they had to care for three of the sick individuals.

7 July - The sky partially cleared. I also had a very good and restful night. However, the wind was primarily from the west and we had to abandon the direct course toward North America and tack mostly toward the south. The ships all sailed in a nearly straight line, but at a distance of about two miles.

8 July - Again a restful night but the wind was still contrary and at nine o'clock, after a cannon shot, a turn was made to the north. Previously I had thought that I would have many things to see in the

The Journal of Lieutenant Friedrich Julius von Papet

ocean, but until this moment I have seen not the least thing other than water.

9 July - There was a promise yesterday evening of a night which would not be the best. I learned that even the sailors can not always foretell what to expect. The sea became rather rough but I have seen it more restless. Today our course was somewhat better but we did not advance much because it always depends on the wind. During the constant isolation and with nothing to see, the time always seems to drag. Toward twelve o'clock it began to rain lightly. Of all the bread provisions which I brought along from Stade and the ship's bread that I bought in Portsmouth, I had the misfortune today to learn that most of it was moldy. For the last few days we have used the zwieback from our provisions, the only means we have in the future to offset the shortage of bread. When the zwieback has lain in warm water for a quarter hour and then been again roasted over a warm coal fire, it can be eaten with pleasure and does not taste bad.

10 July - A day like the previous one, with nothing noteworthy except the contrary wind and boredom. At two-forty-five a turn was again made in response to a cannon shot, and we sailed toward the southwest. During the evening a calm set in and the admiral assembled the fleet so that once again I had the pleasure to see my brother and to speak with him through a speaking trumpet.

11 July - The calm persisted until six o'clock in the morning. During such periods the ship makes very unpleasant and strong movements which go back and forth so that a person believes that the ship will roll over on its side. Anything which is not secured in the cabin rolls about and is busted. I was in no condition to close my eyes. I remained above on deck until three o'clock. The ocean gave me enough scenery to consider. -- It was very smooth and flat and afterward exceptional waves developed. The foam about the ship caused by the ship's movement appeared like fire and then the lightning in the waves, in an area of three square feet, can be seen. At seven o'clock the wind changed and came from the southeast, very favorable for our journey. Toward evening it became calm and in the west, toward which we sailed, a very strong storm arose. The admiral assembled the fleet and did not move from the spot for two and one-half hours, apparently with the intention, in so far as possible, of not

The Journal of Lieutenant Friedrich Julius von Papet

approaching too close to the storm, because with such a course of action the storm might pass.

12 July - The wind changed during the night and came from the northwest. It rained hard during the night. During the day we had considerable wind and clear weather.

13 July - During the evening it became so stormy and the wind mixed with rain was so strong that no one was able to stay on his feet. This was also the most restless night that I have yet had. Previously during such strong movements within the cabin, I was able to recover on deck, but now the exceptionally heavy rainfall made that impossible.

14 July - This morning the ships were widely scattered. The admiral fired a number of cannon shots so they could reassemble. The wind remained westerly, occasionally mixed with some rain, and the movement of the ship made it especially difficult to enjoy our coffee.

15 July - The wind swung to the northwest. During the morning we learned from our mate that a frigate coming from America had passed the admiral's ship and that the commander of the frigate had visited with the admiral's ship for three hours. Toward noon it became stormy and during the afternoon so strong that we will never forget this day. Such a tossing about of men and possessions, much of which was destroyed, I have never seen nor experienced. My [Captain] Ahrend suffered the most, because, as he wished to rest a bit and was on his cape, which lay on the floor, and lay by the always open doorway, a large crock filled with beer crashed through the doorway due to the violent movement and shattered. Beer, bits of crock, everything flew onto the cape and thankfully my friend suffered nothing more than a shock and a small cut on his hand. All but the lowest sails were taken in. The waves beat violently over the deck and all precautions were taken against a full storm. Now the night closed in and it did not clear up. Worry was to be seen on every face. On the deck there was a bell by which the sailors were called to meals and rung to signal the four-hour changing of the sailors' watches. Now it happened that a wave tipped the ship so far on its side that it was partially in the water. The clapper beat so sharply in the bell that it rang as loud as when the bell is rung in the middle of the night in Braunschweig to signal a fire. How this can completely cheer an individual, can easily be understood, as people in Braunschweig had

The Journal of Lieutenant Friedrich Julius von Papet

always told me this voyage would be like a fun cruise. Despite all the back and forth movement, I remained on deck all night because it was impossible for me to remain in the cabin. Toward morning, thank heavens, the wind abated, the air became brighter, and the waves settled down.

16 July - By nine o'clock the wind was again from the west, and therefore from the direction we wished to go. A ship met our fleet. The admiral sailed toward it, spoke with it, and thereafter we assumed that it was an English merchant ship coming from Jamaica with a cargo of sugar. During the evening we counted all twenty of our ships and the wind was from the northeast. The pleasure was generally felt because this wind is the best for our voyage. However, our Captain Noss said that he was not sure how long it would continue. He was right, because on

17 July - it swung to the west again and the wind during the evening was mixed with rain, so strong that even our captain conceded later that within a half hour it was nearly a full storm. Toward morning it eased somewhat. It must have been almost four o'clock in the afternoon when we met a French three-masted merchant ship. The admiral ordered it to give an account of itself by means of a cannon shot, and it immediately lowered all sails and the admiral spoke with it as he sailed closely past it. We had a very sad and restless night, one disturbance after the other and no one was able to get any sleep. The wind blew with the same strength the next day but with the difference that it came from the northwest and it was no longer rainy.

18 July - Today, because of the still constant motion of the ship, nothing could be cooked. Until six o'clock the ocean was exceptionally rough. It appeared no different than when a person looked up at the Harz Mountains. The waves beat vigorously over the deck and a few times I was drenched by them. When such a mountainous wave beats against a ship, and as often happens three follow one after the other, the most dangerous is generally the second one. This morning Ahrend counted all twenty ships, toward evening however, he found not more than eighteen. At this time the ocean and the wind were more peaceful. Our captain promised us a night more restful than the previous one. Although I felt just as strong movements, which did not hold back the tiredness, I was in no condition to remain in bed.

The Journal of Lieutenant Friedrich Julius von Papet

19 July - This morning the wind came from the northwest by north. The wind was a bit weaker and the sea smoother. The horizon however, did not promise us the best weather. There were eighteen ships together, and I had the misfortune to see that of the two missing ones, the one on which my brother was, was included. At nine-thirty the admiral, by means of a cannon shot and using a flag, indicated that the ships were to assemble near him as he wished to speak to the commanders. Therefore every ship lowered a sloop and every ship's captain reported on board to the admiral. Upon their return, we learned that the admiral required an advisory report from each one as to how many sick there were, and how much water and provisions remained, and then ordered that issues of such on all the ships were to be made with the greatest care and economy. Furthermore, we were informed that the English fleet had defeated the provincial fleet and had shut their admiral and four ships in the harbor at New London. The admiral had also announced that if the winds continued contrary, he would seek to sail more to the south. While the captains were on board with the admiral, he signaled the second frigate with a cannon shot that it should go back in search of the two missing ships. The ships lay to for a good five hours at this time. The captains and the frigate returned without having seen the missing ships. It is not consoling that at nine o'clock this morning our captain had still seen the ship *Vriesland*, and assumed that during the change of course, which we made at that time, it had taken another course. Under certain circumstances that ship can sail further, since it sails well and can make use of more sails. Possibly it will arrive in Quebec before we do. At least it is my hope that it will not be long until I see and greet my dear brother. At five o'clock another turn was made, to the north, and once again we had very strong wind and rain from the west and could do nothing other than expect another restless night.

20 July - Our discontent increased. It was as rough as on the fifteenth, but with the difference that we were aware of the unpleasant movement at this time. I do not know how it happens, but ordinarily when we drink coffee or eat our noon meal, it is always the roughest. It is necessary to balance glasses, everything and still it seldom occurs without damage. The wind blew very hard the whole day from the west and the ocean continued to show us its well-known-to-us frightful mountains and valleys. At five-thirty we again turned toward the southwest. Still we could not count more than eighteen ships, to my great disappointment.

21 July - Throughout the night we received occasional very strong shudders, so that I got out of bed several times to check everything for myself. Our mate gave me the best assurance so that I then quickly fell asleep due to tiredness. The wind blew strongly from the northwest. Our cook complained constantly about the effort which was required in order to keep our food over the fire. At four o'clock in the afternoon the admiral again assembled the fleet and the ship *Margaretha Alida*, which had been released but still did not sail well, was again tied to and towed behind him. After eight o'clock, when it was completely dark and the wind arose, blowing very strongly from the southwest, the captain took in some of the uppermost sails. It is astonishing to watch the sailors clamber up the great mast, lay themselves over the spars, and tie the sails down. They hold on then only with their feet, standing on a line. I must admit above all that I can not understand how they can find men who will face such dangers. On the other hand, they are well-paid and money must be the greatest inducement for these people. While the sails were being taken in, and something of its speed was being lost, two nearby ships, which had been behind us, passed our ship. This made our captain very angry and he said they did it with hard work and only to incite fright and worry, but at the same time by such a maneuver they were as much at risk as we were. He took note of the ships and when the opportunity arises, will report it to the admiral.

22 July - During the morning we had very dark and foggy weather. It was possible to see only the admiral and seven ships in the distance. On orders from the admiral the entire fleet had to be constantly in the admiral's lee. If they watched this closely, then all could assemble near the admiral or scatter at any time. We lay to until ten o'clock when the sails were mostly raised and the rear most crosssail was so turned that it caught the wind and slowly drove the ship ahead. This is called drifting by the sailors, so that the ship furthest back had time to catch up. Finally, we counted all eighteen. The *Margaretha Alida*'s towline must have broken because we saw it was again free from the admiral. The fog continued intermittently until eight o'clock, a condition which made it necessary for every ship to exercise the greatest caution so as not to ram another. Toward nine o'clock the sky cleared. The first quarter moon shone so brightly that it was nearly possible to read by the light, and we saw a clear horizon such as we had not seen for a long time. The wind seemed to shift to the north.

23 July - We appeared to be threatened with rain this morning, but at nine o'clock it brightened and toward eleven o'clock, on a sign from the admiral, the ships again lay to so that he could assemble the fleet. Several ships sent boats to the admiral, apparently because he had ordered them to do so. We do not know why. The wind was northwest by north and we again went westward, and therefore made progress toward America. The beauty of the day sweetened the previously bad weather.

24 July - This morning the wind was from the southwest and at five-thirty we turned toward the northwest. At nine o'clock the wind began to blow very hard again and to promise rain for us. Above all, I must say that according to the expression of the old sailors, we found ourselves in a region where the weather changed every moment. About one-thirty the admiral assembled the ships which were at a very great distance.

25 July - This morning the wind blew hard from the west. The storm bells could again be heard and once again we sailed between mountains and valleys. At ten o'clock, upon a signal from the admiral, we turned toward the southwest. Toward evening the wind abated somewhat and we were at least promised a restful night.

26 July - During the night, at midnight, the wind swung to the northeast, the favorable wind, which we had not enjoyed during our entire trip. All the ships, even the admiral's, had the upper sails unfurled, which are the topmost ones. However, we sailed so well that even without those, we still sailed faster than most. The wind continued all day. It was unfortunate that the ship *Margaretha Alida* held up our advance. Toward evening the admiral lay to again to slow so that the above mentioned ship could catch up. The night was again clear and the ocean calm and nearly flat. The lanterns, which the admiral displayed on the braces of the masts every night, so that the ships would be aware of his course, could be seen clearly at all times.

27 July - The ship *Margaretha Alida* was still very far behind this morning and the ships still sailed slowly. The wind was very weak and still did not blow from the best direction. At eight o'clock it seemed to blow from the east-northeast and after a few hours it fell completely calm. However, therewith we had the most bright and beautiful, sunny day, that we had had while at sea. We believed, because the ocean was calm and smooth, that we would see fish enough. However, not the least one came into our view, except for muscles and ocean insects, a few of which we caught in a bucket.

28 July - The past night was so peaceful that I could not have slept more peacefully on land. The wind had become somewhat contrary for our voyage. It blew from the west-southwest, but was very soft and the sky very bright. At two-thirty we met a Spanish frigate of sixteen cannons and at six o'clock a large, three-masted French merchant ship. The admiral ordered each, with a cannon shot, to speak with him, and went on board each one. This evening was very beautiful. A glass of punch was quietly enjoyed and made us contented.

29 July - For the most part, all eighteen ships were together. The wind was southwest and we adhered rather closely to our course, although we progressed only slowly. The most unpleasant aspect was that today we received the report that three men on our ship were sick with scurvy. Because this illness is very contagious, they were at once isolated and all possible steps taken to curtail its spread. Taken together such steps were never better nor more certain than on land. We enjoyed a most pleasant evening. The full moon shone so beautifully that it filled our thoughts with the special thoughts about God and his omnipotence. A bright and beautiful sky also creates and restores an awakening in the soul and a peaceful feeling. I write this by moonlight and my soul is so filled with thankfulness to my gracious Creator .... so full of feeling .... but for which I can only offer thanks.

30 July - This night I had a severe headache, which was so bad that I could not remain in my bed. For our noon meal the previous day I had eaten dried cod, with which our ship's captain had made a sauce, and it is possible that I ate a bit too much. Therefore, I got up at twelve o'clock and went walking on deck for an hour, after which I felt better. In the future I will let this condition serve as a warning to be wary of all hard foods as there is no opportunity here to get the necessary exercise. During the night I noticed that we held our course very well with a southwest by south wind. At twelve-thirty the admiral fired a cannon shot to notify the rearmost ships to raise more sails so that they could catch up. Toward morning the progress slowed again and the wind was from the south-southwest. We saw nothing of the eclipse of the moon which was to occur between the 30th and 31st, because the sky was cloud-covered. Today it is five weeks since we left Portsmouth, and according to our captain's calculations we have still not sailed half way. A situation which in my view, considering the length of our voyage, causes many unpleasant thoughts. According to our captain's remarks, were our ship alone, we could certainly have advanced 100 miles further, but so far the other ships have definitely held us back. The distance which we have covered so far must nevertheless not be insignificant, because taking the time into consideration, it is now eight o'clock here while in Braunschweig it is already after ten o'clock.

31 July - During the night the wind suddenly swung to the north, having been previously in the southwest. The ship was thus turned about so that the blast awakened nearly everyone. The force of the wind necessitated the ship immediately reducing all the sails. The ship steered toward the east and during this time all the ships disappeared from our view, so that I also believed that we would not see the admiral again until we reached Quebec. However, this morning we were almost the first ship to regain him and a few hours later we counted fifteen ships. At eight o'clock the ship began to be driven to the east and therefore moved in the opposite direction from what we had to go in order to join the other three ships ahead of us. At ten o'clock we saw the other three at a distance. At a signal from the admiral the other frigate was sent to encourage them to sail more quickly. At one o'clock all eighteen were together and we sailed very well on our course with a north-northeast wind. During this time it was evident that our ship sailed better before the wind than all the ships in the fleet. Our ship and the admiral's, ours with twelve sails and the admiral's with fifteen, left all the ships behind and to our rear. At seven the admiral again began to reassemble the ships which in part had fallen behind.

1 August - After a restless night we had a calm sea this morning, and bright weather. We proceeded very slowly however, and the wind was nearly impossible to pinpoint because it blew first here, then there. Toward noon there was a complete calm. Many small boats sailed to the admiral from the ship on which Colonel Specht sailed. Many cannon shots were fired, apparently to celebrate this day, the birth of

The Journal of Lieutenant Friedrich Julius von Papet

our truest Lord of the Land, [Charles, Duke of Brunswick], whose graciousness we celebrated on our ship as fully as possible. There was certainly no one among us who did not then wish with all his heart to once again see him in the best of health and happiness.

A small English frigate answered every shot which came from the ships on which our troops were to be found. The entire fleet displayed the English flag until sundown. Toward evening, because of the beautiful day and the celebration, everyone was happy. However, I had such a discontent that this day was made unforgettable for another reason, also. The wind swung to the southwest.

2 August - Today we could also hold to our course rather well. At nine o'clock we saw an unbelievable number of fish, which our captain called terreneinen. They were of the shape and size of about a 24 pound carp. They swam together for a way, are edible, but taste somewhat oily. At five-thirty a boat came to our ship from the admiral, in which a sub-lieutenant came to deliver an order written in German to our major concerning the future signals. With this opportunity, our major requested satisfaction from the commodore because Boutler, who had charge of issuing rations, had over-stepped his authority by hitting one of our soldiers. That officer promised to report it to the admiral and an hour later the admiral sent his first lieutenant, who delivered Boulter to the complete jurisdiction of the major. The ship *Good George*,[16] on which Major von Ehrenkrook sailed, received two shots from the admiral because of several mistakes. Because the ship's captain was opposed to paying for them, the head of the steering rudder, which was there as a decoration, was taken off and delivered to the admiral's ship as security.

3 August - At eleven o'clock during the night our fleet met four large ships. The admiral had to fire six cannon shots and the second frigate two cannon shots to get them to come in to be examined. One ship appeared, from the construction, to be a frigate, but we did not know what kind of ship it was, because its flags were indiscernable in the darkness. The wind remained from the southwest today and after such a fine day, a fine night was to be hoped for. Toward evening there was a complete calm and we barely moved from the spot. After several days we learned that the four strange ships were English merchantmen, coming from the East Indies.

The Journal of Lieutenant Friedrich Julius von Papet

4 August - The calm held throughout the night and because of the heat I had very little sleep. I spent most of the time on deck. About eight o'clock a thick fog set in so that it was impossible to see twenty yards. At ten o'clock it cleared again and the eighteen ships were spread far apart. The heat and the calm continued and at evening a storm was to be seen in the distance. It dissolved into fog again and the wind seemed to want to come from the north.

5 August - Since twelve o'clock the wind has come from the east-southeast. We sailed rapidly and the sky was completely covered with thick clouds. For some time I have said that I hoped, as 5 August was my birthday, to celebrate in the St. Lawrence River. This was known by my comrades as well as our old mate. Both parties surprised me with their congratulations at a pleasant place and I can truly say that they did everything to make this a happy day for me. According to our captain we are still 200 miles from the St. Lawrence River, but if the wind remains as it is, by all indications we will soon see solid land.

6 August - The wind and weather remain favorable for our journey. Furthermore, our captain now says that in the region in which we now find ourselves, there should be no storms. We found it necessary, also, to have reason to praise and thank our gracious God most sincerely. The wind today was southeast by south; about noon, southwest by south. At two-thirty the admiral sailed away from the fleet toward a strange ship to the north. In less than two hours we lost sight of the admiral. Apparently the strange ship had no desire to be visited and therefore sought to escape the admiral's ship. Nevertheless, we continued on our course as before.

7 August - The wind was from the southwest this morning. The admiral had returned at nine o'clock. At the same time a boat went from our ship with the English commissary Fongles, who was responsible for the rations on our ship, to the agent Reckin, in order to report to him that many of his rations had spoiled. At nine-thirty the same returned with the news that the agent, during the first calm weather, wished to inspect the spoiled rations, a sign that the Englander took this very serious. On the ship where Mr. Reckin was, they had had two deaths as the result of scurvy. At ten o'clock the admiral again slowed because the *Margaretha Alida* had fallen behind again and was in no condition to keep up with us. At two-thirty a strange ship came into sight, which was sailing about four miles off to

The Journal of Lieutenant Friedrich Julius von Papet

our right. The admiral ordered the second frigate, by means of a cannon shot, to sail toward the other ship. It therefore left the fleet and sailed toward that ship. All of us doubted however, that it could bring it back because it did not sail well. It returned again in a few hours without having overtaken the other ship. At this time our captain told us that every ship was careful not to run into a fleet, as by so doing, it would initially be delayed on its course and also, in the chain of events, men whom they had on board would often be pressed [into naval service].

8 August - The splendor of this morning caused me to rise very early and to drink my tea on deck. The wind was southwest by south and therefore very favorable for our course. Seven ships were far behind. Therefore the admiral lay to at eight o'clock. Both frigates sailed away to the left of the fleet at eleven o'clock, apparently because they had seen more strange ships. The admiral gave a signal for the fleet to stay on its course. Nevertheless, a light English frigate, on which was the agent Reckin, followed the admiral. The fleet remained therefore alone, without those who could lead it. Our captain was not pleased with such a prospect. He assumed the Englishmen feared, because we were near the coast of America, more than they wished us to know. Because we assumed we were most likely off the Grand Bank of Newfoundland, the captain prepared the lead for taking soundings. At seven o'clock the captain had the lead cast and found no bottom at 105 fathoms. (A fathom is figured to be six feet.)

9 August - The wind was still from south to southwest. The admiral and the other ships, which had sailed away with him yesterday, were back with us this morning. It was very hot and the air very sultry. At eleven o'clock there was a wind calm and a great many storm clouds gathered on the horizon. Abut three o'clock they dispersed and on the other hand, the wind swung to the west-southwest and was very contrary to our course. Today I heard a very special expression from our mate. In our cabin, just above the door, a compass hangs on the overhead according to which we can determine our course and whether it is good or not. Because I keep a close watch on it and fully understand how it works, I saw that the ship suddenly departed from its course. I went out and asked the reason for this so sudden change, whereupon the mate told me he had "caught an owl". After some specific questioning, I learned that the sailors, when they sail by the wind, must be very careful that the wind does not fill the sail from ahead. Should that happen the ship immediately starts to turn and the "owl" is then caught. As laughable as this expression is, that is how dangerous it can become for a ship when it is surrounded by ships and has insufficient room in which to turn because it takes some time before it can return to its desired course. At nine o'clock the sky became brighter, but almost no wind was noticeable.

10 August - This morning the wind was just like yesterday, from the west-southwest, but it was also very weak and we expected considerable heat today. At eight o'clock the admiral began to roundup and assemble the fleet. Many ships which were too far ahead, including ours, had to fall back closer to the admiral's ship.

11 August - Still the same wind, but it blew somewhat harder and then became very blustery. The ships were widely scattered but all eighteen still together. At eleven o'clock we again sailed between mountains and valleys. After half an hour the wind suddenly swung to the northeast and blew so strong that had our captain not been on deck, and had the sails immediately lowered from the middle mast, we certainly would have lost our jack and middle mast. Both bent like the bow of a fiddle when the wind struck. The sails were then shortened and it began to rain very hard. At one o'clock the wind shifted to the west and the weather again cleared. Today our ship was in the lead and as the other ships approached closer to us, we saw that the English ship *British Queen* had lost its middle mast in yesterday's storm. Toward four o'clock it again rained hard. At ten-thirty we had the greatest scare. The wind suddenly shifted to the north so that all the ships were tossed about. Three ships were close to the admiral, which caused the admiral's ship to run against the ship called *Three Friends* with its bowsprit, and both ships were in danger of destroying one another. In the darkness of the night the cry was heard, "Holy Jesus, help us!" Shortly after that outcry, a frightful cracking, so that it was easy to think that with this shout in the night, that our comrades, whom we were unable to help, must be given up as lost. Our ship's officers are always attentive during the night to insure that the ship is clear of the others so that it can turn about completely and without danger. Our captain at once steered away to the east, from our course, so that we became completely separated from the fleet.

Shortly after this sad event, the admiral fired four cannon shots as a signal that we should continue on the course we had now taken.

12 August - Toward three-thirty, as day was beginning to break, we began our return course toward the admiral, whereupon we became aware of the damage which the ships had suffered. The ship called *Three Friends* was missing the mizzenmast and the upper portion of the gallery on the port side, and the admiral, the blind yard on the bowsprit. A boat went from the admiral to the other, the damaged ship, and remained there a long time before it raised a few sails. Because the admiral would not abandon such a ship, we believed he would do everything possible to keep the eighteen ships together. The wind was from the north-northwest and all the ships managed to have repaired the damage to the ship *Three Friends* by ten o'clock. If men were missing therefrom, during the night, we are still unaware. At two o'clock the wind settled in the north-northeast and we proceeded rapidly. At five-forty-five the second frigate fired a cannon shot for the rearmost ships to raise more sails at once.

13 August - This morning we learned that we had made good progress. The wind was from the north-northwest, all the ships, with the exception of a small two-masted English ship, were together. The latter was rather far behind and therefore we had to take in our sails. At eleven o'clock the wind shifted to the north and we proceeded a bit slower. Toward six o'clock it changed to the northeast and was more favorable. At that time our captain had the lead cast. However, no bottom was found, even at 105 fathoms. The ship *Three Friends* again was sailing with all sails and we could see by the repairs that it had been damaged on the port side of the cabin and the stern area. At six-thirty the admiral positioned his ship on the left side and lowered a boat, which went to the ship *Three Friends*, apparently to pick up the work crew which had been put on board, and to return them aboard his ship.

14 August - At midnight the wind died down and was very weak so that we made little headway. At ten o'clock the wind shifted to the southeast and the ship sailed a bit faster. At twelve o'clock the admiral again brought the fleet together. At four o'clock it rained and that continued throughout the night. At ten-thirty in the evening many fish were caught from on board our ship, which during the darkness, as we sailed, left such a bright streak of light behind, that it appeared as if sparks flew about in the ocean.

15 August - This morning the wind was from the northeast and blowing very strong. The sea was very rough. The bell could again be heard and when the lead was cast, no bottom was found. The ship sailed with only two sails and still went so fast that it frequently went six miles in four hours. We learned today, for the first time, the difference of how little one feels from the waves when sailing with the wind. As well and as rapidly as the ship sailed today, we had not experienced before. At three-thirty we saw a strange two-masted ship to our left. The admiral signaled an order that the ship *Three Friends* was to sail toward it. The *Three Friends* sailed from the fleet toward the other ship at once, and the second frigate, sailing at the rear of the fleet, also followed. The wind continued favorable this evening. Toward six o'clock we sailed with fewer sails to allow the two departed ships to catch up with us again. It was very cold this evening so that a fur would have felt very good. The feeling in the air and the sunset did not foretell the best for our troops.

16 August - It was a better day than any of us would have expected. At seven o'clock the admiral gave a signal that he had found bottom. This was indicated by raising a red flag, and when he saw that the ships were alerted, by raising their transport flags, reraised and lowered his flag according to the number of fathoms of depth he had found. He did this five times, with each time figured at six fathoms, and therefore he had thirty fathoms. Our captain also cast the lead and found thirty fathoms. Therefore we were on the Grand Bank of Newfoundland. The bottom consisted of white sand mixed with black pebbles. At eight o'clock we tried our luck at fishing. It was not long until we caught three cable jaws of about ten, eleven, and twelve pounds. They were caught using a piece of goose meat [as bait], which our major had had killed. When the fishing is to take place, the ship must lie perfectly still. After half an hour we had to set sail again and therefore fishing came to an end. Toward evening when we were to draw together, we thought of doing more fishing, so our captain had six good hooks made. The wind was east-northeast and we were sailing well. The cable jaws tasted very good to us, and I can safely say, that I ate a most delicious fish. We also saw a few of the large caselots and grampus, which were as big as our entire ship and which spouted a great stream of water into the air above them. The fishing for cable jaws was unsuccessful this evening. The ship sailed too swiftly.

17 August - A very foggy morning so that almost all the ships rang out the field march by ringing [their bells] and the admiral fired a cannon shot every half hour. At nine o'clock the weather cleared and we encountered an English schooner engaged in fishing. It was ordered to speak by a cannon shot fired by agent Reckin, as he was in the van at that time. Shortly thereafter we learned that this fishing boat had provided the news that the English General [William] Howe had restored the province of New York completely to its duty and that in Canada several skirmishes had occurred resulting in many provincials being captured. The wind was southwest by south, still quite good for our voyage, but it was also very cold and our fishing for cable jaws was also unsuccessful this morning. This evening a heavy fog set in making it impossible to recognize any other ship. Therefore the admiral fired three cannon shots as a signal that the ships should lay to. At seven-thirty it cleared off again and our ship was at a distance from the fleet. Within an hour, however, we had rejoined after raising all the ship's sails. As we were not far from land, having fog about us is not good. It is supposedly very frequent in this region at the present time of the year.

18 August - Toward twelve o'clock at night, the wind blew hard from the southwest. The sails were shortened and on our ship everything was unpleasant. About one o'clock a heavy rain began and it continued until six o'clock this morning, when the wind swung to the northwest and was directly contrary again. A thick fog moved in again at seven o'clock. We lowered the sails and drifted. Our captain cast the lead and found bottom at seventy fathoms, a sign that we had passed the Grand Bank. At eleven o'clock it again cleared and we then saw that the entire fleet had sailed past us and we were the last ship. At two o'clock we could clearly distinguish Cape Race on Newfoundland. We then sailed with the northwest wind directly toward the bay which Cape Race and Cape Pine enclose, so that it seemed as if the admiral had the intention to lay at anchor with the fleet at that place. At seven o'clock we turned toward the west and again sailed to the southwest. The admiral signaled with three lanterns in the form of a pyramid to order the ships to assemble near him

The Journal of Lieutenant Friedrich Julius von Papet

because he intended to take another course with this wind. Immediately after this signal the wind became calm and because the ships, as a result of the signal, were very close to one another, the ship *Three Friends* again had the shock of colliding with a two-masted English ship. Our ship nearly had the same fate, also, because during a calm, care and work are necessary. It is almost necessary to give the ship over to chance. God had looked out for us this time because when the danger was greatest, a bit of air entered the sail and freed us from the danger. I knew nothing and heard nothing about this until morning, because during that time I had slept rather well. At twelve o'clock the wind swung and remained from the northwest.

19 August - This morning it was still the same. The ships were widely scattered. At one o'clock we turned toward the northeast and made as little headway as previously. These turns were made three times during the afternoon. Finally, at nine o'clock the wind shifted to the northeast, to our greatest benefit. The admiral fired a cannon shot to alert the ships to raise more sails and to continue on the correct course with this favorable wind.

20 August - The wind was from the north this morning and therefore still usable. At eleven o'clock it shifted to the northwest. At two o'clock we turned toward the north toward Placentia Bay. During the previous night we had advanced so well with the favorable wind that we were beyond Cape Pine. Toward four o'clock we caught sight of Marie Island and its cliffs. And at seven o'clock we turned from the land again and sailed to the south-southwest. God grant that this tacking may soon come to an end, because many of our troops have numerous symptoms of scurvy. During the night, at twelve o'clock, we again turned to the north. At three o'clock in the afternoon the ship *Helgegonde* [*Christiana*] fired two cannon shots as a signal it wished to speak to the admiral, who during the course of the evening lay to near that ship. Next morning we learned from Major von Barner that Captain Thomae, aboard that ship, had been very sick for four weeks and had a relapse from an accident which he already suffered in Wolfenbuettel. However, it now certainly appeared that he had requested the admiral's doctor.

19 August [Obviously this should be 21 August, although the person who page numbered the manuscript also repeated page numbers 80 and 81.] - This morning, as we had wished, the wind came from the northeast and we could again follow our desired course. The wind remained alternately from the northeast and southeast today, but it was weak and we passed Marie Island and saw most of the coast of Placentia Bay. It was full of cliffs and hills and of the latter there were a few on which only bushes were standing. At four o'clock we were observed by an English frigate of 30 to 36 cannons, which was apparently cruising in the local area to check on the fishing. It sent a boat to our commander and by all indications must have had considerable news to impart.

22 August - This morning the wind blew from the south, but very weakly and to our right we saw many rocks sticking out of the water. The land, which we had seen yesterday evening, could no longer be seen, a sign that even with the slow sailing, we had still made some headway. Toward noon, with a southwest wind, it was very foggy. We sailed very close to the coast of Placentia Bay, where we saw a great many fishing boats lying. Our captain displayed an English flag to try to determine if any fish could be bought from them. Some of them tried to approach us, but it was not possible because of the admiral and because of the fog. At seven o'clock the fog was so thick that the bells had to be rung on all the ships, drums beaten, and a shout raised. Our captain was very attentive due to the night and the nearness of land. Toward eleven o'clock, during the darkest night, it showed us how many reasons there were for that. We received from the south, from the solid ground, from America, such a severe storm as I have never experienced in Europe. A more frightful, frightening night I have never experienced at sea. The danger which a person faces during a thunderstorm, of being struck or being knocked down, is thereby more than doubled if the person is sailing in a squadron. It was so dark that no land could be seen and the howling of the wind and rain made it impossible to carry on a conversation. Ships sailed to both our left and our right and these could not be recognized except when lightning flashed. Thunder and lightning at sea are far more frightening than on land. The lightning is seen double, first in the sky and then also in the water. Our ship, by the grace of God, suffered not the least damage, although the lightning ran across the whole deck, and our captain and the entire crew earned our highest praise. In a night as dark as this one was, they did almost everything that could be done. It was eleven o'clock at night when I arose to go on deck to

observe the strength of the storm. There was constant lightning and it could be clearly seen that this storm was weakening. Therefore the captain told me that I could lie down in peace and without any worry. I did so and slept until one-thirty when in response to the captain's commands and all the preparations for a storm caused me to go on deck again. The approaching storm could be seen in the distance. Lightning and the howling of the wind were frightful to see and hear. All sails were securely tied, even the lowest great tack on the middle mast. It is noteworthy that ordinarily the sailors can foretell a storm with thunder and lightning by means of a light which generally appears at the tip of the mainmast. Because of that, in former times, this was believed to be the appearance of a guardian angel; now however, it has been learned that such light comes from the heavy pitch which is on the lines and ropes and even on the tip generating electricity. This light was also visible today and the captain and chief mate assured us this morning, on their word of honor, to have seen it and to have made their preparations accordingly.

23 August - This morning our troops saw nineteen ships together. Please God, let it be the *Vriesland*, which has caused me much concern. We saw one ship which had lost its forward-most sail and a portion of the jack spar. Toward eight o'clock it again became foggy and the admiral reported his location each hour with a cannon shot. It cleared again at eleven o'clock. During the afternoon, off to the right, we saw the Peters Islands [St.Pierre and the Miquelons], and were therefore beyond Cape May and sailing with a good wind so that we should reach Cape Ray by tomorrow and enter the Gulf of St. Lawrence. At five o'clock we were again in the midst of fog, which is always to be expected in this region when a southeast and west wind alternately blow. At seven o'clock it cleared and the wind was from the southwest.

24 August - The past night was quite peaceful. Because of the contrary wind two turns were made. This morning the wind was west-northwest and not really useful for our voyage. At three o'clock we caught sight of Fortune Bay. It was at a distance of five miles and looked much like the Harz Mountains in Germany, but consists primarily of many valleys and bare hills. At five-thirty the admiral assembled the fleet because three ships had fallen too far behind during the night. Today we had rain and good weather alternately, but made little headway and as it grew dark, the sky became overcast with thickening rain clouds.

25 August - We continued to sail with a weak west wind, along the coast of Fortune Bay today. At three o'clock we turned toward the southwest by south, away from the coast in order to gain the depth so that with a later turn toward the north we would be able to enter the channel of the Gulf of St. Lawrence. Toward six o'clock the admiral began to drift with the ships again, and several times a boat went back and forth to the ship *Helgegonde [Christiana]*.

26 August - We have not yet been able to pass Fortune Bay because of the contrary winds. This morning we were at the place where we had been yesterday evening. We make little headway with the tacking because the wind comes just from the direction that we wish to go. The wind was from the northwest. Ordinarily it is difficult to enter the channel with favorable winds. There have been cases in which it was necessary to tack at the entrance for seven weeks or even longer. Because of our increasing number of sick, this caused us much concern and sorrow. Praise the Lord! Toward evening our prayers were answered. The wind shifted to the northeast at seven o'clock and the entire fleet, which had been assembled by the admiral at six o'clock, sought to use this good wind as long as possible.

27 August - During the night the wind shifted to the east and was even better for us. This morning we saw that we had passed Cape Ray and Cap Angiulle and therefore had entered the Gulf of St. Lawrence. At nine o'clock we already saw Brion Island; at five o'clock in the afternoon we could see Brion Island clearly. The good wind advanced us five and one-half miles every five hours. At seven o'clock we passed close by that island. It could more correctly be called a rock rather than an island. I believe that the largest of them, because there were at least four, was not a German mile [about six English miles] in circumference. We passed it at a distance of half of a quarter hour [about one-third of an English mile][17].

28 August - The east wind continued favorable for our journey. As at this time of year the Gulf is generally covered by a persistent fog, we can not thank providence adequately for providing such good wind and few storms during our fortunate entry. This morning we had the displeasure of seeing that three ships were missing. The admiral sent the second frigate to look for them. Even though we could assume they had suffered no damage, still their absence definitely held up our good progress. At three o'clock we saw the coast of America on our left, as well as the islands lying before it. Our captain believed it to be Cape Gaspe. At five o'clock, without waiting longer for the ships which remained behind, all possible sails were set on all the ships in order to sail past this cape during the daytime. However, the wind weakened so much toward evening that on

29 August - it was necessary this morning to tack because the wind had become contrary, from the northwest. The second frigate with the three ships was with us today and we counted nineteen with one strange ship still unrecognized. At five o'clock the wind came from the southeast again and we made some headway. The weather was incomparable and the sea smooth.

30 August - This night we not only passed the previously mentioned cape but also Cape Roussiere. Because of the northwest wind we again had to tack close to land. The weather was like yesterday, beautiful and hot. About nine o'clock the wind shifted to the south and we made a little headway. The present and actual coast of America or Nova Scotia was far better and more fruitful to see than that of Newfoundland. Today we learned that the nineteenth ship in our fleet was the ship *George and Molly*, missing since 17 July. Toward evening, about six o'clock, the admiral assembled the fleet.

31 August - We continued to tack because the west wind still blew hard. We made four course changes and we soon neared the coast of Cape Levesque; soon we turned away from it again, and it continued in this manner, to and fro, without much further progress. The weather was as in Germany, but already a bit cold.

The Journal of Lieutenant Friedrich Julius von Papet
In the St. Lawrence River

1 September - The wind blew constantly during the night from the west. Toward six o'clock we again turned toward the land which we had already had in view yesterday, and about ten o'clock it blew somewhat weaker. Please God, may it soon shift to our advantage because some of our sick are so bad off that one man from our company has already requested the last rites. Toward four o'clock our tacking took us away from the solid ground of America, toward the coast of the northern part of Anticosti Island. At seven o'clock the wind swung to the north and to our favor. Although our ship had to sail close to the wind with the wind, nevertheless it brought us directly into the St. Lawrence River.

2 September - We could clearly see by the hills, which were to our left and right, that we were finally in the St. Lawrence River. This morning the wind shifted to the northwest and we began to tack once again. At eight o'clock we came to a place where the difference between the river and the sea water were clearly distinguishable. The contrary wind persisted all day and throughout the night. We saw on

3 September - this morning that we were still at the same place which we had seen yesterday. Toward evening it became calm and we could anticipate that there would be a wind change.

4 September - With a fresh east wind we sailed twenty miles today, but it rained hard and toward three o'clock became so foggy that we remained at anchor for the first time in ten weeks, off Nova Scotia. According to our captain we did not have the best place in which to anchor. At flood tide there was seven fathoms of depth and at ebb tide, only three and one-half. We were only a musket shot from the shore of the coast which was overgrown with an impenetrable growth of trees and low shrubbery. It is surprising that here in America good clear weather can be expected with the west winds. That is just the opposite from what it is in Europe.

5 September - The anchor was raised at seven o'clock, upon a cannon shot being fired by the admiral, and at eight o'clock we set sail with a weak east wind and clear weather. At eleven o'clock the wind became calm and the squadron made no forward progress. From here to Quebec it is reportedly only 45 miles, but also the most dangerous [miles]. Toward evening, at a mile from the previous position and in

The Journal of Lieutenant Friedrich Julius von Papet

ten fathoms of water off the mentioned coast, the anchor was dropped. The sky was blanketed with storm clouds which mostly moved away and from appearances, we can anticipate a restful night. At nine o'clock the northern lights were more brilliant than I have ever seen; such are seen here almost every evening, as the further north a person travels, the stronger and more frequent the northern lights become. Several ships had put crews ashore in small boats. They often fired shots and made a great fire. The admiral fired several cannon shots to let them know that it was necessary to return aboard ship.

6 September - This morning a thick fog set in and the wind came from the direction which we wished to sail. It was southwest. Both remained that way and we can remain here a long time. Nine ships, which had carried our first division to Quebec, passed our squadron at four o'clock. We gave letters for Europe to one of those ships. From those ships we heard the news that two of our regiments lay at Quebec and the others had occupied Montreal. To my great pleasure and comfort I also learned that thirteen days previously a large Dutch ship with German troops had arrived, which it was not necessary for them to name. It most certainly could be none other than that on which my brother was. Today we had the first death aboard our ship. He was a member of the Leib Company and died of a burning fever illness, which he had partially brought on board the ship. According to maritime practice, he had to be kept for one hour in his berth and then he was brought on deck, sown tightly in a hammock, and because we lay at anchor and were close to the shore, on

7 September - during the morning, taken on land by an officer and a detachment of men and buried in a very proper place. Before his death, this had been his only wish and the satisfaction and pleasure of all our soldiers concerning this, can not be overstated. The entire coast is overgrown with a nearly impenetrable pine and fir forest. There are also linden and birch trees which are no different than those in Europe. The soil must be very rich because the grass and other weeds, such as reeds and wild plants, grow very tall. Deer tracks were seen frequently. This moved our major, as we remained lying at anchor due to the wind calm, to go ashore on this coast. Not two hours later however, the admiral gave the signal to set sail as the wind became favorable for us and from the southeast. Within an hour our boat was back on the ship and we immediately set sail. Our major brought various plants with him, all of which were fully similar to those in Europe, and he no longer had misgivings that he had not known previously that such excellent water was to be had on this coast, from which we could have profited and been refreshed. The good wind did not last long and at ten o'clock a complete calm returned. At eleven o'clock the admiral gave the signal to anchor. However, as soon as the anchor was lowered, we discovered that the place where we had drifted was too far from the fleet and the anchorage there would not hold the anchor. It required a great amount of effort to raise the anchor and because the shouting and commotion on board had roused me from sleep, I arose and personally gave a hand in order to make my contribution. Three hours passed before the anchor was again lowered, and that had barely happened when I received the unpleasant report that our company had suffered another death. Because of the distance from land, the appearance of the weather, and because our captain had to make six course changes in order to find a place to anchor, this dead individual was lowered into the sea at three-thirty at night in my presence, on orders of our commander.

8 September - Toward four o'clock our captain finally found the place where he lowered the anchor at a depth of fifteen fathoms. We remained at anchor the entire day due to contrary wind and had advanced about two miles from the previous anchoring place. Today we had numerous visits from the ships *Ostriut* and *Bonifacius*.

9 September - At seven o'clock the admiral gave the signal to raise the anchor and we began to tack with a southwest wind. Toward evening we noted that in that manner we had advanced nearly five miles, but had the unpleasantness that the admiral's ship was nowhere to be seen. Our captain allowed the ship to drift all night and toward morning, on

10 September - we saw the fleet in the distance. Several ships, including the second frigate, had lain at anchor on the left bank of the coast. After tacking back and forth we finally advanced far enough so that at ten o'clock we were able to anchor where the water had a depth of thirteen fathoms, a half mile from Nova Scotia and not far from Burnabe Island. During the time when France had the sole occupation of Canada they generally took the route along the north shore and this is to be noted on most sea charts. The English have discovered the present route the most comfortable because on this last one, conditions generally allow an anchor ground to be found. On the other hand, there are few such locations along the north shore. Because of the frequent calms and contrary winds it is necessary to be ready to anchor at all times or to lose due to the ebb tide what has been gained with a good wind and the flood tide. From the *Bonifacius* we learned that the admiral had sent a pilot to it and several other ships. Therefore, our captain lowered his boat in order to see if along the present coast he could get a pilot. I entered the boat and we traveled to the most pleasant and most eye-catching house. The boat landed at a place where there were nothing but shoals sticking out of the water and which necessitated the greatest care in approaching the shore. Nature seemed to have insured quite exceptionally through this wall, that the flow of water would not wash away the shore, because these cliffs stretched along the bank and were in layers at this place. The colony, which was here, consisted of Frenchmen who called themselves forgotten ones and all were properly polite people. We found wheat and grain fields standing already for harvest and almost all garden vegetables which we have in Germany. The women were very nicely dressed and everything in their homes was neatly maintained. It was our intention to buy some livestock, but everyone of the colonists had lost most of their stock during the previous winter. As the wind swung to the east, our captain hurried to return aboard his ship as no meat could be obtained here. We settled for some potatoes and cabbage with which we could provide nourishment for our sick. At five o'clock we again set sail after the captains of all the Dutch ships had discussed together allowing Captain Wilson of *Bonifacius* leading them until they could halt and obtained pilots for themselves, who, according to the inhabitants, were all on Bic Island, where an English frigate lay for our protection. Toward evening it became calm again and all the Dutch ships also anchored.

11 September - This morning the wind mixed with rain blew very hard from the south. At eleven o'clock it weakened and we sought to make some advance by tacking. At five o'clock the ebb tide set in and as no advance was to be made by tacking, we anchored in fourteen fathoms of water. On our charts we could see that our ship and two others had advanced two miles. On the other hand, two ships had fallen far behind. I have seen clearly today that on three ships three different winds blew. Some to a disadvantage, some to an advantage. Today we had our third death. He was from Major von Luecke's Company and was also buried at sea during the night.

12 September - The wind today remained from the west just like yesterday evening and we remained at anchor not far from the island. At ten o'clock the anchor was raised and we tacked. At four o'clock we anchored again, and at five o'clock we received a pilot from a naval officer from the guard frigate which had its post near Bic Island. The pilot was born at Quebec and had already taken a ship from our first division to Quebec. At the same time the naval officer delivered the order to go under sail at ten o'clock tonight with the flood tide. This was done and the wind was quite favorable. However, this morning

13 September - it was so light and finally so contrary that with the ebb tide we lost the progress we had made during the last three days, and at four o'clock lay at anchor. Of all the ships, we were the last one. It rained nearly all day and was especially cold. Today, to our sorrow, we had our fourth death. He was a member of the Major's Company.

14 September - About eight o'clock, as the wind was rather favorable, the anchor was raised and we passed through the entire channel which separated Bic Island and the firm land of Nova Scotia, partly due to the good wind, partly due to the flood tide. At daylight we saw the frigate of 24 cannons, which guards the channel and provides cover for us. We advanced so far today that we again joined up with nine ships. At four o'clock, with the start of the ebb tide, we again lay at anchor. About five o'clock our boat went to the mainland in order to make some purchases because the pilot said there were two occupied homes there. At seven o'clock the boat returned. It brought back potatoes, four smoked salmon (a sort of lachs), six head of cabbage, some peas, and what was best, beautiful fresh water. There were six houses there, all wretched huts, two of which were occupied by Indians, who, in part, looked very old and dirty. In the others lived French people who conducted an ordinary business. From the huts all kinds of necessities can be purchased, but in part, most of the merchandise had been taken by the other ships.

15 September - At three o'clock in the night we raised the anchor and went under sail with a fresh east wind. About five o'clock it began to rain very hard and at eight o'clock it was again so foggy that it was

The Journal of Lieutenant Friedrich Julius von Papet

difficult to see Basque Island, which we passed on our left. At eleven o'clock we passed Pomme Island and at eleven o'clock, Verte Island. Near the latter we had to pass one of the worst places, as there are not only many shoals in the area, but also the great stream Saquenay enters the St. Lawrence, which can only be passed with a good wind. Our ship swept past. From ten-thirty to twelve-thirty we had a full storm and at no time during our entire trip did we have stronger winds. At twelve o'clock we were already past the Isle of Cores. Our captain was initially prepared to drop anchor there because of the violent storm, but as the storm abated somewhat at twelve-thirty, we continued to sail and sought to reach the island of Coudres, which is still seven miles away, yet this evening. At one o'clock we saw the three little Belleice Islands off to our left and many shoals to our right. At two o'clock we could clearly see the south coast and the colonies established thereon. Stretching toward Quebec they were in the following order: 1) the colony of Kamouraska 2) la Riviere Ouelle 3) Ste. Anne 4) St. Roch 5) Jean Jean 6) L'Islet 7) le Cap 8) St. Aumont 9) Berthier 10) St. Vallier 11) St. Michel 12) Beaumont 13) Pointe Levis. At seven o'clock in the evening we lay at anchor for an hour at Coudres in sixteen fathoms of water. At several places along this coast, we saw residences and developments. Today we advanced 21 miles.

16 September - At five-thirty we set sail with a northwest wind. Within a half hour we passed the colony of Eboulements on the solid coastline and anchored in the narrow channel which is cut between the coast and Coudres Island, at eight o'clock, because of the ebb tide and the complete wind calm. Our boat immediately went to this inhabited island and brought back water, potatoes, four fresh turkeys, and fresh kohlrabi. All of the people were polite and sociable. Colony had been there for twenty years. There were also establishments there established in the spring. At two o'clock the frigate which had the responsibility for us, gave the signal to raise the anchor because of the flood tide, and within an hour, we passed the small place of le Pais, named St. Paul, which not only had a good situation, but was beautifully built. With a northwest wind we traveled about six miles by this afternoon and also anchored at six-thirty in sixteen fathoms of water. We could already see the Isle of Orleans.

The Journal of Lieutenant Friedrich Julius von Papet

17 September - We raised the anchor at five o'clock. We had to tack because of the contrary wind. This and the flood tide enabled us to go forward so that we passed the little islands of Bisle Grunde, les aux Roi, and le Dame, off to our left, and the Isle of Orleans lay just ahead of us. At ten o'clock we again anchored and so close to the mainland and the hills of Canada that we could almost have fired a pistol that far. At two o'clock we raised the anchor and then passed one of the most dangerous areas, where we had to pass close between two sandbanks lying before the Isle of Orleans and the smallest island of Rotts. Fifty feet too far to the left or right we could go aground. The ship *Helgegonde* [Christiana] did that because it steered too far to the left. However, with the flood tide it can float free. The depth of the channel changed moment to moment; four, five, four, and three fathoms deep. A shame that it was such foggy weather, because we sailed close by the island of Orleans, with the island to our right. It is beautifully developed and presents the most beautiful view in the world. There one sees in a very large plain the most beautiful and vivid surrounding fields and gardens. We saw three churches, the l'Eglise English Francois, St. Jean, and St. Laurentz, which were well-built even by European standards. At seven o'clock in the evening, as it was already getting dark and was foggy weather, a frightful situation again came about. A ship, the *Anne and Catherine*, which was sailing ahead of us, forgot to notify the following ships soon enough, nor did it hang out a lantern on the mizzenmast. Our ship was under full sails and nearly rammed the *Anne and Catherine*'s bow with our bowsprit. There was hardly the space of a hand's width between them as we passed by and our captain immediately let go the anchor. Although he could have sailed for another hour except for the incident with that ship.

18 September - The anchor was raised at five o'clock. It was still very foggy. We sailed with a weak wind and the flood tide, still between the coast of Nova Scotia and the Isle of Orleans on our way to Quebec, and past the parishes of St. Jean and St. Lorentz. On both sides the land was as nicely developed as one can find only occasionally in Europe. At ten o'clock we reached the end of the Isle of Orleans and then we saw Quebec and the waterfall of Montmorency. The first presented itself as exceptionally beautiful and from a distance looked nearly like Cleve on the Rhine, except that

Quebec is larger and the surrounding area is more beautifully built up. Above all, all of us had to concede that none of us had ever seen a more beautiful view. The waterfall fell 100 feet, straight down, and created a cloud of spray. We had to take our ship to the outermost part of the roadstead which the Isle of Orleans made for Quebec, because the start of the ebb tide prevented us from reaching Quebec. About five o'clock we raised the anchor again and sought, by tacking and with the flood tide, to enter the roadstead where the other ships lay together. At seven-thirty we attained this goal and anchored in nineteen fathoms of water.

19 September - This morning the ships which had been behind us, arrived. In the harbor we found in addition to our two frigates, the warship *Isis* of fifty cannons, [Captain Charles Douglas], and the *Tristan* of 28 cannons, [Captain Skeffington Lutwidge]. Captain Douglas, who had commanded in the harbor, had gone to Lake Champlain, for which reason Captain Jacobs, who led our division, assumed command. The ship *Vriesland* to my regret has not yet arrived at Quebec and we are beginning to worry. Concerning this it is positively reported that the ship *George and Molly* first noted it missing here in the harbor. It is also possible that it will arrive in a few days. This afternoon we were visited by the Quartermaster General Gerlach from Quebec. We learned from him that he had come directly from General [Sir Guy] Carleton in Montreal in order to lead us further along. In a few days we will go to Trois Rivieres on our ships and debark there. The first division arrived here already on 22 May. A great difference from our boring voyage.

Quebec, 1776

20 September -Today I went to Quebec, in part to shop for various necessities, in part sight-seeing. The governor of Canada, who usually has his office in Quebec, had already gone to Montreal with a corps [of the army]. He is very well liked in Canada, by the citizens of Quebec as by all the colonists, even the native savages are exceptionally well-satisfied with him. Our Dragoon Regiment lay at Quebec as did the Prince Friedrich Regiment and Lieutenant Colonel Baum was the commandant. Quebec lies on the high side of the mainland and as it is on a hill and is built about 100 yards up the slope, it creates an amphitheater appearance with its massive churches, cloisters, and houses, built of stone. A sort of citadel lies on the highest point. The neck of land is not much in evidence, although it provides a good field of fire for defending the harbor area of the city. On the land side the city is fortified, on the river side however, it is open. As the point of land of the city is built up from the banks of the river to the outer heights, it is divided into a lower and an upper city. It consists of several thousand large and small houses. All, even the smallest, houses are built with stone, have very strong firewalls, very large chimneys, very high but narrow windows with large glass panes, and all are covered with wooden shingles or boards. The churches and public buildings have the same roofing, which gives a yellow appearance when new, green when somewhat older, and black when very old. There is a danger of fire to most of the buildings as well as the need for repairs if damaged. All the houses look good externally, however, most are poorly built. The rooms are quite large and solid enough, but in reality made of large nailed-together boards, and very seldom covered with plaster. In one house, where I bought my wine, I saw the same covered over with beautiful wallpaper. Nevertheless, I am amazed to encounter very good paintings, among which even a Voltaire is to be seen. In the rooms there are large iron draught furnaces which generally are removed during the summer.

The cathedral church is large, but without much decoration, and has a wooden floor and a roof of the same. All the other churches are built in the same manner. The bishop in the city has the title of monsignor and his seat is in the cathedral church. On the high altar there is a large armchair under a canopy. The Jesuit college is to be converted to barracks. There are now only three [priests] from the order still here, who are to retain their positions until they die. The inhabitants of the city consist primarily of French, some English, and a few Germans. Luxurious dress and carriages are not to be seen here as the streets are narrow, very steep, and unpaved. Therefore such are not only difficult to travel, but also very dirty, and many two-wheeled chaises and small carts are to be seen in the city, and the small, compact horses hitched thereto trot up and down the hills with ease. Loads which are not too heavy are occasionally seen in carts to which large dogs are hitched, traveling from one place to another.

The Journal of Lieutenant Friedrich Julius von Papet

Of the necessary foodstuffs, meat, vegetables, wholesome fruit, and good wheat for bread, there is no shortage here. Trimidera and a French red wine are as expensive as can be imagined. The latter is supposedly not the healthiest and easily intoxicates; as to the first one, however, which is similar to the Malaga, I had to pay two guineas, two shillings prior to anchoring. Smoking tobacco is bad; coffee and sugar are expensive as in Europe. A sort of beer, called Epinette [spruce beer], is brewed by every inhabitant from the buds of a tree which is similar to the tamarind. It is more black than brown in color and sweetened prior to drinking, as a rule. This beer is considered the best cure for scurvy. Today all the sick from all the ships were taken on land to the large hospital Gitterinnen, a stone cloister, where we hear they will be well-cared-for.

21 September - On this day there was nothing noteworthy, except that the ship lay with two anchors because of the strong winds and that we received reports that the Dragoon Regiment is to move forward with us.

22 September - This morning we received orders to go under sail with the first good wind, but there is little sign of that. This afternoon we had visitors from Quebec, from the Prince Friedrich Regiment.

23 September - In compliance with the orders we would have set sail already today, but because of the contrary wind this was impossible and we remained here.

24 September - This morning we saw that after raising the anchor, the flood tide had carried us fifty yards closer to the city. At ten o'clock we advanced with the flood tide again and moved so far that we were able to anchor close to the castle. The Dragoon Regiment embarked in boats today and is also to go to the army.

25 September - Today we received the order that part of the troops were to debark here at Quebec. The von Barner Regiment began to do that today and immediately began a march on land to cantonment in Trois Rivieres. At the same time our company received the order to occupy the place of the still missing troops of the Specht Regiment.

26 September - The landing took place at seven-thirty in the morning and because our captain raised a flag on the jack mast, so many boats came from the other ships, that it took less than two hours until we were finished. On the shore at Quebec we found small carts

The Journal of Lieutenant Friedrich Julius von Papet

and a chaise, each of which was hitched to a horse, waiting for us. The first carried our and the company baggage and the latter was just for us officers. The company then marched through Quebec and through the St. John Gate leading to the parish of Ste. Foy, which lay at a distance of one hour. On this side the city is very well-fortified. Outside this gate there must have been a suburb, which was visible by the fire locations there. The area and the route along which we marched presented a splendid view. At eleven o'clock we arrived at Ste. Foy. At first the area was very disagreeable to our soldiers. The company received five houses. Our host was a polite individual and had three not entirely unpleasant daughters.

27 September - The march led to Pointe aux Trembles, which was six French miles from the former place. This was a very tiring march, not only because of the distance, but also because of the bad weather as it rained the whole day. We were carried across the Carouche River on a raft, first the company, then the baggage. Two carts could be taken at one time and then the chaise. Then we passed the parish of St. Jean and had to cross the channel, created by the ebb tide backing up in the St. Lawrence River, on our own, and we arrived that evening at six o'clock in quarters. The company had nine houses. Our host was not only very polite, but as far as one could see, well off. However, I have noticed that the more polite the people, the more pay they expect.

28 September - During the previous night I received orders from a non-commissioned officer who came from Quebec. He brought the joyful news that the ship *Vriesland* had arrived at Bic Island and that all the officers thereon were in good health. At eight o'clock we marched away and after a four hour march, we passed the parish of Eqireux and arrived at the river called Jacques Cartier, which flowed very fast and turbulently. We were transferred across in two small boats. This transfer took a full six hours because the baggage had to be unloaded from the carts and then reloaded on the other side. Half an hour later we entered quarters in the parish of Cape Sante. In our quarters we encountered a sick man and four small children, whose moaning and crying out granted us little sleep during the night. Still, I have never been in quarters where I had to put up with four little children. The company shared fifteen houses.

The Journal of Lieutenant Friedrich Julius von Papet

29 September - We departed at seven-thirty and marched to Deschambault, crossing the little river of Port Neuf, over which a small wooden bridge was laid. Not far from the St. Lawrence River, which was in view during nearly the entire march, lay a warship, which was apparently meant to protect the river. At twelve o'clock noon we entered quarters and ours, compared with the previous ones, were like a palace. We had a day of rest in this parish. All the parishes which we have passed lie along the St. Lawrence River, and those we have seen and where we have been quartered, those of Pointe aux Trembles and Deschambault, are the largest, being at least seven and one-half miles in length.

30 September - There was such stormy weather throughout the night that because of the howling of the wind, we could hardly get any sleep. Now we understood for the first time, how nice it was during such a storm, to be on land. The other four companies of our regiment, which were following us on foot, must have been very miserable yesterday, not only because it rained very hard yesterday evening, but because they were delayed for so long at the Jacques Cartier River also, as we had been, as we heard that those companies did not arrive at their night quarters until twelve o'clock at night.

October 1776

1 October - General march was beaten at seven-thirty. We then crossed two rivers, both of which were named Chevretier, and passed the small parish of Grondines. After we had marched fifteen miles [six lieue - a French lieue equals two and one-half English miles or four kilometers], we entered quarters in the parish of Ste. Anne. The further we go from Quebec, the more beautiful and fertile the land seems to be. I have never seen such beautiful, comfortable, and well-furnished quarters outside of Quebec, as I found in our quarters today.

2 October - At eight o'clock in the morning, after we received our carts, we departed. We had marched two hours when we arrived at the parish church, which was well-built. Just beyond the church we passed the Ste. Anne River, which is exceptionally large and wide. The baggage and the troops were taken across once again, in the same manner as at the Jacques Cartier River, except that it proceeded more quickly here because the boats were larger. From there we continued to the parish of Batiscan, which is also not very big and where we were again transferred in the previous manner across the river which flows nearby and has the same name. This one was larger than the previous one and therefore the transfer took two hours longer. At four o'clock in the afternoon we reached the third river, Champlain, which was nothing compared with the two others, and we were carried across on a raft. All three of these rivers emptied into the St. Lawrence River and the higher we go up the river, the more noticeably it narrows. Not far from the place where we made our last crossing, we entered quarters in the parish of Champlain. All the inhabitants are excellent marksmen. We bought six wild ducks from them for three shillings. There was a man at our quarters who had only one arm, having lost the right arm while hunting. Despite that, he brought two fat ducks which he had shot with only his left arm.

3 October - We marched away at eight o'clock. The wind, mixed with hail, began to blow very hard, so that we had to cover our faces.

Several hours later this wind changed to a steady, uninterrupted, heavy rain, and we had a difficult march. At three-thirty we arrived at the Genoux River, which formed three small islands where it flowed into the St. Lawrence River, and from which the nearby small city of Trois Rivieres gets its name. We were transferred across the river by the same slow process as happened at the previously mentioned one. It took so long that we only arrived at our night quarters in Trois Rivieres at six-thirty. The baggage arrived later because the limited facilities encountered meant that at the end there were no carts available, and our company was always the last one. Near this river, several savages had built their huts. I have personally looked into one for the first time and can honestly say that I have never seen a more miserable dwelling for a human being. These huts are made of poles set together at the top in a pyramid. Over the poles they lay the bark of birch trees, which are woven together, piece by piece, with strips of hide. In one of these huts lay two women, four small children, and several dogs. The women were removing insects from themselves, even looking under their breasts, and the children picked at entrails which were hanging in the hut. One such sight took away the desire to look into the other huts. God! How miserably these creatures live! -- In the summer they put these huts near the river; in the winter they go deeper into the forests with the huts. They live by hunting and fishing.

The Journal of Lieutenant Friedrich Julius von Papet

To accomplish the latter purpose, we saw them placing several boats in the river, which were also made of bark and so skillfully worked together and so light, that such a boat can be carried without effort by one person. Above all, these savages live like animals compared with us, whose residences are kept cleaner than those of the savages which I have found. Our troops are situated very badly in this small city, which consists of about 300 houses, because they are quartered in a house which is called a barracks here. The company which was in the lower level could have a fire. Ours was in the upper level and had as little heat as straw. Trois Rivieres is an open and terrible place, lying close to the St. Lawrence River, and I have not seen the least sign of defenses.

4 October - As it was difficult to bring the carts together, we could not march away until nine o'clock in the morning. The weather had cleared. After we had passed the small parish of Pointe du Lac and had marched fifteen miles, we arrived at our quarters in the parish of Machirte at three o'clock. This parish supposedly is one of the most vigorous and richest. This could be seen already by the very well-tended fields. It reportedly has nearly 300 inhabitants. Our company had only four houses and, considering the wealth of this parish, was quartered very badly.

5 October - We marched away at eight o'clock with beautiful weather. At eleven o'clock we passed a woods in which a great many large trees had been cut down and burned. They lay so intertwined that they looked very much like an abatis, and I understood later from the accounts by the inhabitants that in the previous year they had been used for that purpose against the provincials by the English. Toward noon it was very hot. The air in the woods and the swamps was therefore very foul and rotten. Several times I felt sick therein. At eleven-thirty we passed the parish of St. Antoine, and half an hour later we reached the small de Loup River, which we were transferred across on a very large raft. This crossing went more quickly than all the previous ones. Each time the raft carried a loaded cart and fifteen men from the company. At three o'clock we entered the parish of Maskinonge which a small river of the same name divided into two parts. Our quarters were on the far side and therefore we had once again to be carried across on a raft.

The Journal of Lieutenant Friedrich Julius von Papet

6 October - Today was a day of rest. At one o'clock all company chiefs had to report in person to Colonel Specht, whereupon it was decided that this winter the soldiers should have long overalls, mittens, and hooded capes made. This is how people protect themselves against the cold here, and because of a shortage of blue cloth, brown cloth will be used instead.

7 October - Because the carts arrived so late again today, we could not march on until ten-thirty. We have not had a worse road during our entire march. After we had marched for two hours we reached a woods, which was exactly like the woods in Europe, which are otherwise quite different. Next we marched along a large river called Chenailtre du Nord and on that route crossed two small rivers, which entered it, on rafts. About seven-thirty we reached the border of the parish of Berthier. Other times our company always was assigned the first houses and formed the left flank. Today this was different and we were placed in the middle, among Colonel Specht's Regiment and therefore had to march the length of the parish, until seven-thirty, before we arrived at our quarters. From what we hear, we are to be transported from here in boats coming from Sorel.

8 October - At eight o'clock we saw the boats arriving. One of those handling the boats reported to our and Captain von Plessen's Company that he had been sent with twelve boats by an English captain, to take the companies and their baggage to Sorel. However, because we had specific orders from the colonel to send all boats arriving here to his headquarters, we could not take them, and they had to double back. At twelve-thirty we finally received our boats, which we should have had at seven o'clock. In the meantime, between six and seven o'clock we heard heavy cannonading several times. Several days later we learned that a warship had saluted Commodore Douglas. The company received eleven boats, plus two for baggage. Our soldiers had to assist with the rowing. At three-thirty, after having proceeded for two hours on the water, we arrived at Sorel in rainy weather. We passed the St. Lawrence River where at least thirty three-masted ships lay, near Sorel. The baggage remained in the boats and all of it from all the companies was then loaded into four boats. Here the troops received bread for three days, and we received orders to march into quarters in the parish of St. Ours, which was seven and one-half miles from Sorel. The bad road, which can be imagined, and the continuous heavy rain made the march so difficult that even I found it nearly impossible to continue on. We had no carriages, nothing had been provided for us, and even if we had such, most of the time we would have had to proceed on foot. Then night set in and the rain steadily increased. We continued through a thick woods and we had to wade, up to our knees, in mud. Finally Colonel Specht passed us on his way from Sorel, and when he saw the impossible conditions through which the soldiers had to march on this dark and rainy night, he ordered us to take quarters in the first houses we would come to. We did that and received for our purpose, four small huts.

I and Ahrend found these unsatisfactory, and although he wanted to remain there, I convinced him to tell the host of those houses that he should take us, not far from his house, to a more spacious one. Therefore we set out. The road was so bad, that we soon regretted not having remained in our first quarters. It was not possible to see your hand before your face, and we were often in danger of sinking out of sight. Added to all that, the house he was taking us to was already occupied by Colonel Specht's Regiment. Therefore there was no other course of action, except that he take us on to the next one. A stick of wood, which he lit and which kept going out, took us directly back to one of the houses which was already occupied by our company. These were such poor people that they did not even have light nor [lamp] oil. In one room (which only had the name), among eight children, three cradles, and a broken stove, we made our straw [bed] with hay. A knapsack took the place of a pillow. I was so tired that I immediately fell asleep, as soon as I lay down. It must have been in the middle of my slumbers that I came too close to a cradle in which a large youth lay. That one began to pass his water out of the cradle and he nearly soaked me through and through. For my Ahrend things were even worse. Several children scrambled about on his body and not far from him deposited their bowel contents. Above all, it was a night that I will never, in my whole life, forget. The crying of the other children kept us from closing our eyes. We heartily wished for morning and on

9 October - at six o'clock Ahrend already had general march beaten and then at seven o'clock we marched. At nine o'clock we entered the parish of St. Ours, where we should have been yesterday evening. Colonel Specht personally welcomed us and had the foresight to bring a carriage for us and to send a cart for the soldiers' knapsacks. We marched from there to the parish of St. Denis, where we arrived in quarters at one o'clock. In this parish we met a detachment of eighty men from our first division. It consisted of men from our Grenadier Battalion and the Hesse-Hanau Regiment. They lay in the lower part of the parish, in quarters near the church, had a watch of one officer and twenty men, and seemed primarily here to control the frequently encountered disaffected.[18] This kind of occupation we had to assume for the upper part of the parish. True, we were alone in the best quarters. However, because all our baggage had been left behind in our four boats at Sorel, many of the most urgently required necessities were missing, which were necessary for eating as well as for dress. The latter was especially needed as today we still had many traces from yesterday's den of assassins.

10 October - Our baggage was still missing this morning. At eight o'clock Colonel Specht visited our quarters, with the intention to make arrangements [to replace] various items because of the shortage of baggage. I personally received the order also, upon his return from the English church of St. Denis, to be prepared to lead those boats on to Chambly. He returned at nine o'clock and I had to leave at once. One of the boats had arrived at Captain Plessen's quarters and the other three could be seen in the distance. In two hours they were all here. The company marched already at ten o'clock, and I had the most exact orders to first unload the meat for the company and then the officers' baggage (for each company two wagons) from eleven wagons. However, I received only seven wagons, and because three of them were needed for the meat, only four were available for the officers' baggage. With the rest of the baggage in the boats, I then started, and from that time was the commander of four boats. I ordered the other three to follow me. From the militia captain, who is to be found in each parish, I obtained two pilots for each boat, one of whom was to give directions and our soldiers had to row. In my boat, I also rowed. My boat went so swiftly up the Chambly River (because on that river the boats from Sorel were always rowed by us), that I caught up with my company at five o'clock at the parish of St. Charles, where it had to be transferred across. After marching two hours they entered quarters in the parish of Beloeil. As it was already the onset of night, I and my boats had to lay to as it is very dangerous to travel further on the Chambly River at night.

An hour and one-half later my other boats arrived and I quartered all the troops from the four boats in four houses, left a guard on each boat, and hope with daylight tomorrow to reach Chambly by evening, which is still six hours from Charles. We saw the parish of St. Denis today. Many inhabitants wished to go with us to the army in order to fight against the rebels. They were in their usual clothing which consists of a long, white, woolen waistcoat. They also carried a musket, as well as powder, horn, and balls. They were all handsome and determined individuals. They carried their baggage with them in small carts. The parish of Cariola provided forty men plus a captain, who led them and, as I later heard, the surrounding parishes provided the same number, or even more.

11 October - I sailed with my boats at five-thirty and reached the parish of Beloeil at eight-thirty. I acquired pilots there and it cost much difficulty. Instead of eight I got only four because all the people for the most part had been commandeered with their carts by the army and fifty of the young men had also gone to fight with the army. I reached the parish of Chambly at three o'clock. I allowed the boats, as much as possible, to sail to the quarters of the company commanders and departed at once in a coach along the road in order to report at the colonel's quarters. This took one and one-half hours. He was not in. He was visiting an English colonel, who commanded a detachment here at Fort Chambly, as a guest. It took me less than an hour to go there. En route I could see that there had been a camp here. I had to make a detour around a small lake made here by the Chambly River, on which was a fort built of stone. After making my report, I had to return the same way alone because the owner of the coach, as the result of the considerable jolting, developed a very strong color, and even lost the ability to speak. I left him behind at a house and drove away. The fort is of little consequence. Against an attack by savages, without cannons, it is probably strong enough, but certainly not against regular troops.

12 October - Today we had a day of rest. Tomorrow we will enter the camp at Fort Chambly. From all appearances, that will be the place I saw earlier. We have orders to be there at ten o'clock tomorrow and the baggage will be delivered to the lake and the fort by the same boats which I commanded. Colonel von Ehrenkrook moved into the lowest part of the parish of Chambly today with the other four companies of our regiment in order to establish the camp together with us tomorrow. For the time being our company will remain with Colonel Specht's Regiment. *Vriesland* debarked at Quebec on the sixth. My brother remained there with the sick while the rest are now lying at Trois Rivieres.

13 October - At daybreak the baggage was loaded onto the same boats which I had commanded and brought to Fort Chambly. We moved it into camp. On our left wing the fort stood before us, on the right hand a woods, and behind us, the small lake. The tents were set up in a different manner than was practiced by our company in Germany, where the two rows otherwise stood in a depth behind one another. They now stand along the length of the front. Today to my great joy, I received a letter from my dear brother from which, at least, I learned that his illness was nothing of consequence. Today I went on watch with the colors, at the age of nineteen, for the first time.

14 October - Today we received twice confirmed news that the rebels on Lake Champlain suffered a double loss. Previously they have always had a superiority in that against the approximately twenty frigates of their flotilla, we could only oppose them with small vessels. For the past week however, our side has fitted out a large swimming-battery and several frigates of thirty or more cannons. They have already captured a rebel frigate, shot two to pieces, and their great military adventurer, Colonel [Benedict] Arnold, had been captured.[19] This evening I went on picket duty with a captain, two officers, and fifty men.

15 October - This morning I received the news from a non-commissioned officer who had been sent to the Montreal alms hospital with four sick individuals, that the Senior Cashier Goedecke considered it necessary to discuss such and to buy various things. Therefore, would I try to go to Montreal the next day. This afternoon a report was received to the affect that the rebels had lost three frigates and had run six aground. The rest of their fleet has been closed into the Bay of Cumberland.

16 October - Ahrend and I traveled in a carriage to Montreal. It is about twelve and one-half miles from Chambly. The road and the region, which we passed through, was bad. Not far from Montreal, we had to allow ourselves to be transferred across. Montreal lies on a fertile island made by the St. Lawrence River. On the land side the city is partially fortified, but not at all on the river side. On the side from which we approached, we had to pass through a suburb before we reached the city proper. We found it to be occupied by an English detachment. The whole city consisted actually of two long but narrow, main streets. Other than that, the houses are built more beautifully and larger than those at Quebec, and the streets are not as dirty. But just to buy something, everything is more expensive than at Quebec. The least valuable coins known to men are the piaster and the Portuguese. They are seldom able to make change for those coins, and if it is necessary to buy something at less than those prices, the purchaser must have the necessary small coins with him.

It was my intention to buy a beaver skin fur, because the fur trade is actually centered here. However, in part everything had already been sold and the least thing that was still available was so expensive that I lost all desire to buy one. According to some accounts, German merchants supposedly have become rich through the fur trade and have made their fortune here, and even in an unallowed way have grown rich. Almost all items made of fur are brought to Montreal to be sold by the savages. All the savages who live in the vicinity of Montreal have grown rich as a result. When they marry among themselves, the dowry which they give to their daughters consists of the finest furs that they can provide. Therefore, the merchants who had a knowledge of the savage language have taken the daughters in marriage and thus obtained the furs. By so doing they receive gifts from the entire tribe. For a time they have stayed with their new wives, but then left them sitting alone and then repeated the process with another tribe, without terminating the first marriage. I have been told that this has been done by many individuals who were married in Germany, and who even had their wives with them. In this way they have been married two, three, or even more often among the savages, who have accepted it as a great honor when these pious married men occasionally marry their dependent daughters. Personally, I have not seen any savages, although there are many here. We met our Goedecke, who also complained about the high costs. As we only had a one-day leave, we could only remain for a few hours. At three o'clock we were already on the opposite shore and arrived back in camp at eight-thirty. The night and the bad road often made it necessary for us to walk.

17 October - It rained hard during the night and the whole day. A courier from General [Sir Guy] Carleton brought us the good news today that the general had taken possession of the strong Crown Point on the lake.

21 October - I have the pleasure to report that I received a pleasant piece of news this morning. On 27 August, General Howe attacked the rebel army and totally defeated it. He made prisoners of three generals, four colonels, eighteen captains, 43 lieutenants, eleven ensigns, one aide-major, thirty sergeants, and 1,800 privates. Three to four thousand rebels were wounded and left on the field. We lost one colonel, three captains, twelve officers wounded, and 330 dead and wounded privates. The night after the battle, the enemy withdrew leaving his entire camp and the artillery therein. General Howe then took possession of the city of New York where he made various sick and many others prisoners. This information was sent to us today by General Carleton. This afternoon we also received the very welcome order to enter winter quarters. According to rumors, it is very difficult for the carts and other vehicles to transport the necessities on the roads and therefore the local troops here in Canada have done everything possible this year. Tomorrow the cantonments as far as the other side of Trois Rivieres are ended and pending further orders are to have quarters in the parishes of Champlain, Batiscan, and Ste. Anne.

22 October - After both of our regiments received bread, meat, and rice for three days, we struck our tents at nine-thirty and marched to the parish of Batiscan at ten-thirty. This march was very unpleasant for me because I had the flag detail and, as there was a shortage of carriages, had to walk the entire distance of not less than twelve and one-half miles. All the baggage was transported in boats and because it was down stream, it arrived at our quarters before we did.

23 October - The march continued to the parish of St. Denis. We moved out at seven o'clock. The boats, from which the baggage was first unloaded, carried the company across the Richelieu River, and we arrived at our quarters at three o'clock. There was still a shortage of carriages today, also.

24 October - At seven o'clock we moved out and marched to quarters in the parish of Sorel. The people there were very poor and not the least thing could be bought for money. I had such a disagreement with Ahrend about the purchase of lights and he opposed me in such a manner that I was nearly forced to forget he was my friend. An unusual apathy on my part kept me under control today.

25 October - We marched onward toward Sorel at seven o'clock today. However, the issuing of bread and meat for ten days delayed us so long that we did not leave until ten o'clock. The company received four boats with which to be taken over the St. Lawrence River, where we then entered quarters, where we had previously lain, in the parish of Berthier. Our troops had to row themselves across.

26 October - We could not march away before ten o'clock because of the difficulty in getting the carts together. During our march we had such a thunderstorm at twelve o'clock as no one in Europe has seen, even on the hottest summer day. We marched into the parish of Maskinonge and the road for most of the way was worse than on 7 October. At seven o'clock we arrived in our former quarters and the baggage arrived at nine o'clock.

27 October - We marched onward to the parish of Yamachiche and our previously occupied quarters. Toward the end of our march it began to rain very hard and the road became exceptionally bad.

28 October - Our march continued to Trois Rivieres. One-third of a company of Colonel Specht's Regiment, which already occupied that place, marched out prior to our arrival, taking with them the heavy baggage which had been on board the ships *Liable* and *Three Friends*.

29 October - Colonel Specht with the rest of his regiment marched into winter quarters in the parishes of Champlain and Batiscan; our company remained in Trois Rivieres in order to rejoin our regiment, which is due here today. As a result, we also had a day of rest. Personally, I was ordered by the lieutenant colonel to go to the parish of Cape Madeleine to obtain carts for the next day's march. I set out and was carried across the Genoux River in a boat. From that point to the parish of Cape Madeleine I had to walk for an hour and one-half. I obtained no satisfaction from the militia captain, even to get one cart, as the Specht Regiment had taken all of them. He promised to send all of them to me tomorrow, if they were returned. I remained overnight with the captain. I found him to be a very polished gentleman, who gave me a cordial welcome.

The Journal of Lieutenant Friedrich Julius von Papet

30 October - Already at four-thirty I began my return on foot along the road to the parish of Champlain. No carts had as yet returned. I had been walking only a few hours when I met a coach and seven carts on their return. I took the first for my own use in order to continue my journey and ordered the latter to go to the Genoux River. In the parish of Champlain the militia lieutenant allowed me the pleasure of eighteen carts and gave me a ride in his own coach to the parish of Batiscan, to Colonel Specht, where I requested the use of the carts for the next day's march. The militia lieutenant had left his sick wife behind, and due to concern, returned after lending me his coach, which I had to drive. Colonel Specht was somewhat angered, but promised me the use of the carts for our regiment's march tomorrow. With an order from him to Colonel Speth I set out on my return as I wished to return the coach to the militia lieutenant. I fortunately met Captain O'Connell with a mail coach at Champlain, and he was so kind as to take me with him to Cape Madeleine. I delivered my order and after two hours arrived at my quarters with the company that night.

31 October - The company marched at six o'clock. Within the space of seven hours we crossed the three rivers, Champlain, Batiscan, and Ste. Anne and entered into our winter quarters in the parish of Ste. Anne at three-thirty. The company had seventeen buildings, but two of them were not to be occupied. Captain Ahrend and I shared quarters. As we were crossing the second river, the Batiscan, I had the pleasure to embrace my dear brother. The day before he had left Quebec with a group of convalescents to return to quarters, and God be praised! I met him again in good health. Our baggage still had not arrived today, and we had to get by as best the quarters allowed.

November

1 November - Our baggage finally arrived at noon today. Our quarters were close to the Ste. Anne River, and seemed quite satisfactory for the winter, but as they lie nearly two hours from the main road to Quebec, we never see anyone and we find ourselves in a true wilderness, completely surrounded by a thick forest through which no white man can move. So little is said here that it seems to me as if we were banished to Siberia, and here this is called winter quarters.

The Journal of Lieutenant Friedrich Julius von Papet

4 November - I visited the quarters of all the companies. I found most of them in poor condition and I could almost say it was impossible for our troops to survive here in these in part dens of assassins during such hard winters. I had taken my host's rifle along and shot a wild duck on the way. However, as it fell in the middle of the river and I had no dog, I could not get it.

23 November - We were originally told that there were absolutely no fish here in the winter time and yet today we were offered the chance to buy a very nice fourteen-pound salmon trout. We paid two and one-half shillings for it. This evening my Camsel [servant ?] returned from a visit to my brother. I had sent him to buy food in Quebec. As my brother, in his parish, had the opportunity to read the gazette from Quebec, he sent the information that it contained a report of 13 October. General [William] Howe had totally defeated the rebels. It continued that General [George] Washington now found himself at General Howe's headquarters.[20] The rebels immediately thereafter surrendered and requested permission to hold a general congress and this was granted. It stated further that the Americans desired to make peace if the King would only grant certain conditions. In this newspaper there was also an address extended to General Carleton from all Canadians, upon his arrival at Quebec. This contained the clearest proof as well as love and the best wishes of the Canadians for General Carleton.

December

2 December - At seven o'clock in the evening we received the order to march tomorrow to the parish of Grondines. Due to the illness of the regimental quartermaster, I was ordered to go ahead with the quartermaster sergeants and the guards and to report with them to the lieutenant colonel at six o'clock. General march was to be beaten at the company at eight o'clock.

3 December - At five-thirty I was at the lieutenant colonel's quarters with all the quartermaster sergeants and the guards. Those from the two companies on the other side of the Ste. Anne River had much difficulty crossing the ice. I was ordered to meet the Quartermaster General, Lieutenant Gerlach, who was to give me further orders, initially at Grondines. I met him at eleven o'clock and

The Journal of Lieutenant Friedrich Julius von Papet

began preparations for quartering the regiment at Grondines for one night. The companies each received twelve houses, and during the day I had to walk twenty miles. The quarters extended to the end of the parish of Deschambault. About seven o'clock in the evening I returned in a coach to Captain von Schlagenteufel's quarters. His company was with those in Grondines and would remain so the next day.

4 December - I set out for Captain Ahrend's quarters which were with the company in the parish of Grondines and were to remain there today because our companies had only 44 houses in the parish of Grondines and a part of them, as a result, were quartered in 23 houses in the parish of Deschambault. During the previous night much snow had fallen. The man, who had brought me to his house in a coach, used a sled, which people in this country call a gig, to take me very quickly to the captain's quarters. We traveled the nearly four miles in half an hour. The sled allowed us to travel not only in comfort, but also more quickly than in our coach, because the compartment in which we sat was built on the runners close to the ground. As soon as I arrived at the captain's, we visited the quarters in order to prepare a written report concerning the quarters. Among the 67 houses which the companies occupied, I found about twenty which in part were empty or because of poor condition could not be used. After we had traveled back and forth for about twelve miles, we finally returned to my quarters at four-thirty.

11 December - Our regiment is spread out in such a manner that our company is on the right wing and forms a front in the parish of Grondines and a small part of the parish of Deschambault. Next comes Captain Ahler's Company and it is assigned the other houses in the parish of Deschambault for its quarters. The companies of the lieutenant colonel and Major von Luecke, and the staff are quartered in the large parish of Cape Sante.

Captain von Schlagenteufel's Company is located on the other side of the St. Lawrence River on the south bank, in the parish of Ste. Croix. It took considerable effort and a full day before that company could be transferred across, because there was heavy ice on both banks of the St. Lawrence River and the middle has not yet frozen over. It was also my brother's lot to be with Captain von Luetzow's Company on the south shore of the river, in winter quarters in the parishes of St. Pierre and St. Jean. Therefore we are separated by the river and until it is completely frozen over we will have no opportunity to visit one another. Supposedly the quarters on the south shore are better because the inhabitants living there have suffered little, or not at all, from the war. However, considering the social situation, much is regrettable. As the company is now more widely scattered than previously, the arrangements for religious services are such that it must be conducted in each company. For our company this will be held on Wednesdays. This is to begin next week and for us the church in Grondines is to be used. Today we bought four rabbits. They cost one shilling, six pence. They are caught in traps just as we do, and they taste very good to us.

14 December - The reports that our quarters would become very quiet proved to be unfounded today by an order which suddenly arrived from General Carleton. Accordingly we were to be ready at all times to march. To that end, the regiment is to practice, as soon as possible, getting its equipment ready for marching, and because the German troops are not accustomed to marching in snow, we are to practice that. For that purpose rackets [snowshoes] are to be made in Quebec for all the troops, and as soon as they are ready they will be issued -- a completely new maneuver for us. Most Canadians have these rackets and walk on snow very quickly. These rackets have the form of those things with which the shuttlecocks are hit in Germany, but with the difference, that the netting is woven more closely and is made of catgut. They are fastened under the shoes, but all the grenadiers assure me that these rackets can not be used with our type of shoes or boots. Therefore, if we are to use them, we must wear the same light shoes that are worn by the Canadians. Nothing has been said about that.

20 December - If I were not looked over by Providence, it could have been very unfortunate for me today. As I have tried on several occasions to drive one of the local sleds for myself, I did the same on this sunny day, also. On my return I had to pass down a large hill close to the St. Lawrence River. The passage there is narrow and the road was only wide enough for my gig. Coming up the hill however, was a horse running at a full gallop. I was unable to stop and unfortunately had to yield to another gig going up hill, which had taken the middle of the road. My horse broke loose, the forward part of my gig rose in pieces and, thank the Lord! I and the rest of the gig flew over the oncoming vehicle without harm. The crackling of the boards frightened my horse. However, I had kept hold of the reins and continued on the road quite well for about 2,000 yards before it threw me over. Then my horse sprang to the left and fell on an open area where the pickets all stood in this fashion. [Von Papet sketched a picket fence at this point.] A picket from the open area caught my chin and another my right thigh, and suddenly I and everything that I had with me lay on the ground. My horse moved on to the next house rather slowly and, as I saw him standing there and that my chin was only slightly bloodied and I could still walk, the host took me from his house to the sled and we began then to fix it up. I got into the sled alone again and drove on, but as my horse ran away again because of a barking dog, I took a grenadier from the first and closest house and he then had to drive me to my quarters.

Journal of Lieutenant Friedrich Julius von Papet

January 1777

1 January - Deep thoughts! Many wishes! and a thoroughly warm, sentimental feeling for my beloved fatherland.

2 January - Rather warm weather so that it seemed as if the weather were about to break. All the Canadians assure me that this is something strange for them.

3 January - A conduct list was prepared on all the residents. Were they armed or unarmed? Had they been loyal to the King during the past year? Did they have acquaintances among the rebels; and under what circumstances? These questions were asked by our company and submitted after detailed inquiry.

4 January - During the evening I had the unfortunate incident that an English ensign and an English merchant from Quebec, en route to Montreal, were to be quartered by me, *sans facon* [without ceremony]. To avoid any difficulties, I agreed with that and in the end we got along quite well.

5 January - At seven o'clock in the morning my friends departed. In the afternoon I strolled to Ste. Anne to visit Lieutenant du Roi,[21] and wrote from that place to my brother, from whom and whose company I had received no news. I also heard a great amount about the politics occurring at headquarters in Quebec, that is about General von Riedesel, Brigadier Specht, and all the officers of our corps while there. As I was not present [at headquarters], I will let others discuss such matters.

6 February - Nothing of importance, except that we received leave today to go to Trois Rivieres.

7 February - We departed at six-thirty in the morning. Captain Ahrend's host drove us in his coach and we were made three piasters poorer by his generosity. From Ste. Anne we traveled on the ice along the shore of the St. Lawrence River in the post coach to Champlain, where we had previously lain in quarters. We ate our noon meal from what we had brought with us. At two o'clock we continued on our way. We found many places where the river had only about fifty feet of ice on which to drive. The confining space in the coach made us very uncomfortable, otherwise the route was very good and we arrived at Trois Rivieres at five o'clock. The road on land is much shorter, but because of the heavy snow, which the wind had blown into drifts in

Journal of Lieutenant Friedrich Julius von Papet

places, was far more uncertain. The many bends in the river made the first route almost three hours longer. We took lodgings with the Senior Cashier Goedecke and found him not to be in the best of health. He had nettle rash and until today had taken nothing for it. The following day

8 February - we were introduced to the general by Lieutenant Cleve. He met us with the greatest display of politeness and invited us to be his guests for the noon meal. At eleven o'clock we attended the parade. It was conducted by the general's brigade every fourth week by 200 men on the parade ground. This was in the barracks yard. The changing of the guard occurred here daily and, when not too cold, exercises were also conducted.

This morning Captain O'Connell gave a dinner and we were also invited to attend. At first some games were played, followed by a very magnificent feast, which resulted in many toasts to our health. This nearly destroyed our good intentions. Initially we planned to return [to the company] the next day. We had even made all preparations to do so, but it did not help us. The general pressed so strongly, that it became completely impossible to refuse staying for one more day.

9 February - Early in the morning the general sent to our quarters and invited us to the noon meal. After eating I played a game of chess with the general, then taro, and after the meal, we took our leave, very much affected by the many kindnesses shown to us.

10 February - We returned at nine o'clock. It was very warm and gave the appearance that there would be a thunderstorm. The road was also not the best because the flood tide came in at this time and the water rose so far above the ice that we encountered many waves which rose almost two feet above the bottom of the coach.

At five o'clock in the afternoon we were back in our quarters and truly very tired. In Ste. Anne they anticipated the arrival of General Carleton, for which an honor guard of one captain, two officers, and fifty men had been assigned.

4 March - We were informed by a letter from Cleve that the four companies of our regiment on this side of the river were to be under arms at Deschambault at nine o'clock Thursday because General Carleton, on a tour to Montreal, wished to inspect all the troops. During the night we received orders from our lieutenant colonel for the company to fall out on the sixth so as to assemble at the lieutenant

Journal of Lieutenant Friedrich Julius von Papet

colonel's quarters at Cape Sante at eleven o'clock in the morning. However, as this was a march of twenty miles, the captain decided to assemble the company at Deschambault on the fifth, and therefore we moved out during the afternoon of

5 March - at two o'clock and the company assembled at Lieutenant Modrache's quarters and was quartered in twelve houses. Personally we remained in the lieutenant's quarters and I had a very restless night so that I was unable to close my eyes.

6 March - We fell out at six o'clock and all the companies of the regiment were at the assigned place already at ten o'clock. General von Riedesel also arrived at this time and each company had to conduct special exercises for him and actually in three ranks. Next the entire regiment was aligned two men deep and on orders from General Carleton eighteen inch intervals were taken between the men on either side. At one-thirty his excellence finally came, alighted on our right wing and passed down the front. We presented arms, the music played and saluted. We then marched off by files. (The company in two files), and marched past him with dressed ranks. As nearly a foot and one-half of snow lay on the ground, it was not the best for marching. We then marched away from the previous place and everything went as well as could have been done on the parade ground at Braunschweig. We then marched past the general again in rows and he observed each one closely. General Carleton has much in his appearance which is very similar to our Colonel Jerusalem; a proud bearing, taciturn, but at all times decisive. Afterward we marched immediately to our quarters. General Carleton apparently did not remain in our colonel's quarters very long, as within half an hour, together with General von Riedesel, he passed us on our march, and as we have heard, they stopped to eat with Brigadier Specht and the following day inspected Specht's Regiment. We arrived at our quarters at seven o'clock. On this day I suffered excessive pain from standing. Just as we were eating, my brother, whose company had been transferred across from the other side this afternoon, came to arrange a good time for meeting tomorrow, at the meeting ground.

7 March - The brigadier's regiment assembled at Ste. Anne and took a position on the ice on the river. They were inspected by His Excellence just as they were. During the past night, at eleven o'clock, General von Riedesel set out to notify the other regiments that His

Journal of Lieutenant Friedrich Julius von Papet

Excellence wished to inspect the entire army, as far as Montreal. My brother came this afternoon as planned and ate with us. His company passed here en route to its quarters at two o'clock.

17 March - Today the brigadier's regiment was mustered, by companies, by Captain Edward Foy.

18 March - We held a review. Captain Foy had notified us the day before that the company was to assemble at the church in Grondines, because that would make the trip from Ste. Anne easier for him, as he could then travel on the ice. At nine-thirty he arrived. The troops were individually mustered and the entire review took less than a quarter-hour. From our company, he went on to Deschambault, and then on to Cape Sante.

April

7 April - At nine o'clock in the morning one storm followed another. There was constant thunder and lightning. I have never seen such changeable weather. Two days ago the strongest cold and now a strong thunder storm such as occurs in Germany only in August. The storm seemed to come from the region of New York. It rained hard here, and there was still snow on the ground. Two savages passed by here today from Quebec. They were from St. Louis, three miles above Montreal. They visited in Captain Ahrend's quarters. They knew his name and had been sent to the captain, by the lieutenant colonel, from Cape Sante. One spoke some French. Upon their entrance they shook hands with everyone and were very friendly. One had painted his face completely black and had a piece of silver hanging from his nose. The other, however, had painted his head from the left eye to the right with several diagonal stripes. Both of his ears were slit in various places and painted red, and he spoke some French. He made us understand that he had the position of an officer among the savages and was being sent to Montreal at this time with an order for his tribe from General Carleton. As ugly as these savages appeared, that is still not the case, because the one is considered the most beautiful who can paint himself the most beautifully. We gave them a glass of wine and a piece of roast veal. They appreciated that. Upon their departure they asked for money [to buy] drinks. We gave them a little something, also. The captain's host did not like that, because he said that money is not well used by the savages and when they are drunk, they can commit the greatest atrocities. General Carleton never gives them money when he wishes to make them a present, but instead offers them an item of clothing or some such other necessity. Furthermore, their natural savagery makes it necessary that all merchants are forbidden to sell the savages rum or other strong drink. The savages have always committed the most gruesome custom of scalping their enemies and, when they are drunk, even their friends.

Scalping is done in this manner. They use a knife to cut the skin around the head and then take hold thereunder with the thumb and pull that piece from the head. They have a special talent for this and it happens in only a moment. This piece of skin is then hung from their ears as a sign of honor and those of the tribe who have not taken a scalp are not respected. This was the reason why they often secretly scalped even their French friends. During the previous [Seven Years'] war, when the savages were allied with the French, the government frequently had to save the captive Englanders by paying the savages ten to twenty livres. There is not much to say about their courage. They are only to be feared when attacking. A single cannon shot causes 1,000 savages to flee, and in an open field three Canadians can always drive off thirty savages.

26 May - We received the report from the staff that each company was to receive two batteaux in which the troops were to practice rowing. This is very necessary not only because the St. Lawrence River is very full of rocks, but also many accidents occur which could be prevented by a knowledge of boat handling. A few days ago a boat carrying provisions for the brigadier's regiment, from Trois Rivieres, collided with a two-masted ship which lay at anchor at night. A soldier of the major's company drowned as a result. Today my brother planned to return to his company. However, the strong wind caused me to disapprove and the men with the batteaux had to wait until next day.

29 May - The order also arrived that the German brigade was to move closer together. Therefore the brigadier entered quarters with his regiment at Cape Madaleine, Champlain, and Batiscan. From our regiment, Major von Luecke had to cross from the south side of the river today and will apparently take over command of all of the companies. Today the Canadians also celebrated, just as we do, only not as magnificently. They call it *Fete de Dieu* [Corpus Christi]. This afternoon I made a trip to our militia captain to arrange various details concerning tomorrow's march. The guy who drove me in a chaise, constantly drove like a madman and when I returned home, I was not in the best condition.

June

2 June - Today we received information as to the amount of baggage the officers can take with them.

3 June - The Company marched out at three o'clock. All the baggage was carried in the two batteaux which had been delivered to the company. After we crossed the three rivers of Ste. Anne, Batiscan, and Champlain, the company entered quarters in the last two houses in the parish of Champlain, completely soaked by the very rainy weather. This evening I received the news that I was to be assigned to a detachment. This detachment consisted of German troops including Lieutenant Colonel von Ehrenkrook, six captains, twelve lieutenants, 48 non-commissioned officers, and 600 privates, and was to remain as a covering force in Canada.[22]

4 June - My friends in the company marched already at three-thirty to Point au Lac. I and Lieutenant Bohemeyer remained lying here with the detachment.

The farewell from my friends was, as it had to be, painful and touching. Captain von Schlagenteufel, who had been ordered to the detachment from our regiment, arrived from the south side in four hours. At two o'clock I received orders from Trois Rivieres to report there at once. Therefore I took a coach for me and a cart for my baggage and reported there, to the lieutenant colonel, at six o'clock in the evening. He had chosen me to be the regimental quartermaster for the detachment, took me on his table [made him a part of the commander's suite], and from this time I have no other duties. This night my brother had his lodgings with me. He had escorted the heavy baggage here, and probably will escort it further.

5 June - Our detachment received the order from our regiment to move here to Trois Rivieres. The officers were assigned quarters in the city, the soldiers, however, were all quartered in the barracks. Here in Trois Rivieres can now be found the war chest, the detachment from our regiment, and Major General von Riedesel, and two men per company as baggage guards from all the companies of the entire corps. The baggage is on the barracks grounds, arranged by regiments and under the charge of Lieutenant Dove. Because General Riedesel has not been well for several days, he only departed from here with his suite this morning, at seven o'clock.

6 June - The detachment from the Specht Regiment remains at Cape Madeleine; that of the Prince Friedrich Regiment at Rivieres au Loup; the Chasseur Battalion at Yamaska; and the Grenadiers at Laroroit. Today a report in French was sent to General Carleton.

7 - 9 June - Considerable activity concerning provisioning and paying out of moneys received.

10 June - The German recruits from the Scheiter recruiting plan,[23] to be assigned now among the English regiments, and who arrived here yesterday, did not wish to march today.

There had actually been a fight between them and some English recruits. The English strength was greater and the Germans complained about the advantages which those in charge always gave to the English. The officers complained to the lieutenant colonel and requested an escort, which was granted them at once. When they saw the escort they were satisfied and the escort only accompanied them to Trois Rivieres.

11 June - A courier passed through here, who brought the news from General Carleton at Quebec, that an entire fleet with German troops, supposedly our recruits, provisions, and even the relatives of General von Riedesel, have complained to him. The latter has already for some time been settled in General Riedesel's house at Trois Rivieres.[24]

12 June - At about three o'clock in the afternoon, the general's wife and children arrived here in bad and rainy weather. They had traveled from Quebec to Cape Madeleine on land, and from there transferred across in a most dangerous manner in a light canoe. Against all arguments she was determined to follow her husband to the army. They stopped at the local post house. At six o'clock the recruits for our regiment, from the Dragoons, from Riedesel's Regiment, and a part of the Specht Regiment, arrived here in a three-masted ship. A Captain Thomae had escorted them here from Brunswick. As we had no definite orders to allow them to debark here, they will sail on to Sorel tomorrow. Because of the favorable wind, at least twenty ships passed en route to Sorel.

13 June - At five o'clock this morning the general's wife departed, as did the ship. Captain von Tunderfeldt told us today that the report about General Carleton had arrived and that in a few days, he would arrive here to give us further tactical orders.

16 June - The three ships with recruits which had gone to Sorel, returned. They and the equipment for the regiment were unloaded. A company of jaegers from Hesse-Hanau and the recruits were also landed.[25] Captain Thomae, who was in charge of our recruits, was not with them but had gone on to the army at St. Jean. The recruits for the Prince Friedrich Regiment, a part of the Specht Regiment, and those of Major von Barner's Battalion, are to be commanded by Lieutenant [Johann Conrad] Ruff.[26] Pending further orders, all the troops are to be quartered in some [local] houses.

17 June - As the result of a duel between two officers of the Hessian Jaegers during the morning, one of them was wounded. The lieutenant colonel, because of receiving a report of this event, was forced to have one of them immediately arrested. During the afternoon an order arrived from Quebec that all the troops were to be embarked again, and they were to proceed to Montreal. This took place during the evening and with the first favorable wind, the ships will set sail. A letter to General Carleton from General von Riedesel was my last activity for this day.

18 June - The ships set sail.

19 June - Lieutenant Ruff came here with a large part of the equipment from Brunswick.

20 June - All the items which belonged to the Brunswickers were unloaded and given to the care of Lieutenant Dove. About noon General von Riedesel's wife arrived here. She had spoken with her husband at Chambly. She moved into her husband's present quarters, which he had occupied during the past winter. General Carleton also arrived here this evening. He immediately went to the house of the general's wife. We made all the courtesy arrangements, but he forbid the showing of all honors. He took quarters with Militia Colonel Tonnencour and departed on the morning of

21 June - already at four-thirty. From all appearances no changes are contemplated for our detachment.

Journal of Lieutenant Friedrich Julius von Papet

July

10 July - We received the confirmed and happy news from a courier who had been sent through here, that the rebels had to abandon Carillon [Fort Ticonderoga], retreating toward Albany, and that our army had occupied the fort the following day. Additional and more complete details are still lacking.

11 July - Today nearly twenty ships passed Sorel on the river. Since yesterday's report, we find a noticeable change in the behavior of the local inhabitants. They are not only more polite, but far more tractable. There are only a few who are true friends. Resentment is seen in the face of most, and I would not have believed that so many were allied with the goals of the rebels. With the conquest of Carillon their secret hopes have been completely lost.

15 July - Lieutenant Colonel [Carl von] Creuzbourg arrived here.[27] He traveled on land from Quebec. He will wait here two days and if the ever contrary winds persist, he will debark his Jaegers where the ship now lies and lead them further on land.

16 July - Lieutenant Colonel Creuzbourg with Captain Plessen and Lieutenant Ruff went to meet the ship in a canoe. The latter was ordered to lead our recruits here on land. According to a letter from an officer with the army, all the troops are lying within cannon shot of Carillon.

17 July - A commissary came from Quebec with the order that troops left here in Canada, as well as those with the army, are to have spruce beer at the King's cost. Because the water here is bad during the summer, this is very advantageous for our soldiers, as our soldiers frequently fall victim to dysentery now. I had to write to General Carleton to request, if possible, that at least the soldiers on guard be issued fresh meat once or twice [per week?].

23 July - Lieutenant Colonel von Creuzbourg passed Trois Rivieres with three companies of Jaegers and placed them in the houses of the bordering parish.[28] They were all handsome troops and well-armed.

26 July - Those same troops had a day of rest.

27 July - By means of the Janizary music [also called Turkish music - crude, noisy music produced by shrill wood instruments, various drums, triangles, and other percussion instruments] which we

Journal of Lieutenant Friedrich Julius von Papet

have in our regiment and the instruments which remained in the baggage, we set the entire Trois Rivieres into motion. I had created this situation. The pleasure of the general's wife in this was most exceptional.

28 July - It looks as if there will be much to do because of the reports and letters.

29 July - Five batteaux were sent to pick up the rest of our baggage from the ship *Isabella Dorothea*, which was still lying at anchor at Pointe au Trembles due to the contrary winds. Captain Thomae's eagerness to return to Europe created this action.

31 July - General von Riedesel's adjutant, Captain Willoe, arrived here from the army. He is to accompany the general's wife to Carillon. According to a letter from the general the same [assistance] is expected for each regimental officer, who is transporting recruits and baggage to Carillon. No one remains here in Canada except our detachment, and God knows when we will be relieved. Because of an over-abundance of activity, I wish for that with all my heart.

August

1 August - Many warm and sincere wishes for the [long-] life of our most precious Father of our Country.

3 August - The baggage for the general left in two batteaux. A detail from our detachment is to take it to Chambly.

4 August - The general's wife, in company with Captain Willoe, left in a coach this morning at eight o'clock.

5 August - The order for the lieutenant colonel to send on the recruits and baggage, finally arrived from General von Riedesel.

9 August - On orders from the government district of Trois Rivieres, 25 intractable inhabitants were arrested because they had deserted royal service at St. Jean.

10 August - Lieutenant Hertel with two non-commissioned officers and fifteen men escorted the 25 above mentioned to Riviere du Loups, and from there the local detachment escorted them to Berthier and Montreal.

16 August - A detachment of about 300 Englanders, which was to strengthen the regiments, came through here. They were quartered in the parish and will remain here tomorrow.

Journal of Lieutenant Friedrich Julius von Papet

17 August - Nothing new except for much disturbance caused by some drunken English.

18 August - This morning we were rid of our disturbing guests. They marched onward to join the army.

19 August - Captain von Tunderfeldt wrote that in Quebec the talk was that General Washington had arrived at Albany and that very significant news was expected from General [John] Burgoyne in the near future.

30 August - All six ships set sail during the morning. One non-commissioned officer and four men of the von Barner Battalion were delayed because of details and the ship on which they were assigned had already sailed more than one mile [without them]. Therefore, they hastened to get on board, obtained a light canoe from the local inhabitants, and a Canadian luckily took them to the ship with the warning to remain as calm as possible. A young chap saw a line hanging from the ship, grabbed it, put one foot on the canoe gunwale and caused it to turn over. Two unfortunately drowned. The non-commissioned officer and one man fortunately had the Canadian to thank for their rescue.

31 August - After the recruits had marched away, I had some leisure time in which to partially recuperate.

September

1 September - Nothing new.

2 September - A letter arrived here from General von Riedesel. It was dated 20 August. It can be seen therein that once and for all, everything that has been sent to him has arrived. The general acknowledged in his letter that he is well-satisfied with all arrangements made by the lieutenant colonel. Concerning the action of 16 August, he mentioned very little. It is now confirmed that Captain Schick and Lieutenant d'Annieres were killed.[29] The many crimes which our soldiers commit in the gardens of the inhabitants at night has caused the lieutenant colonel to place a guard at the barracks at night.

3 September - On my side, a great deal of work will be necessary to answer the incoming correspondence.

4 - 5 September - Nothing new.

Journal of Lieutenant Friedrich Julius von Papet

6 September - Many Indian chiefs have passed through here aboard ship en route to Quebec from the army, in order to pledge their loyalty to General Carleton. Having been appeased by him, they returned through here today on their way back to the army. The inhabitants had to transport them, two by two, in coaches, on orders of His Excellency.

7 - 8 September - We hear nothing but bad from the newspapers which the local inhabitants support.

9 September - Captain von Tunderfeldt writes much of what is not good news from the army. It is believed that Lieutenant Colonel Baum, Captain von Schick, Riding Master [Captain] Reineking, Lieutenants d'Annieres, Jr., and Hohlenfeld are certainly dead. Major von Barner and Captain Dommes are wounded and Lieutenants Uhlig and Gebhardt are missing. No one of the Dragoons has escaped except Captain von Schlagenteufel and 32 men and the baggage and standards which were left behind in a house, prior to the battle. I learned all this in a letter[30]

10 September - of 24 August which I received from my dear brother and thanks to him, a letter from the senior field cashier of 30 August. The first wrote that he was still well but had to put up with excessive fatigue which surpassed all human expectations. God has graciously protected him this far, but everyone assumes that they are in a perilous situation. He only briefly mentioned the losses of 16 August. They consisted of 21 officers dead, wounded, or captured, and 350 men, and these losses are described as well as the [enemy ?] superiority, and also the poor support when reinforcement was neglected. However, the rebel army continues to retreat, and with God's help the whole province of Albany will soon be occupied. Most of the inhabitants there are very friendly and welcome them [the English army] with open arms.

11 September - I answered all incoming letters and also wrote to Europe.

12 September - These letters were sent away.

13 September - Nothing new.

14 September - A lively traffic at the lieutenant colonel's.

15 September - We dined at noon with the local grand vicar. The captain of the frigate which lies here as a covering force was also present. The courses were mostly unappealing to me and the conversation among us was very boring.

16 September - The lieutenant colonel and I were guests of the captain aboard the frigate. We were picked up in a sloop at two-thirty. In the captain's cabin everything was beautifully arranged. The frigate was called the *Niger*.[31] The captain who commands it is a man of wealth. This frigate has done much damage to the rebels, having captured more than 25 prizes.

19 September - We received the order to immediately assemble a detachment of 300 men, fully prepared to march at once. As, according to the letter from Captain von Tunderfeldt, General Burgoyne crossed the Hudson River on 10 September with his entire corps and destroyed the bridge behind, all communications between us have been cut. God! he wrote, must be British. They will be forced to fight their way through if they are to join General Howe. The army clearly finds itself in the most ticklish situation. A shortage of provisions, unbelievably fatigued, completely worn out, and thoroughly discontented, the entire army looks to General Carleton [for deliverance]. Because the latter assumes that the rebels are able to make a move against Carillon, he wishes to have a 300-man detachment on hand to send there as a reinforcement, if necessary. This detachment is assembling at Riviere du Loup and is to be commanded by Captain von Zielberg.

Prince Friedrich [Regiment] is to supply one captain, one officer, four non-commissioned officers, and sixty men; von Rhetz, one officer, four non-commissioned officers, and 58 men; von Riedesel, Specht, and Hesse-Hanau are each to supply one officer, four non-commissioned officers, and sixty privates. A total of one captain, five officers, twenty non-commissioned officers, and 298 men.

Tomorrow or the day after, General Carleton is expected here. Obviously he wishes to inspect everyone himself to insure the necessary measures for the security of Canada.

20 September - Orders were sent to the various detachments, new uniforms and equipment were issued to the soldiers and everything put in the best order.

21 September - The general arrived at one o'clock in a batteau from the corps at Madeleine. An honor guard was ordered out for him, consisting of one captain, two officers, and sixty men. Upon his

Journal of Lieutenant Friedrich Julius von Papet

arrival a salute and drum rolls was rendered. I and the lieutenant colonel received him at the river. The general's conduct and satisfaction with Lieutenant Colonel [Obviously there is a copying error at this point as the subject matter changes drastically from a mention of the lieutenant colonel to von Tunderfeldt, who had the rank of captain.] [From Captain] von Tunderfeldt we received a reliable list of all the casualties of 16 August, which Captain Gerlach had received on the subject from the captured Major von Maibom. At three o'clock the general departed. The entire detachment from Cape Madeleine arrived here today and the officer with the sixty-man detachment marched on to Riviere du Loup.

22 September - The local detachment from the von Rhetz and Riedesel Regiments also proceeded to Riviere du Loup.

23 September - Captain von Tunderfeldt wrote from Sorel that, as instructed, he had already sent orders to Captain von Zielberg to march with his [Zielberg's] detachment. Therefore, he will depart on the 25th, have the Hesse-Hanau command join him at Berthier, and then after receiving the promised batteaux from Brigadier [Francis] MacLean, cross at Sorel and continue on to Chambly. According to the report from Captain von Tunderfeldt, our army, and it follows, we also, are in a very sorry situation. Carillon reportedly has been recaptured by the Bostonians after our army marched on. If the report is factual, our losses can not be offset, and God knows, if Canada will not then also be lost. Thus the mistake of a [blank space] is made worse.

24 September - Captain Thomae at Yamaska received the sharpest orders to be alert. At the same time, I wrote to Lieutenant Governor Cramache [requesting] 5,000 ball cartridges and also powder, for our recruits.

27 September - It is surprising how the local inhabitants display their sympathy with the rebels. One of them insulted me today by already forbidding me to freely enter his house when, as a soon-to-be prisoner, I should pass Trois Rivieres. Then, because he has many good friends among the rebels, he would join them. It would be in my best interest to leave. The rest of the detachment of the Prince Friedrich Regiment, under the command of Lieutenant Harz entered here today.

29 September - The order was brought here by a courier today that the rest of our detachment should be ready to march. The same was given to the detachment at Yamaska. From these, a detachment of one officer and twenty men was to be sent to St. Francois. Accompanied by Canadians, the detachment, on land as well as on the rivers, is to make a reconnaissance deep inland. For the first Colonel Tonnencour received instructions to order the militia captain to pass the order to Captain Thomae. At the same time, I prepared a notification for the remaining detachment to be ready to march.

8 October - At eleven-thirty General Carleton and his suite arrived here in a coach. The honor guard had to fall out immediately. They ate at noon with Colonel Tonnencour and at three o'clock set out for Ste. Anne in batteaux. While they were entering the batteaux, a courier arrived from Quebec with the report that he had arrived in a warship of fifty cannons, which brought many dispatches. Possibly we will also receive mail from Europe.

9 - 12 October - Nothing new.

13 October - The frigate [Triton], which lay here all summer as a covering force, sailed to Quebec, where it will spend the winter. The frigate's captain is employed on board a frigate of 24 cannons on Lake Champlain.

24 October - Captain von Tunderfeldt reported to us that Lieutenant Colonel Breymann was killed by his own grenadiers after he had killed four of them. --- Sad events that we dare not dwell on! - - - Still no definite, current information concerning the army has been received by General Carleton. All this unfortunate intelligence is received through special reports.

25 October - Nothing new, except rumors and sad misgivings about the fate of our dear colleagues! Dear God! What sad events they might have to see and endure! --- My poor brother and Ahrend - -- As some from Captain Zielberg's detachment were to have been sent to Chambly, Captain [Friedrich Ludwig] von Schoell was also ordered to go there.

26 October - In the evening an English Captain [Alexander] Frazer, who had also been made a prisoner, arrived from the army. On the following morning

27 October - I learned from his remarks the confirmation of the loss of the entire army. This captain is taking dispatches from General

Burgoyne to General Carleton. This afternoon 150 English soldiers arrived here from Quebec, en route to Montreal and St. Jean. They were quartered here and remained on

28 October - lying here.

29 October - At eight o'clock the English departed.

Under the present circumstances, as our entire army is in ruins, there is already a rumor that Carillon has been lost and the Prince Friedrich Regiment has also been captured. Such a sorry situation I have never experienced in my entire life. With the thoughts about the sad fate (which I already know) of my dear brother, friends, and my dear countrymen - who find themselves under a completely double-dealing nation - it is necessary to face the possibility that a person might also be caught up in battle and captured.

30 October - Nothing new, except that nearly one-half foot of snow fell today. During the evening a deep freeze occurred so that many Canadians passed on the road in light gigs. Captain von Tunderfeldt wrote today describing the totally unfortunate events concerning our army. It was on 16 October that General Burgoyne concluded a convention with the rebels. Accordingly, 1,800 English and about 1,500 Germans were made prisoners of war. These were immediately escorted to the region of Boston. Two hours after the convention was signed, the news arrived that General [Henry] Clinton was actually only thirty miles from Albany and had taken Fort Montgomery by storm. At the same time, news arrived that General Howe had thoroughly defeated Washington twice. However, I believe that all these successes can not offset our loss.

November

1 November - Today I actually saw the signed convention. I have no doubt it will soon be available in Europe.

9 November - We received the disposition from General Carleton as to how the German troops are to be assigned winter quarters. All the Germans (including those returning from Ticonderoga, who have all come back after destroying all those fortifications) are to be under the command of Lieutenant Colonel von Ehrenkrook. The districts from Sorel to Berthier and from Trois Rivieres to Terrebonne are designated for their winter quarters. All baggage is to be sent to Trois

Journal of Lieutenant Friedrich Julius von Papet

Rivieres again and Lieutenant Dove will be in charge of it. Captain Foy is to return to London in a few days and will take our letters with him.

10 November - I wrote to Major Dupre, who is to assign quarters and completed orders to the officers assigned to the baggage detail.

11 - 12 November - Nothing changed.

13 November - Lieutenant Colonels Praetorius and Creuzbourg received orders to move into winter quarters. The first received the district from Sorel to Beloeil and the latter is to march ahead of the other to Berthier. The remaining officers of the detachment and those with the baggage are to march here. Captain von Zielberg is to rejoin the regiment.

23 November - An English artillery company, which came through here, is marching to Quebec. They are to be quartered here today. The detachment from the Rhetz Regiment under Lieutenant Bodemeyer also arrived here this afternoon. Lieutenant Bodemeyer is to arrange their quarters in the parish of Trois Rivieres tomorrow.

24 November - Today we learned, for the first time, that all the troops were moving into their assigned quarters today. An exceptionally large snowfall occurred today.

12 December - Punishment for a deserter from the Riedesel Regiment was carried out. He ran through 100 men six times. A report from Captain von Tunderfeldt noted that Lieutenant Colonel von Creuzbourg was now in the parish of Repentigny. The most pleasant news for my purse was that the order was issued in Quebec detailing payment of forage money to the troops for 165 days.

Journal of Lieutenant Friedrich Julius von Papet

January 1778

1 January - It is common throughout all Canada, that people, who wish to extend best wishes to another, go to visit them and kiss everyone whom they meet in the house.

Due to various reasons I have not followed this custom but, to put it briefly, I have followed good German customs in my own billets. My thoughts today were all turned inward on my own dear family, my friends, and my beloved fatherland. That God might hear my wishes for all of these.

3 January - Toward five o'clock the brigadier returned from his visit to Quebec. He had been received and treated with many kindnesses. Then much later three rebel officers were brought here by an English officer. Three weeks previously they had been captured by a patrol near Ile aux Noix. Supposedly they had letters to General Carleton from General [Horatio] Gates. Early tomorrow morning the escort officer is to take those officers to Quebec.

4 January - Many orders concerning discipline and the designation of alert assignments.

5 January - A general order from Quebec for everyone to be prepared to march.

6 January - This order was passed to all of the troops.

7 January - Except for the arrival of Lieutenant Colonel Praetorius, nothing special.

8 January - Lieutenant Colonel Praetorius presided over a hearing for Captain Thomae. During the afternoon there was a festive dinner at the brigadier's. Toward evening the Bishop of Quebec arrived here. Upon his arrival and as he passed through each village the bells were rung. He is on his way to Montreal.

9 January - During the morning the bishop visited the brigadier. He greeted each one of us with a kiss and thus made a good impression. He is not only a fine individual, but his speech and manners were exceptionally polite and gracious. The pension which he receives from England provides that the interest he gets is quite generous.

10 January - Many orders, much to do and to be done, caused by three soldiers who sold uniform items.

11 January - Nothing new.

Journal of Lieutenant Friedrich Julius von Papet

12 January - Lieutenant Colonel Praetorius started his journey back to Berthier.

13 January - The order came from Quebec that for every ten men, a snow shovel should be made and for each like number, an axe would be delivered. The troops were to be held in readiness to live in the woods in huts. The three officers mentioned as coming from the rebels, supposedly intended to get some of the prisoners exchanged. However, General Carleton will have nothing to do with such an idea. The departure of the auditor ended all further plans. As of today

14 January - the whole detachment of the Rhetz Regiment is to be assembled on the ice on the river, from here to Trois Rivieres, including all the men from the local barracks. I placed an order for the snow shovels with a resident of Becancour, as directed.

16 January - An order from Quebec designated all troops which are to march. From the leading elements to all of those who are to follow, one after the other. Included in the order was that each regiment was allowed one sled, the brigadier two, and the commanding general-in-chief four, only for transporting baggage. All remaining officers were to pack so light that they will always be in a condition whereby they can carry their own baggage. Yesterday evening a courier (Captain LaMotte) arrived here from Niagara with the news that General Howe had completely routed the rebels and that General Washington was dead. We expect General Carleton in the next coming days. Major von Barner is to assume command over all the detachments from the Brunswick regiments.

[For an unexplained reason the diary skips from January to 5 March. Possibly during this time the author was sick.]

March

5 March - Early in the morning at eight o'clock, General Carleton arrived here quite unexpectedly. I was summoned at once and after breakfast he gave us the order to march with all the detachments, except those at Yamaska, to St. Ours by way of Sorel, because the rebels were marching against St. Jean. Therefore all detachments received march orders today. The barracks at St. Francois was reinforced by Lieutenant Hannemann. Tomorrow the senior field cashier will travel in safety and I and the brigadier will also follow the detachment tomorrow.

6 March - Everyone marched at five o'clock, except for those ordered to remain with the baggage at Trois Rivieres, and proceeded to Little Machiche, the first night's quarters. At twelve o'clock noon the brigadier and I set out in a carriage. I left all my baggage in the care of my host. I took nothing but a leather knapsack with some underthings and four [illegible word], and during the evening we entered Rivieres du Loup where we met Major von Barner at the home of the militia captain. The major had suffered another misfortune, when thrown out of a sled a few days earlier on his way to Montreal. The end of his spine and all of his old injuries were further aggravated thereby, so that it was impossible for him to take on the command of the detachment. Therefore, he will go to Trois Rivieres and await further developments. The brigadier's baggage was left behind today and not delivered.

7 March - We went from Rivieres du Loup to Sorel. En route we encountered the detachments of the Riedesel, Specht, and Dragoon Regiments. Already on the morning of 6 March General Carleton had arrived at Sorel, and during his stay he was completely satisfied with the defensive preparations. At Sorel we stopped at the quarters of Captain von Hambach, inspected his preparations, the blockhouses, of which there were two with the barracks standing between them, and then spent the afternoon with him. The blockhouses which have been built here are for defense against the Indians, without cannons, but very well built and those located at Sorel have an advantageous situation so that 150 men can defend themselves against an attack by 1,000. They are made of wood and in each there are two six-pound cannons. The detachments arrived at Sorel at two o'clock and after being inspected by the brigadier, were quartered in the surrounding houses of the parish of Sorel. General Carleton had left behind at Sorel an order for the brigadier to reinforce Captain von Hambach with an officer and thirty men, which were necessary [to support] a warship lying there. We entered St. Ours at five o'clock in the evening. The brigadier's quarters were at the entrance to the parish and in proximity to the quarters of the Hessians.

Quite late [in the evening] a merchant, who had a store in the brigadier's quarters, returned from St. Jean, having left that place at seven o'clock in the morning. He imparted the news that everything was still peaceful at St. Jean. It was assumed therefore that the rebels had other plans and for now had decided not to attack us.

8 March - This morning the entire brigade was alerted to the arrival of the brigadier and his staff. All the various detachments assembled this morning in the parish of St. Ours. I directed the march orders (assigned the watches and patrols). A letter from Captain von Tunderfeldt came during the afternoon with the order that the detachments were to stop their march, and, if the weather permitted, were to return to their previous quarters. Therefore I issued the necessary orders this afternoon. The brigadier is to visit Lieutenant Colonel von Creuzbourg. However I have reason to prevent that occurring.

9 March - We moved out at eight o'clock in the morning toward Sorel and continued today on to Rivieres du Loup, where we spent the night in the previously occupied quarters. The commanding officer and thirty men were withdrawn.

10 March - At three o'clock in the afternoon, in unpleasant weather with much snow, we arrived at Trois Rivieres. My batman on the previous day had taken it upon himself to meet me there, but during the night lost his way on the lake and had to spend the entire night on the lake. This damaged his eyes and caused me much embarrassment. All the inhabitants were exceptionally pleased about our return. We met Major von Barner at Trois Rivieres and now he will remain here. Most information indicates that the enemy is possibly quite near. Captain von Tunderfeldt wrote from Montreal.

11 March - Many orders were sent out to some of the detachments. I advised Goedecke in Quebec of our return and hope that he will soon return.

12 March - The Rhetz detachment finally arrived here with its command of 100 men and all the detachments moved into their former quarters. Many of the men had received damage to their eyes. Even the officers had not avoided this damage. The glare from the snow could certainly be the cause, as such damage is rather common in this country. At any rate, most of the men's conditions are already improving. It began to thaw today and toward noon it rained heavily.

13 March - The thaw continued. It was very warm and the St. Lawrence River is high. Today I sent a carriage and two attendants to

Quebec to bring Goedecke back here. General Carleton is expected back here soon.

14 March - A transport went from Quebec to Montreal with money, escorted by one non-commissioned officer and six men from the local garrison. The water in the St. Lawrence River is so high that it is nearly impassable.

15 and 16 March - Nothing new.

17 March - Captain von Tunderfeldt informed us of a small skirmish which reportedly took place near Crown Point. Supposedly from our side the MacLean Regiment suffered one officer and six men killed and eight wounded. A strong patrol had been sent there and it had advanced further than it had been ordered to do. In a few days His Excellence is to pass through here en route to Quebec. Concerning the [a series of dots is recorded here] there are many complaints which he will forward to Montreal.

18 March - A detachment of one officer, two non-commissioned officers, and 25 men was sent to the parish of St. Pierre because the inhabitants do not wish to carry out His Excellence's orders. The senior cashier came from Quebec today. This noon Major von Barner hosted a large dinner.

19 March - General Carleton came through here this afternoon. I and the brigadier immediately greeted him and he was very pleasant. He was interested in everything and asked if there had been further problems with our soldiers' eyes. As Captain von Schlagenteufel was still suffering therefrom, his concern went so far that he sent his personal physician Kinaday [Kennedy] to visit him. Major von Barner was also present and took the opportunity to mention that our nation should be considered separately from the English. -- We informed the general about everything here.

20 March - General Carleton departed for Quebec at five o'clock in the morning. At his departure he ordered that the command at St. Pierre be strengthened so as to consist of two officers, four non-commissioned officers, and sixty men. Lieutenant Bodemeyer, who was ordered there, reported that the militia captain and most of the inhabitants who were in his area admitted their errors and had promised better behavior. Despite that, the reinforcement was sent.

21 March - The reinforcement marched away. The entire command now consists of men of the Rhetz detachment. An English

Journal of Lieutenant Friedrich Julius von Papet

naval officer passing through here mentioned a deserter who had passed through St. Jean.

27 March - We received information that most of the inhabitants of Terrebonne revolted, had taken up arms, and driven an English command out. The brigadier received orders therefore to take 300 men from the detachment and send them there. These were taken from the Riedesel and Specht detachments. Captain von Plessen was given command over all of them and was given instructions to be alert and to take all necessary precautions so that this uprising could be held in check. At the same time, Lieutenant Colonel von Creuzbourg was ordered to go there with all his Hessians and Jaegers and to assume command over all those troops. All of this is to be carried out in the most secretive manner and I therefore had to take the necessary steps.

28 March - Still, everyone knew where the troops were marching. Therefore everything is very unsettled, except for the brigadier and me. The day began with a strong thaw and travel on the ice became dangerous.

31 March - Orders came from Quebec that the 300 man detachment under Captain von Plessen was to return to its former quarters from Terrebonne. However, they were to remain in readiness, as soon as the road to Quebec had improved, to move into the garrison at Quebec. The inhabitants of Terrebonne have returned to a quiet situation. Nevertheless, Lieutenant Colonel von Creuzbourg and his Jaeger Corps are to remain there.

April

9 April - The day began very picturesquely. The ice flows (in a periphery of one, two, three, or even four lieus) [a lieu equals almost 2.5 miles] built up hills of ice on the Trois Rivieres side which were astonishingly high. At a glance some appeared to be thirty to forty feet high, and when they gradually collapse they leave the most beautiful after effect behind. To the eye of a German, such as I, something quite rare. To me it could certainly be no more astonishing than when one tells me that such great ice flows often push ships away like pieces of wood. The von Riedesel and Specht detachments arrived in Machiche today.

Journal of Lieutenant Friedrich Julius von Papet

15 April - The march of 300 men to Quebec was confirmed today by a report received from Captain von Tunderfeldt. It will consist of the detachments from Riedesel, Specht, and the Dragoons.

16 April - The rest of the Riedesel detachment, under Lieutenant von Pincier, marched in here. The reason being to put this detachment in a proper and march-ready condition.

21 April - This morning the Specht and Dragoon detachments marched in here and were quartered wherever possible in the city. During the afternoon all the officers were invited to dine with the brigadier.

May

19 May - We finally heard that a ship had arrived at Isle au Coudres. It came from Cadiz with a cargo of wine and salt for corn for some merchants in Quebec, and brought the news that everything was still peaceful in Europe and that 300 royal transport ships had departed from the ports of Portsmouth and Plymouth and would soon arrive here.

June

6 June - Today the 2nd division of Sir [John] Johnson's Corps, commanded by Major Mackbey, arrived; all fine men, well-equipped, and most were from Albany. They were quartered here and will continue their march tomorrow. Many among them speak German. The major is a fine man and much loved by his men. During the afternoon Captain von Schoell and Lieutenant Siefert arrived here in a carriage to prepare the baggage which is to be sent to the Hanau Regiment. On 4 June a misfortune struck the detachment commanded by Captain von Hambach. During the firing of a cannon on the King's birthday, Corporal Wiedmann was seriously injured when the gun accidently discharged during the loading. He lost the thumb and two fingers of his right hand and it may be necessary to amputate his left arm. The regimental surgeon Bernt, of the Prince Frederick Regiment, was immediately sent to attend him.

9 June - This noon there was a large group at the brigadier's. In accordance with orders, Captain Willoe returned to Quebec. From

Journal of Lieutenant Friedrich Julius von Papet

that place General Carleton assured us of his satisfaction concerning the items to be sent away. As a proof of his concern for the German troops, just as for the English troops, one pair of shoes, one pair of stockings, and a French elle [about one-half yard] of blue cloth for winter boots are to be delivered as a gift and I am to submit a list of all the German troops in a few days. This is understood to mean the non-commissioned officers, hautboists, drummers, and privates. A ship which arrived from Domingo, loaded with sugar and rum, brought the news from that place that since 21 April there was still no state of war existing between France and England. An express order from His Excellence forbids all manner of reports, lists, or other information about the local situation being sent in letters with the baggage to Boston. All letters from the troops were first to be sent, opened, to the brigadier.

30 June - [Inserted in the middle of the 1 July entry.] A letter from privy councillor Feronce [a blank space follows] said his prince had promoted him to lieutenant colonel. The brigadier, despite my opposition, did not wish to make this promotion known to the brigade. I nevertheless placed this in orders in such a manner as not to make it a complete declaration, so that the brigadier was not entirely pleased with me.

July

1 July - In general orders of 27 June all the troops were notified that it was His Majesty's intent to transfer the government of Quebec Province to Lieutenant General von [sic] Haldimand from His Excellence, Sir Guy Carleton. We are to go to Quebec tomorrow to greet the new governor.

The ship with the baggage set sail this morning. At three o'clock in the afternoon we departed for Quebec in a batteau.

Toward six o'clock the wind became contrary. Many storms came together so that it was necessary to land at the parish of Ste. Marie in order to protect ourselves from the strong waves which the river generated and the frequent rain. The closest house became our quarters. Personally I was inconvenienced during the night in a room filled with an astonishing number of lice, so that I was in no condition to remain therein, but wished to wait for daylight on the steps by the fire.

2 July - We took two carriages for us and our servants and arrived after frequent changes and continuous heavy rain at the post station at Pointe au Trembles. The brigadier wished to continue onward, but all the post coaches had departed prior to our arrival, which was fine with me, as on this trip I had become thoroughly soaked, so that I could almost no longer go on.

3 July - We departed at one-thirty in the morning and arrived at Quebec at eight-thirty in the morning. It was difficult to obtain any kind of quarters. We finally acquired some through the courtesy of a person name Brendis, whom the brigadier knew. After changing our clothes we went in company with all the officers of our corps to General Carleton's levee at the castle St. Louis in Quebec, where in the anteroom we already met General Haldimand. The brigadier and I were introduced to him. He spoke with us at length and inquired about everything most exactly. His Excellence understands spoken German, but speaks only a little, using French most of the time. If he is as old as his predecessor, His Excellence, General Carlton, he does not show it. Still, for now it is wise to give the new governor our full support. We were invited to dinner at noon by His Excellence General Carleton, and at three o'clock we went there together. The meal consisted of 24 dishes and everything was served in the English fashion. Among the ladies present were General Carleton's wife and her older sister, Major Carleton's wife. General Haldimand conversed often with the brigadier in broken German. After dessert, both ladies excused themselves. For half an hour there was drinking, during which the bottle was passed around and everyone had the opportunity to drink as much as he wished without proposing any toasts. We learned that the Hessian recruits and our baggage from home had already sailed toward Trois Rivieres on the ships *Nancy* and *Favorite*, and with the good winds would arrive soon. After dinner, together with Captain von Plessen, I inspected the ship wharf and the magazine. There is presently a warship of fifty cannons in Quebec harbor, which is commanded by Commodore Douglas, three frigates, and almost 150 merchant ships. The first will take General Carleton and his family back to England. The transport and merchant ships, which have come from England, are heavily armed. All merchandise which has arrived is again nearly as expensive as in the previous year, and that is because everything must be insured. Toward evening I watched the English parade and I must say that our troops do not make such an impression. Their entire pay is used for that purpose however. Each captain is so to speak, a merchant. The soldiers receive no cash but everything is spent on uniforms that he must accept. We ate our evening meal in our quarters.

4 July - Before the levee, just like yesterday, we again ate with General Carleton. On 6 July two ships are to be sent to Halifax to get news from that place as to how the negotiating has progressed with the provincials. It is assumed, that everything here depends on that news. Most people in Quebec believe that peace with the Bostonians is as good as concluded. On 7 July General Carleton will move to the country home of Lieutenant Governor Cramahe, about five miles from Quebec, and then three weeks later he will depart for England. Primarily I know for certain that General Carleton does not desire to leave Canada. He appears more downcast, because as open as he was, this change was unwanted. After the dinner we took our farewells and will return to Trois Rivieres tomorrow. From 7 July on, General Haldimand will preside at the dinners and during these days will also move into the castle St. Louis. From the castle there is the finest view in the world. It lies on the citadel and has a view of the entire port with all its ships, the Ile d'Orleans, and on the far side, the well-built-up region of Pointe de Levi. There are currently 150 iron cannons on the ramparts. A recently brought-in ship, a privateer, is a small two-masted ship and according to everyone's accounts, who have seen the inside, quite advantageously equipped for defense, as well as for offense. It has two rudders and reportedly can sail well with almost any wind.

5 July - We departed Quebec at five o'clock in the morning in two carriages. We entered Grondine at six o'clock in the evening and entered in our former quarters of Captain Ahrend. All the inhabitants of the place showed an unusual amount of joy to again see me in good health. However, the news which I now could give them about my brother and Ahrend was very unpleasant for them. They overwhelmed me with many compliments, were very friendly, and I was unable to get away from them until twelve o'clock at night.

Journal of Lieutenant Friedrich Julius von Papet

6 July - We departed at five o'clock in the morning. A strong storm overtook us at Ste. Marie at eight o'clock. We therefore had to wait for half an hour in one of the local houses, because of the heavy rain. We arrived at Trois Rivieres, without incident, at one o'clock. The Hessian recruits had already marched toward Terrebonne, where a captain from Lieutenant Colonel von Creuzbourg's Company is to lead them.

15 July - This order was sent to Lieutenant Colonel von Creuzbourg. At the request of Captain von Tunderfeldt I sent an inhabitant to Montreal today to bring horses, which the captain had purchased, to Quebec. This noon Ensign Sternberg arrived here with five batteaux and fifty men of the Prince Friedrich Regiment. They will pickup the items sent here as well as the baggage which came from Germany. Also, today, at the request of His Excellency, a list of all the craftsmen among the German troops was ordered. There are many reasons to be dissatisfied with the Prince Friedrich Regiment. The complaints are to be answered by Lieutenant Colonel Praetorius on 16 July.

Late entry for 14 July - On the orders of His Excellency 29 men of the Hesse-Hanau detachment are to be joined with the 31 Hessian artillerists to make a sixty-man unit. They are to march here to Trois Rivieres first and then receive the orders to march to Quebec.

16 July - Today one of the English detachments which remained here in Canada, while the main regiment marched with Burgoyne's army, marched through here en route to Quebec. All the privates were quartered with the regiments stationed here.

23 July - The required artillery detachment, consisting of two officers, four non-commissioned officers, one surgeon's mate, one drummer, and sixty privates of the Hessians, marched in here and were quartered in two barns.

24 July - The artillery detachment remained here today. As no answer came from Quebec today, and as it was preferred that the detachment get to Quebec sooner rather than later, it will continue on its way using the designated march route. That was the brigadier's belief, because he apparently wished to be rid of this detachment for some other reason. I gladly made the suggestion that with the departure from here, they could wait until the 28th for their next day of rest. However, my suggestion was not accepted. We received the

Journal of Lieutenant Friedrich Julius von Papet

news in a letter from Quebec, that General Carleton would embark on Sunday, 26 July. All our letters will go with him. Therefore, General Haldimand will soon establish his government.

25 July - The artillery company marched at three o'clock in the afternoon toward Cape Madeleine and according to the proposed march route, will enter Quebec on 2 August. They took the two deserters from the Specht Regiment, that were here, with them. The auditor of the Prince Friedrich Regiment left here at the same time.

26 July - Nothing new, except that the batteaux sent by Captain von Hambach for his part of the shoes sent here, departed.

27 July - This afternoon the brigadier received the order from two English officers passing through here that he was to allow the artillery company sent from here to return to Trois Rivieres. It has reached the point just as I said it would on 24 July. This detachment [of artillery] is to remain here until it receives further orders, and should do so and then exercise with two cannons coming from Montreal. The order for their return was immediately sent with an express.

28 July - During the afternoon the detachment returned here. They had already been alerted before our order, from Quebec, for their return. They were quartered as best possible. Because the barracks, due to the great many lice, must be repaired, all of the men were quartered in the city.

August

1 August - An order for the Prince Friedrich Regiment to give the artillery detachment an officer, one non-commissioned officer, and fifteen men. This last order was necessary because the 200-man detachment of Captain von Schoell was so strong, but had only one officer. Ensign [Friedrich Ludwig] Kaempfer was sent already today to Captain von Schoell's detachment.[32] Frequent and heavy storms.

2 August - This evening I had a small dispute about the provisions with the lieutenant colonel. The non-commissioned officer of the Prince Friedrich Regiment was recalled by the regiment on orders for sound reasons.

7 August - The officer sent from Cape Madeleine arrived here today at ten-thirty and reported to us that His Excellency would arrive here in one hour. He arrived at eleven-thirty and stepped out down at the water. We greeted him and led him to the street, where all the local garrison and a part of the militia paraded on the dockside. His Excellence excused himself for not being able to accept the brigadier's invitation this time as he had already accepted the hospitality of Colonel de Tonnecour. He entered the latter's house and everyone paid court to him. Then he went with the adjutant to the local new cloister and performed the conventional visit. Later the brigadier visited the beautiful garden and then the curate. Colonel Tonnecour was pleased to invite all of us this morning. However, everyone could not accept because they had all been invited by the brigadier. Therefore Colonel Tonnecour was not occupied. The brigadier put out fifteen dishes. Captain von Tunderfeldt received several truths today, especially from the brigadier as well as from Lieutenant Colonel von Barner. His Excellence inspected the barracks, the barracks' garden, and noted everything. Colonel Tonnecour did not come out well at this opportunity. He had put on the fanciest coat, while all the other militia were properly attired. This made him suspect by his own nation. At three-thirty His Excellence departed toward Machiche, where he will spend the night at the home of Seigneur Guichi. Due to an officer's oversight, upon his departure the brigadier was unable to make his farewell compliments as should have been done. After this departure we took a pleasure ride in a carriage.

18 August - One thousand Indians, who are now to assemble at Montreal, caused us considerable unrest. Because they are no longer needed, they have become very restless. They were assembled by General Carleton, but now we wish to be rid of these restless guests. Today's letter from Captain von Tunderfeldt finally provided us with the news that the Indians were pacified by General Haldimand and sent away with many gifts. His Excellence next requested an exact list of the present quarters situation for the troops. As such is to be submitted quickly and the previous pleasure of such a task fails me, the list will cause me much effort. Lieutenant Colonel von Barner ate with us today. During the afternoon a visit by the grand vicar and Father Theodor of Becancour. The latter wishes news if the Gulf is now fully occupied by four French frigates and many privateers. A bad situation for our recruits, whom we daily expect. We grope our way because we still haven't the least interesting information from Europe and are completely in the dark.

Journal of Lieutenant Friedrich Julius von Papet

21 August - The local commissary received orders to attend to his duties by having magazines with sufficient provisions for 1,000 men for one year. These are to be distributed on this side from Rivieres du Loup to Ste. Anne, and from Yamaska to St. Pierre on the south side. If they should consist of German or English troops, is still not known. The quarters list, as ordered, was submitted today.

31 August - Punishment was carried out this morning, in part for theft, in part for theft which failed. Concerning this, inquiries had been conducted according to the articles of war by the Prince Friedrich Regiment. Afterward Corporal Grube of the Dragoons was demoted and must run a gauntlet of 200 men, twelve times. Corporal Grube of the Light Infantry Battalion the same [brothers ?], the other privates according to their crimes. This afternoon Captain von Tunderfeldt passed through on his way from Montreal to Quebec. When the 2,000 German troops, which have already reached Bic, seek to enter at Quebec, he will be there to present the further orders of His Excellency for them and to make all necessary arrangements. He dined at noon with the brigadier and told us that we would soon be ordered to march and to camp for some time at Sorel. Lieutenant Colonel von Barner, who recently has gone to Montreal will try to make all the necessary arrangements. Supposedly war with France has not yet been declared, but we will soon receive news from Europe. At one-thirty Captain von Tunderfeldt continued on to Quebec. The lists and reports, as well as a French extract of the orders issued by the brigadier pertaining to the previous year's winter quarters, the ordnance carriages, and the harmony with the inhabitants, were completed today.

September

1 September - All the above were sent to Montreal with Captain le Maitre.

2 September - Toward noon the English Lieutenant Colonel [Barry] St. Leger, with eight companies of the 34th Regiment, arrived here, some in batteaux, and will be quartered tonight with them. Toward evening Lieutenant Colonel von Barner arrived. He had much to tell us about how good we would have it in the future under

General Haldimand. On the seventh the lieutenant colonel will go to Sorel.

7 September - Sir Johnson's Corps passed here in batteaux today and will proceed to Sorel. It is General Haldimand's intention to have the main depot and principal concentration of troops at Sorel.

8 September - Finally, according to a letter from Captain von Tunderfeldt, part of our recruits as well as the Anhalt-Zerbst Regiment commanded by Colonel [Friedrich] von Rauschenplat,[33] who had formerly served as an ensign in our service, have arrived at Quebec. Supposedly our recruits number 470 and were escorted here by Captains Stoeter, Weiss, and Ruff, and Lieutenant Confes. There are many sick who must go to the hospital in Quebec. The letters and news from Germany has not yet arrived. According to Captain Stoeter [the shipment amounts to] thirteen non-commissioned officers, one surgeon's mate, ten drummers, 394 privates, thirty children, and 21 women.

9 September - Many inhabitants from all the parishes who were ordered to Sorel to work, passed through here. Barracks are being built for 2,000 men.

11 September - Two officers who escorted the English troops here arrived on their way to Quebec and then to return to Europe. They ate at noon with the brigadier. Reportedly the French fleet of Mons. [Charles Hector, Comte] d'Estaing has been seen at New York. As Admiral [Richard] Howe took and armed the transport ships in order to attack, the French fleet quickly raised sail and went to sea.

15 September - Our long-awaited recruits for the regiments Prince Friedrich, Rhetz, Dragoons, and Riedesel, and 48 for the chasseurs arrived in a small and a large two-masted ship. Captains von Stoeter and Ruff and Lieutenant Confes were with them. All were landed at twelve o'clock and quartered here in the city. I looked through the letters which I received from Europe. We were all very pleased as the orders we received had depressed us. All the officers ate with the brigadier and we discussed the news from Europe. I entertained them during the evening.

19 September - I finished briefing the officers, after which they are to brief the recruits. At the same time the plan for the new organization and structure of the battalions arrived. After this, the commanding officers ate with the brigadier. During the evening

Captain Ruff gave me and the senior field cashier a description of everything that has been taking place in Braunschweig, and we nearly went through every house. An order to the Prince Friedrich Regiment, according to orders from Europe, is to reorganize the regiment. According to that order, the Stammer Company is to be deactivated and the men transferred to the other four companies and reinforced by the 44 recruits. Many officers and non-commissioned officers must be transferred from that regiment to the von Ehrenkrook and von Barner Battalions.[34] From these two latter, the accounts are to be balanced.

20 September - We all ate together at noon with Lieutenant Colonel von Barner. My duties did not allow me any free time so everything that occurred and that was discussed, had to be learned elsewhere.

From Quebec to Sorel, all boards which are in stock are to be purchased by an English engineer because they are urgently needed to build the barracks for 2,000 men at Sorel.

21 September - His Excellence's answer arrived, whereby the brigadier is fully authorized to draw the detachments together so that the two new battalions may be formed. His Excellence is fully satisfied with this reorganization. The solution to both the last points of the accord was rejected.

22 September - March orders were sent to Captain von Plessen at Quebec and to Captain von Hambach at Montreal. The first is to go to Montreal and the latter to Grand Machiche. Today I also wrote several letters to Europe, to Lieutenant W. and to Secretary K. The evening was spent socializing with Captain Stoeter.

23 September - During the morning all the recruits stood inspection with weapons and those assigned under the recently received plan were transferred to Lieutenant Colonel von Barner. Those men will now camp in the parish of Trois Rivieres.

24 September - I gave the Barner Battalion adjutant the briefing after the camping roster of the recruits had been prepared. During the evening visiting Lieutenant Colonel von Barner.

25 September - The brigadier's company was formed from the Rhetz detachment. Many letters to Quebec and one to Mons. le Maitre, as well as one to my uncle the privy councillor. According to a letter from Captain von Tunderfeldt, the detachment at Quebec is to move to Cape Madeleine on 1 and 2 October.

Journal of Lieutenant Friedrich Julius von Papet

28 September - Captain von Zielberg and Lieutenant von Reitzenstein arrived here. The first is to receive the Dragoon Company and the latter is to lead the 44 men of the recruits of the Prince Friedrich Regiment. Captain von Hambach reported this noon that he has arrived at Grand Machiche with his detachment of grenadiers. He received orders to quarter them beyond Pointe du Lac and when the company is reinforced by the 38 recruits, together with his company they are to relieve Captain Thomae at Yamaska.

30 September - The 44 recruits for the Prince Friedrich Regiment were delivered to Lieutenant von Reitzenstein, and are to be escorted to the regiment.

October

1 October - Captain [Francis] le Maitre, His Excellence's deputy general adjutant, arrived here to see how far the brigadier had advanced with the formation of the new regiment. Everything was explained to him and he ate at noon with the brigadier. At the same time, Captain von Plessen reported that he had arrived at Cape Madeleine from Quebec with the first division of the detachment. A letter to Europe to my dear sister.

2 October - I gave my report concerning the full state of the Brunswick troops to Mons. le Maitre.

Lieutenant Wolgast was sentenced to four nights in arrest because he was insubordinate to the brigadier.[35] Colonel von Rauschenplat and Captain von Tunderfeldt arrived here. They dined with the brigadier and after the levee continued on to General Haldimand at Sorel. Concerning the promotion for Colonel von Rauschenplat, General Haldimand has not yet concurred.[36] No one knows whether Brigadier von Ehrenkrook will lose anything if it is approved. The Dragoons of the Quebec detachment moved in here today. A copy to the Duke of Brunswick.

5 October - The Dragoon Companies of Captains von Zielberg and von Schlagenteufel were formed and everything went smoothly and according to the approved plan. Toward evening Colonel von Rauschenplat returned to Sorel and he will continue on to Quebec tomorrow. He brought letters for the brigadier. An order to the regiment concerning a request sent to Europe.

Journal of Lieutenant Friedrich Julius von Papet

7 October - The brigadier ordered the company of Captain von Plessen to Cape Madeleine. Therefore we departed at nine o'clock this morning in batteaux. Captain Stoeter, the senior field cashier, and the auditor accompanied us there. We found the company of the former detachment of the Specht Regiment in such exceptionally good condition, that the brigadier had occasion to be especially well pleased. We dined at noon at the local post house and were treated to all the best by Captain von Plessen. We returned at about four o'clock and arrived back at Trois Rivieres toward evening. My headache caused me to go to bed early.

14 October - Today His Excellence is to inspect the Hessian troops and will apparently then go to Montreal for a few days. The lists of Lieutenant Colonel von Barner were delivered to me today. During the past night Vice-corporal Senf of the Barner Battalion and three dragoons deserted. Nothing is left undone in an effort to catch them. Two batteaux with 26 convalescents came from Quebec. They will go to their regiments immediately. This evening two batteaux from Sorel were delivered to us against receipts. A small surprise to me.

15 October - Captain Foy is to inspect the von Hambach Company at Yamaska and St. Francois. We were pressed on all sides. The commanding officers' baggage left for Quebec today in two batteaux and the officers will follow on land in a few days.

16 October - Captain Foy mustered the companies at la Bergne and Nicolet. All our things, which are being sent to Europe, must be given to the commanding officers and those things will be sent to Quebec with the post tomorrow.

Captain von Tunderfeldt wrote to us, that such had to be done quickly because the ships returning to Europe will sail in a few days. I still wrote a letter today to my dear sister and with the letter sent some souvenirs from here. This evening there was a great social dinner at the brigadiers. We can await the neglected thanks for the recruits in the coming days. The mustering of the Prince Friedrich Regiment conducted on the twelfth of this month, during a steady rain, caused Foy to show great pleasure.

17 October - The officers departed at nine o'clock in the morning. God grant them a safe and speedy return. Shortly after their departure, Captains Foy and von Tunderfeldt arrived in order to muster the brigadier's battalion. They thought they would immediately find the troops under arms because they had informed us with a letter from la Baye to that effect. However the letter never arrived. Therefore those assigned to the company were immediately commanded to come here and to be ready to be mustered this afternoon. Captain von Plessen's Company at Cape Madeleine is to cross so as to arrive here at the same time. After eating, both companies and the general staff were mustered and Captain Foy was especially pleased with the brigadier's company of the Rhetz detachment. We then went to meet Captain von Plessen's Company at the crossing and the muster was conducted near the crossing. Foy was also exceptionally well pleased with this Specht detachment. Because it was too late to inspect Captain von Zielberg's Company at Pointe du Lac, the mustering of that company was postponed until eight o'clock tomorrow morning and scheduled at the post house in Pointe du Lac. In addition to the muster rolls, which Foy took in duplicate, I had to prepare his ideas in a battalion report and conduct a briefing at the same time for the von Barner Battalion. We then dined with the brigadier and Captain Foy was entertained with a European style punch.

18 October - The brigadier and I went on ahead to Pointe du Lac. We found the company had marched to the post house. At nine o'clock Foy and Tunderfeldt arrived and the company was mustered. After the muster Foy finally had the opportunity to eat breakfast with us and to enjoy the taste of a glass of warm wine. Satisfied with all of this business which followed quickly one after the other activity for me, at twelve o'clock we again arrived in Trois Rivieres. Foy and Tunderfeldt wanted to return to Sorel this evening.

21 October - His Excellency stayed overnight at the post house at Cape Madeleine and departed again this morning in a batteau for Quebec. This tour on the water does not please His Excellency's adjutant, specifically Captain von Tunderfeldt. Furthermore, His Excellency takes more with him than under the government of General Carleton. General Haldimand does not favor much formality, but rather large numbers and is content when he can sit peacefully and smoke a pipe of tobacco in front of his fireplace.

28 October - Reportedly there are ten ships with troops from Halifax in the river heading for Quebec. They are coming from New York and it is said that our exchanged prisoners, including officers, non-commissioned officers, and privates of Burgoyne's army, who were captured before the Convention, are on board.

November[37]

11 November - The staff watch established in the brigadier's battalion stood guard mount for the first time. Now all companies must provide their share of men.

17 November - A courier passed through on his way to Quebec. He was coming from St. Jean and brought news from the expedition which Major Carleton had made beyond Lake Champlain. The detachment had consisted of 300 Englanders, 200 volunteers, and 60 Indians. He went as far as Kingsbury and destroyed and burned everything along that route. It was evident from the houses destroyed here and there on the lake and for some 25 miles up the Ottenbruck River that the rebels from time to time had collected food and forage for 8,000 men. This as well as the houses was left in ashes from the fires and the entire region from St. Jean to Kingsbury was made a waste land. Women and children were exiled to New England but he brought back all the menfolk. A 100 man command at Fort George was made prisoners also, with a loss of only one man. On the return across the lake, one batteau with its crew was lost. This expedition was therefore to our advantage, well carried-out, and apparently this destruction puts difficulties in the rebel's plans, if they had the intention of paying us a visit. Sir Johnson plans to conduct a similar raid with a like detachment along the route to Oswego.

24 November - The report was forwarded. An inquiry concerning wood and light [candles] for the watches. We finally received the news from Quebec that the ship *Nancy* is at Halifax and had been forced by a severe storm to anchor there. Two English officers who had made their way on land from Cape Gaspe brought two letters to Lieutenant Colonel von Barner, one from Lieutenant Colonel von Specht and one from Captain von Gleisenberg. The first wrote that he had been exchanged already in April but had to remain in New York until October. He had sailed from there on 17 October with Captain von Gleisenberg, Cornet Count Foender Haeberlin, and about eighty men, and twice had been as far as Anticosti, from where he had been driven back to Halifax, and finally forced to spend the winter at

Journal of Lieutenant Friedrich Julius von Papet

Lueneburg, 100 miles from Halifax. Our corps is scattered throughout America and will surely be in a condition too poor ever again to be united. Above all it appears that things are going very badly for our prisoners and those included in the Convention. Many of our privates desert, take service with the rebels, and then desert again in order to get to the English army. Therefore, service with the rebels must not be very pleasant. Lieutenant Colonel von Specht, like all the others, has lost everything and describes himself as naked and destitute. The command to Vercheres, consisting of two officers, four non-commissioned officers, two drummers, and fifty men of the Prince Friedrich Regiment was ordered by Brigadier [Henry Watson] Powell and apparently because the inhabitants there have refused to be ordered to work. Lieutenant Colonel von Barner's joy at Lieutenant Colonel von Specht's release is exceptionally great and it is a pleasure for him, an embarrassment to the brigadier, and occasioned many remarks from both parties.

I say nothing and only think.

28 November - The captives, 39 men, one woman, and one child, taken by Major Carleton's detachment on Lake Champlain, arrived here. They were brought here by an English officer, and one officer, five non-commissioned officers, and 24 of our men. These poor people were very miserable to see and have lost their spirit as well as in part their wives and children, who have been sent to New England.

29 November - These captives were escorted on to Cape Madeleine at ten o'clock in the morning by one officer, five non-commissioned officers, and 24 men. That command will escort them all the way to Quebec and will bring back to us from there, if possible, the desired ammunition and convalescents. The suggestion was sent to His Excellence with the escort. A visit today by Seigneur Guichi to the brigadier. He also dined with him.

30 November - Captain von Tunderfeldt communicated to the brigadier, on orders of His Excellence, that Lieutenant Colonel von Specht had written and also brought with him a list of the troops. His Excellence desires that the Brunswick troops be dressed this winter against the cold with a blanket [coat], just like all the others, because it will certainly be needed by the troops this winter. Therefore, he will have everything delivered which serves that purpose, but the brigadier must request of the Duke that he pay for these items and be responsible when, on the other hand, the troops are at a disadvantage without them. A great embarrassment for the brigadier that providing the necessary clothing for winter in this climate is not included in the treaty for the troops, and therefore no adequate instructions as to what to do or not to do in such a situation.

The acquisition of such items for the corps will cause an expenditure of at least 7,000 Reichsthalers for the Duke, which is the reason it has been put off.

December

19 December - The order came from Quebec that the troops could remain in their quarters. Captain von Hambach received a quarters assignment from Quartermaster General Carleton and so must be ready to march. The Prince Friedrich Regiment received the good parish of Vercheres for its quarters and so will be able to accommodate an entire company. Lieutenant Colonel von Creuzbourg hoped to occupy the parishes of l'Assomption and Repentigny with his jaegers and the Ile Jesus with Captain von Schoell's detachment. In Quebec it has been learned that General Clinton had embarked with 15,000 men at New York and sailed against Boston. The French have supposedly taken the Island of St. Domingo from the English.[38] There had only been two companies as garrison there. An English deserter from the 34th Regiment was brought here under arrest.

20 December - Captain von Hambach received an order to be prepared to march.

21 December - Many orders and the inspection of the condition of the quarters of the von Ehrenkrook and von Barner Battalions.

22 December - The orders and letters were dispatched. Today there was a court-martial, whose president was Lieutenant Colonel von Barner, concerning the desertion of a dragoon.

Journal of Lieutenant Friedrich Julius von Papet

January 1779

1 January - On 31 [December] I made many wishes concerning my dear fatherland. God grant that those wishes might be fulfilled and that I might soon be freed from the necessity of often repeating those wishes in such a far distant place.

2 January - I and the brigadier paid visits to the local officials. Today there was a thaw.

3 January - Captain Sander arrived at noon and joined us for lunch, which showed the true proof of our host's living style.

4 January - An auction was held to dispose of the possessions of the dead officers. The items sold at very high prices. Toward noon Lieutenant Colonel Praetorius arrived. During the evening many persons visited the brigadier.

5 January - The rest of the reports and lists were sent to Quebec. I sent two piasters to Lieutenant Colonel von Creuzbourg against receipts. The suggestions sent to His Excellency have still not been answered. In response to a general order, each month a list of the already expended ammunition and how it was used is to be submitted. I had to pay as much at the auction for blue and white cloth for a uniform as I would have had to pay in Germany.

6 January - Lieutenant Colonel von Barner suddenly came in after dinner and a bitter dispute developed between him and Lieutenant Colonel Praetorius-----not however, coming to blows. I can say nothing more about it, except that I wished not to have been a witness thereto. It was finally settled by a friendly agreement, after both sides had been fully clarified.

7 January - Militia Captain Schmidt returned from his trip to Quebec. During his visit with the brigadier, he was asked again about his affair with Captain von Hambach and the full particulars. It appeared that the latter was not as innocent as he had said. He was promised all possible satisfaction.

8 January - A serious complaint was received from Quebec concerning Lieutenant Herlet's detachment. Captain von Hambach's reply, as well as the accompanying letter from Lieutenant Colonel von Barner, had not been well received by His Excellency and he clearly indicated his displeasure with several remarks in Lieutenant Colonel von Barner's letter. Now, due to the heat developed, the situation

Journal of Lieutenant Friedrich Julius von Papet

becomes more important than would have been thought initially, and not altogether as we had wished and hoped. Today I carried out an order to appease His Excellence.

9 January - Lieutenant Colonel Praetorius and Captain Sander departed this morning for St. Charles.

10 January - His Excellence's answer was passed on to the lieutenant colonel and he immediately ordered Captain von Hambach to report here so that this situation could be more thoroughly investigated than it had been previously.

11 January - Many letters to Quebec. My batman took such a fall today that his right shoulder was completely dislocated.

12 January - After eating, the brigadier and I and Goedecke took a pleasant ride in a carriage to visit Captain von Plessen at Cape Madeleine. Toward evening he returned with us.

13 January - The sale of items belonging to the dead officers was completed. Lieutenant Wolgast reported that an inhabitant from Nicolet heard from a rebel wood-cutter, who had come here and then disappeared, that the rebels were making many snow shoes with the intention of paying us a visit during the month of February.

14 January - Except for much easing of the conscience, nothing new.

15 January - An order concerning winter quarters for both the von Ehrenkrook and von Barner Battalions finally arrived, accordingly the following are to be occupied:

von Ehrenkrook Battalion

In Riviere Batiscan and the parish of Batiscan - Captain Zielberg

In the parishes of Champlain and Cape Madeleine - Captain von Plessen

In Trois Rivieres - the brigadier's company, with a command of one non-commissioned officer and 100 men, which is to be relieved every four to six weeks by the four companies of the battalion

In the parishes of Trois Rivieres, Pointe du Lac, and Grand Machiche - Captain von Schlagenteufel.

von Barner Battalion

In the parishes of Kinchien and Vaudreuil - Captain von Hambach
In the parish of Riviere du Loup - Lieutenant Colonel von Barner
In the parishes of Maskinonge and Sormiere - Captain Thomae
In the parish of Culbert - Captain Rosenberg

Journal of Lieutenant Friedrich Julius von Papet

From the last three companies, a command of one officer, two non-commissioned officers, and thirty men is to go to St. Francois, and one officer, three non-commissioned officers, one drummer, and 40 men is to go to Nicolet and la Baye, and are also to be relieved every four weeks. In the assignment of the quarters for the von Barner Battalion, the confirmation by His Excellency is still awaited. Today the brigadier received a letter from Chaplain Fuegerer,[39] of the Prince Friedrich Regiment, in which he cloaked all his infamous actions under the influence of drunkeness. That letter, the most individualistic one of its kind, will be put aside as a future proof that he cared as little for us spiritually as bodily.

16 January - I completed preparing the orders for winter quarters for the two battalions so that the von Ehrenkrook was to enter them on 18 January and the von Barner on 19 January. New witness - concerning the character of ones conscience - to complete understanding. Avarice and ingratitude.

17 January - Nothing new.

18 January - The von Zielberg Company marched through on its way to Batiscan where its assigned quarters were, and the von Schlagenteufel Company marched from here to Grand Machiche and Pointe du Lac. Today I personally paid for my room being wall-papered.

19 January - In orders today, Colonel von Rauschenplat was designated a brigadier in the army, and Captain [Carl Friedrich] Piquet [or Picquet] was named brigade major. Captain von Hambach arrived here today. Toward noon it became very cold and the temperature fell to a minus thirty degrees.

20 January - An accident was reported by an express from Captain Thomae that during the march across Lake St. Pierre eight men and two women froze to death and additionally many individuals had frozen hands and feet. Supposedly Thomae had been warned by the inhabitants not to undertake this march during such extreme cold, nor could the inhabitants be motivated to move the provisions. Therefore, despite being bound to do so by orders, without these conditions, this march concerned only the movement into winter quarters at Saathe. This was indicated by the first news from Canadians, who reported the most. Therefore, nothing was neglected here in the way of helping these unfortunate individuals with medicines, and on

Journal of Lieutenant Friedrich Julius von Papet

21 January - the local doctor departed at once for Riviere du Loup in order to learn personally the exact details. Today I wrote to Lieutenant Colonel von Barner that the brigadier saw it as necessary, because of this precipitous and ill-considered march, to call Captain Thomae to account and the lieutenant colonel apparently can and must, from all indications, because of his persistent illness, give up command. As to my obligation, because I was asked my opinion, I recommended what I would advise so that it would not be my responsibility, not to interfere with what the brigadier had begun.

22 January - The English doctor returned today and according to the current reports twelve have already frozen to death and nearly thirty have frozen limbs. This misfortune will be investigated to determine if it should be attributed to fate or negligence. I wrote to Lieutenant Colonel von Barner to decide whether or not he could return to his battalion. The brigadier is determined in the latter case, to transfer the investigation and the command to one of the staff officers. If he is actually determined to carry out this decision or to put it into effect, I can not say, but at least I already saw the fickleness of the lieutenant colonel's answer this evening. Therefore on

23 January - I had, in a duplicate letter to him, diminished the determination of the investigation. Today two men died in the local hospital, one from Captain von Zielberg's Company and the other from Captain Rosenberg's Company. Ensign Kolte, who had written to His Excellence, about this affair, without permission, was placed in a 28 hour arrest for that reason. At noon today Captain Rosenberg finally appeared with the complete list of losses of 19 January, consisting of fifteen dead, two missing, fifteen seriously ill, who had to go to the hospital, ten seriously ill at the battalion, and 23 slightly ill.[40] It has been determined that a full investigation about this incident had been held and that this officer was no more responsible than anyone else. For those sick individuals still living the best possible care had been given and it was hoped that most of them would improve.

24 January - Captain Rosenberg traveled back to his quarters area. A written account of this event was requested from Lieutenant Colonel von Barner today and was received this evening.

25 January - Captain von Hambach and Militia Captain Schmidt appeared at the investigation of the von Hambach incident and stated that Captain von Hambach, one non-commissioned officer, and two

Journal of Lieutenant Friedrich Julius von Papet

men had been sent to his house and had threatened him with arrest, and he was able to prove this. Because of Captain von Schlagenteufel's illness, who because of a shortage of staff officers was the acting major presiding at the investigation, no sworn statement could be taken from Captain von Hambach today.

26 January - The incident of 19 January was reported to His Excellence at Quebec. I had to prepare numerous orders and letters to answer. The regimental surgeon of the Prince Friedrich Regiment is to go to Riviere du Loup and St. Culbert in order to see if the sick individuals at those places are being well-cared for by the company surgeon's mates. Toward evening Father Peri came from Quebec and visited the brigadier. They dined together and he was taken to his assigned quarters in the brigadier's coach late in the evening. He is en route to Montreal. An order to the troops in which it was forbidden for anyone to write to His Excellence on his own behalf. The expenses for Ensign Kolte's trip to Quebec are to be advanced from the Prince Friedrich regimental money chest.

27 January - Fourteen of the sick individuals who froze extremities on 19 January were brought here to the hospital from the battalion on thirteen vehicles. All the various statements agree that this misfortune can be attributed to fate. This is all immaterial when the clothing in which we arrived in such a cold climate is taken into consideration, and even more so, that for years and years heavy clothing for this battalion has been lacking, and it is no longer known how this situation and in such circumstances could be prevented for the men who so seldom travel about. Many of the battalion officers are sick and if their health does not improve, the entire battalion will become unserviceable. Never before has a battalion been in such poor condition. If we were attacked by an enemy in this situation, it is certain that we could make little or even no resistance.

28 January - The investigation of Captain von Hambach was ended today and put aside. He was not as guiltless as he had indicated in his first explanation. He paid costs and was sentenced to 24 hours in arrest. Today I sent two minot [a minot is 1.1 bushels] of Alocasia [a herb of the arum family], which are also known among us as green berries, to Captain von Tunderfeldt.

29 January - The answer arrived from His Excellence concerning the report of the 19 January incident. He has reported it to England

Journal of Lieutenant Friedrich Julius von Papet

and is quite satisfied that no blame will be placed on the officers; that they could have a clear conscience. We sent a request to Quebec asking whether or not we could occupy the barracks at St. Francois.

30 January - Lieutenant Colonel von Barner appears to be very dissatisfied. He seems very annoyed with me as the originator who as directed sent him orders. For my part however, I have a clean conscience and am therefore undisturbed. With time all this will be cleared up.

31 January - I suggested an answer from the brigadier to His Excellency's letter of 7 January. He should forward an extract of the investigation of Captain von Hambach and an apology from Lieutenant Colonel von Barner.

February

1 February - The Regimental Surgeon Bernt came from Riviere du Loup and made his report concerning the sick individuals of the von Barner Battalion to the brigadier. According to the list there are six men who lost fingers making them unfit for service. Pity him on whose conscience lies the many unfortunate ones. There is still much that could be said and that now we can be thankful for----! It thawed today.

2 February - The thaw continued and all the reports, lists, and letters were sent off with the post today. According to a report from Quebec the rebels hope to be at Chambly by 28 February. This report still awaits confirmation however.

3 February - Nothing new except for the departure of the regimental surgeon.

4 February - The English Lieutenant [Richard] Walker of Sir Johnson's Corps died here in the hospital.

5 February - He was buried by us with all military honors and the brigadier and all the local officers followed the corpse. There was another bitter cold spell today. Yesterday two Englanders, under arrest, one a sailor and the other a suspicious person, were sent to Quebec.

6 February - An order was sent to Lieutenant Colonel von Barner that the detachment at St. Francois could move into the completed barracks.

Journal of Lieutenant Friedrich Julius von Papet

7 February - Today a soldier from the brigadier's company died in the hospital.

8 February - The auditor traveled to the von Barner Battalion at Riviere du Loup in order to investigate a deserter. He will then continue on to the regiment.

9 February - Many letters to answer for Quebec and also an order on the regiment concerning pay accounts. The letter to His Excellence from the brigadier was answered today and he was completely satisfied with the brigadier's reply.

10 February - A suspicious inhabitant from Machiche, who had spread the report that 12,000 rebels were marching against us, was arrested by Colonel von Tonnecour and on

11 February - escorted from here to Quebec by the aide-major of the militia and a non-commissioned officer and one man. This morning two Anhalt-Zerbst officers came from Quebec. They were sent to see me by Brigadier von Rauschenplat, who wanted me to instruct them in preparing the muster rolls and all other regulations because the [Anhalt-Zerbst] Regiment was to pass in review on 16 February. I instructed them about everything and also gave them a format for the rosters. They ate at noon with the brigadier and returned from here to Quebec in the evening.

12 February - The brigadier and I received our warrants concerning our pay from 23 June to 24 January 1778, 187 days.

13 February - Nothing new.

14 February - During the morning we traveled in a carriage to visit Captain von Plessen at Champlain. We remained there during the day and then departed early on

15 February - very well-satisfied. Upon our return the English Engineer Captain [William] Twiss reported to the brigadier, as he had been ordered to check the local barracks and the Recollects Cloister, where the brigadier is presently residing. He was therefore shown those places. The deserter Corporal Beckmann has been arrested in Quebec.

16 February - The 180-man detachment at this place was relieved. An order was received by the brigade that no rum or cognac was to be sold to the Indians. Reportedly the news has been received from Halifax that the French have captured many West Indies islands from

Journal of Lieutenant Friedrich Julius von Papet

the English, and also that the King of Prussia has twice defeated the armies of the Holy Roman Emperor. I have not been feeling well.

17 February - A strong storm suddenly sprang up from the west at midday. It began to thaw very rapidly and in two hours there were strong gusts of rain with thunder and lightning. Another suspicious inhabitant was escorted to Quebec today.

18 February - The deserter Corporal Beckmann was brought here in arrest from Quebec today. The barracks at St. Francois was occupied on 9 February. There was some frost again today.

20 February - A visit from Captain von Plessen and Lieutenant Sommerlatte. This evening thirty recruits raised at Quebec for the MacLean Regiment at Montreal arrived here.

21 February - They remained here today and received permission from the brigadier to remain here for three or four days and to carry on recruiting efforts with drum rolls. It was reported in the brigadier's house today that he very much agreed with that idea about which there is reason for general agreement.

22 February - Nothing new.

23 February - A sharp punishment was carried out on several soldiers of the brigadier's company for a ruthless beating and for the desertion of Corporal Beckmann, who was demoted to the lowest rank. Captain von Plessen and Lieutenant Sommerlatte paid their compliments today.

24 February - Many letters in order to clarify the current accounts. During the afternoon Colonel Tonnecour arrested two people from Condition, Mons. Latteriere and Jensen, and one from Quebec who had been released from rebel captivity, and delivered them to the local guards for safekeeping. Reportedly letters were found on the first which placed them in agreement with the rebels, without a doubt.

25 February - An escort with money for Montreal arrived here from Quebec. This was escorted onward to Montreal from here by one non-commissioned officer and four men.

26 February - An impertinence toward me by the so-called, and so-designated by the brigadier, Staff Surgeon Iserhof, which circulated widely and for which the reason was easily divined. Toward evening a heavy snowfall.

27 and 28 February - Nothing new.

Journal of Lieutenant Friedrich Julius von Papet
March

1 March - Still the same. A dispute during the noon meal about my duties as brigade major.

2 March - The monthly reports and lists were sent to Quebec. According to the news from Quebec, Lake Champlain is already free of ice and therefore on this side we are secure. The non-commissioned officer returned from Montreal.

3 March - I saw Lieutenant Colonel von Barner moving out again. He had visited the brigadier and plans to return to his battalion again. Today I received my pay as brigade major from 25 June to 24 December 1778.

4 March - Many letters and preparation of orders. Today Magistrate Paby and Mons. Guichi came from Quebec in order to conduct a hearing on the suspicious persons recently arrested here. The first hearing was held this afternoon and because of the request made to the brigadier that the three men in arrest be kept apart by our general, so that they can not speak to one another, it is obvious that it is very serious.

5 March - Two of the arrested individuals were locked up. A visit to Lieutenant Colonel von Barner by the brigadier. The former tried to convince the brigadier with representations to have the matter of the unpaid forage money brought to the attention of His Excellence, but the brigadier was not persuaded to do so. I could offer no advice because I saw that in this arbitrary affair, the representations would be to no avail.

6 March - Nothing new.

7 March - The locked up men in arrest, Jensen, and John Ogs were escorted to Quebec. At noon there were numerous guests for dinner with the brigadier. Several days ago a resident of Becancour reported that during the night three men had broken into his storehouse and taken 100 pounds of tobacco, 100 pounds of bacon, and forty pounds of salt. According to the tracks the men were either soldiers from the Cape or those stationed locally. Therefore all were inspected but nothing was discovered. Part were from the brigadier's company and they had buried the items in the snow on the Genoux River and they still had some with them. The perpetrators were arrested.

Journal of Lieutenant Friedrich Julius von Papet

8 March - I sent an order to Lieutenant Colonel von Barner, as ordered by the brigadier, to inspect the companies at Riviere du Loup on 13 and 14 March.

9 March - The men arrested for the noted break-in were examined by Ensign Reinerding. Many regulations pertaining to pay for the necessary transportation arrived with the post, as well as what the inhabitants were obligated to furnish to the troops in quarters, because there was a long-standing complaint by the host of Lieutenant Colonel von Barner concerning theft and he complained also that he could not support Lieutenant Colonel von Barner in his house much longer.

10 March - The regulations were translated. Toward noon a visit from Captain von Plessen and Lieutenant Sommerlatte.

11 March - The orders received were disseminated to the brigade. The brigadier considered it necessary in carrying on the war, that the carriages be paid for from the regimental chest, which advance would be made good during the accounting for the following six months.

12 March - This order was sent to the entire brigade. Just as we were about to depart for Riviere du Loup, Colonel von Tonnecour delivered a letter to the brigadier from Lieutenant Governor Cramahe that the man in arrest, Latteriere, was to be sent as soon as possible and as quietly as possible to Quebec. As it was assumed he had many accomplices, one officer, one non-commissioned officer, and six men were detailed to take five carriages and drive day and night all the way to Quebec. Before our departure everything was ordered for that escort. We departed in two coaches at one o'clock and arrived at Riviere du Loup at six o'clock. Lieutenant Colonel von Barner greeted us with a very reserved manner. We dined with him and about eight o'clock went to the quarters prepared for us. Mine were bad. The company of Captain Thomae at Maskinonge will be inspected at ten o'clock tomorrow and that of Rosenberg at St. Culbert at twelve o'clock. We will eat breakfast with the first and our noon meal with the latter.

13 March - I had coffee with the brigadier in the morning and at eight-thirty the brigadier, the lieutenant colonel, I, and Ensign Kolte departed, arriving at Maskinonge at nine-thirty, where the company was inspected on the ice of the river which has the same name as the parish. The brigadier was satisfied with the clothing and equipment, as well as with the personal appearance of the men. We ate breakfast at ten-thirty and after changing carriages traveled on a very bad, untrodden road through a true wilderness, arriving at St. Culbert at twelve o'clock, although it was a journey of almost twelve miles. The company of Captain Rosenberg was better than the previous one, in bearing as well as drill. We ate very well and had quite a lot to drink. At three o'clock we returned in three carriages and Captain Rosenberg traveled with us. I took my place with the latter and found myself no longer so strongly shaken. In Maskinonge we had to change carriages because of the tired horses. The militia captain at that place was very attentive to the brigadier and entertained us with a glass of wine (Madeira). Half an hour after leaving Maskinonge the brigadier noted his hat was missing, as it had been left behind in the previous carriage. Despite all arguments, we had to turn back in order to recover the hat. The road to Maskinonge was, as I had assumed and previously noted, in bad condition and the reason that we did not arrive at Riviere du Loup until seven o'clock in the evening. Lieutenant Colonel von Barner had already arrived an hour earlier. We dined with the lieutenant colonel and as we went to our quarters at ten o'clock, the carriage upset and the brigadier, although unhurt, was thrown out. Therefore we continued on to our quarters on foot.

14 March - The lieutenant colonel's company was inspected at ten o'clock in the morning and showed that it not only made a good appearance, but also executed its drill well. After the inspection we paid a visit to the parish priest, a very pleasant individual. All the officers then dined with the lieutenant colonel. After dinner the priest and his brother, Petriman, who had a beautiful wife, paid their respects to the brigadier. Half an hour later they departed. There then followed much discussion concerning relieving the detachment at St. Francois, which I however, refused at this time to resolve because of the pro and contra arguments given. We took our departure from the lieutenant colonel during the evening and plan to return to Trois Rivieres tomorrow.

15 March - We departed at seven-thirty. The lieutenant colonel accompanied us for a few miles, to his farthest quarters. At Grand Machiche we halted briefly at the quarters of Lieutenant Bielstein, who was not at home. We entered Trois Rivieres at twelve o'clock. Nothing new was found. The escort for Mons. Latteriere had departed without incident. The desired accounts had finally arrived

Journal of Lieutenant Friedrich Julius von Papet

from the Prince Friedrich Regiment, as well as a complaint against Ensign Goedecke concerning an indebtedness to a man in Montreal, who had previously served as a musketeer in the army at Carleton.

16 March - The company here was relieved by a 100-man detachment. During the afternoon Lieutenant von Pincier reported that he had delivered Latteriere, the man in arrest, to Quebec and that His Excellence had been very well pleased with the speedy delivery.

17 March - A severe punishment was administered for the theft during the night of a resident of Becancour. Lieutenant Colonel von Barner was here again today and the brigadier himself told the lieutenant colonel about the complaint of his host. From all indications nothing has changed, but the host has gone to Quebec, apparently to lodge his complaint with His Excellence.

18 March - Lieutenant Colonel von Barner gave the brigadier a statement in French as an answer to the complaint by his host, and requested therein that it be sent to His Excellence. This was sent on

19 March - to Quebec. This morning another visit from Lieutenant Colonel von Barner.

20 March - Again a heavy frost and beautiful clear weather.

21 March - The brigadier and I visited Mons. Guichi at Machiche and dined with him. Two Englishmen, who were en route to Quebec from Montreal, joined us at dinner. One was the General Engineer Cornes, who had surveyed this province, and the other was the Paymaster Drumont from Quebec, a still unmarried, young man of twenty years. He had a beautiful sister with whom Captain von Tunderfeldt was much enamoured. We departed again at three o'clock and had returned here already by six o'clock. This whole trip was made on the ice of the St. Lawrence River.

22 March - According to the news which has been received at Quebec from the province above Detroit, Commander [Henry] Hamilton has captured Fort St. Vincent from the local rebels and with the Indians of his command made himself much feared. It is added that the rebels can make no preparations for the coming campaigns and we are of the hope that the same condition will continue. Lieutenant Colonel von Barner's response to the complaint of his host has been well received by His Excellence. The accounts of our corps have been assembled and will be sent to Quebec at the earliest opportunity.

Journal of Lieutenant Friedrich Julius von Papet

23 March - An order to the regiments concerning summer uniforms, as well as an appropriate answer to the somewhat too blunt question of Lieutenant Colonel Praetorius to the brigadier.

24 March - Lieutenant Colonel von Barner lodged another complaint against the senior cashier with the brigadier. The brigadier notified the senior field cashier to prepare a reply. This was directed to the point so well that this time the complaint appeared incorrect and to the advantage of the senior field cashier, with little or no justifiable complaint and merited no further action.

25 March - The reply was forwarded to the lieutenant colonel.

26 March - An order to the senior field cashier to meet with Lieutenant Colonel von Barner concerning the complaint of craftsman Guntermann against Ensign Goedecke. All the reports were received today. Because the officer accounts which had been sent in, from which payment of forage money had to be computed, another had to be resolved, and therefore the brigadier will make a direct representation to His Excellence today. There was a social get together today between the brigadier and Lieutenant Colonel von Barner and we made plans to go to St. Francois tomorrow to inspect the barracks at that place. Because of my duties I am not yet included.

27 March - I decided against the trip. In my place, Lieutenant Bodemeyer was taken. At eight-thirty the gentlemen departed.

28 March - Mr. Guichi visited me during the morning. He had been sent to Quebec by Mons. Tonnecour for His Excellence, because of my complaint from Lieutenant Wolgast about a resident, and from there sent with the task to settle this affair as quickly as and as best possible. During the afternoon the brigadier returned home. The trip had injured his eyes apparently because the snow caused a blindness. I informed him of Mons. Guichi's visit and he discussed it briefly with that individual and everything was taken care of. After I returned home I suddenly did not feel well.

29 March - Many letters, orders, and items to be sent to Germany to prepare. The order was sent to Lieutenant Colonel von Barner concerning Mons. Guichi and that decision, as well as the truth of the circumstances of the complaint against Lieutenant Wolgast.

30 March - All these letters and orders were dispatched. Even yesterday's decision about the complaint arrived today from His Excellence at Quebec for the brigadier. His Excellence is especially angered by the despotic expressions used by Lieutenant Colonel von Barner in a letter about this and other subjects to Militia Captain Auge at Riviere du Loup, and he has therefore ordered that all the inhabitants are to be treated with more consideration and moderation. I made this known to the entire brigade in a general order and directed Lieutenant Colonel von Barner to deliver a copy of his letter and the complaint which resulted. Also, some news, including Burgoyne's capture, arrived with two Canadians from Halifax. They also brought some letters and newspapers. Both the English and French fleets returned to their harbors in October [I believe the copyist misinterpreted the date which he noted as the eighth and it was probably the shortened form of October.] without having made contact. France continues to strengthen itself both on land and by sea. England does the same. Also many French ships have been captured and all the French ports are blockaded. At Munich-Gratz the Holy Roman Emperor had stood behind the defenses; Field Marshal Landon was also entrenched not far from Niemes. The King of Prussia had his camp near Lauterwasser and Prince Heinrich near Niemes. The King's army entered winter quarters in Silesia at the beginning of October [again the copyist error indicates only on the eighth] and there is still no decisive activity between the two armies, but only small skirmishes. It is believed that it will be settled this winter. General Clinton has sent an English and a Hessian regiment to Halifax. General Clinton is still at New York. At Halifax everything is three times more expensive than here. Captain Foy, who serves as the provincial secretary and who is very sympathetic toward us Germans, is said to be suffering from a serious illness and there is little hope of his recovery.

31 March - Yesterday's copies were sent to Lieutenant Colonel von Barner so that he can answer them.

April

1 April - Several excesses were committed by the Surgeon's Mate Iserhof and Captain-at-arms Scheppelmann. Therefore they were arrested.

2 April - An answer, concerning the complaints received, was sent to Quebec, also the letter which contained Lieutenant Colonel von

Barner's apology to the militia captain. The thaw has been very great for several days.

3, 4, and 5 April - Nothing new, except a visit from Captain von Plessen and much sadness on my part because it is now a year and a day since public church services were last held here. Heaven grant that this is the last Easter that I must spend in this place.

6 April - Lanandiere wrote to me and asked that I obtain a soldier from the brigadier's company to work as a carpenter for him. He is a miller and wants to build a grinding mill for which he has already made a model. The brigadier agreed to send a carpenter to him. Because of the warm thaw, the river is running high. The mail from Quebec did not arrive until six o'clock this evening.

7 April - Captain-at-arms Scheppelmann was demoted for three months, after receiving thirty hits with the flat of a broadsword from the company.

8 April - The ice on the river broke. This year the water is fifteen feet higher than last year. It is possible that the ice will jam. Most inhabitants believe that the lower city will be flooded and therefore they have begun to move most of their belongings to safety and to keep their canoes close at hand. This is not uncommon in April when there is much snow and the weather suddenly turns warm.

9 April - Large blocks of ice passed Trois Rivieres. On the bank, where the houses stand, large pieces of ice forty-five feet square and three feet thick were driven against the houses, but fortunately did not disturb the houses. The bank lost at least four feet of earth.

10 April - Still a lot of floating ice, but in small pieces.

11 April - Now the river is wide open and the water has fallen two inches.

12 April - Nothing new.

13 April - The level of the river has noticeably fallen.

14 April - Mail from Quebec, which should have arrived yesterday, finally arrived this morning. Reportedly the road is passable only at the risk of one's life. Captain von Tunderfeldt informed me that the forage money will soon be paid, and paid for the whole year. If that does not happen, the brigadier and I will lose the most.

15 April - The assignment of quarters for the brigadier's battalion, according to the latest order from His Excellence, still creates many

Journal of Lieutenant Friedrich Julius von Papet

difficulties and Captain von Zielberg needs another eighty quarters. Therefore on

16 April - His Excellence will be asked if the captain may be permitted to extend his quarters as far as Ste. Anne. Until an answer is received, the company will remain where it is. Today, for the first time, a three-masted and two two-masted ships passed en route to Quebec from Sorel. It is said that they are going to check the Gulf of St. Lawrence.

17 April - It turned winter again and a heavy snow fell. The mail again arrived very late. Toward evening I received 216 letters from the Prince Friedrich Regiment to be sent on to Germany.

18 April - All the required lists to be sent to Germany arrived from the Prince Friedrich Regiment. The regiment's present quarters are still insufficient and the use of the parish of St. Ours was requested. This noon there was a large group for dinner with the brigadier.

19 April - The situation concerning the quarters for the Prince Friedrich Regiment was reported to Quebec. An order to the brigadier on removing winter clothing and the start of drill.

20 April - The rumor spread here today that the rebels had been seen on the other side of Lake Ontario. Therefore it was said that they had taken Detroit and captured Commander Hamilton and his 250-man detachment. We must wait and see if that is confirmed by Quebec. A two-masted ship passed on its way to Quebec. Eighty Canadians here at Trois Rivieres were ordered to be ready to march.

21 April - The news came from Quebec that Commander Hamilton had advanced as far as Illinois 1,500 miles from here on the Mississippi, with 74 men and had been captured by a strong party of rebels. This Hamilton, on his own and despite being under the commander in Canada, acted without orders. This evening we dined for the first time in a long while with Lieutenant Colonel von Barner.

22 April - Nothing new.

23 April - Captain von Tunderfeldt reported that he has not approached His Excellence to request extension of the quarters assignments, a sign that he has misplaced the brigadier's letter. Therefore the brigadier is intent, without any further request, to send an order to the militia captain.

24 April - I drafted a report to the Duke concerning the local corps and the necessary repairs and sent it through Commissary Sills, and

Journal of Lieutenant Friedrich Julius von Papet

that failing, through a letter to the assistant quartermaster, Lieutenant Barnes, at Sorel. The brigadier is very dissatisfied with Captain von Tunderfeldt, which I hope however, will soon pass. Colonel [Thomas] Carleton came in a sloop from Quebec today, en route to Montreal. He passed unrecognized.

25 April - Due to contrary wind, Colonel Carleton turned around and departed in a coach after having a brief conversation with Lieutenant Colonel von Barner.

26 April - An order to Lieutenant Colonel Praetorius to extend into the parish of St. Ours if necessary. Ensign Reinerding went to the companies of von Plessen and von Zielberg in order to extend their quarters.

27 April - Yesterday's order to the Prince Friedrich Regiment was cancelled to the extent it is to remain as it now is. The arrival of two ships from Quebec, which delivered orders to Commissary Sills to make necessary repairs to the local batteaux. It was announced from Quebec that His Excellence would soon have the troops camping. How this will be carried out by the combined battalions, which have at most 65 tents available, I do not yet know. It was already reported to Germany last fall that there were too few. If His Excellence finds it necessary to camp prior to the arrival of more from Europe, I see no other remedy except that the brigadier have them supplied by His Excellence. An announcement to the brigade concerning seven deserters from Captain Thomae's Company. One of them has deserted here for the fourth time. Colonel von Creuzbourg was informed that he was to obtain the necessary batteaux for his corps from the Assistant Quartermaster General Mr. Maurer at Montreal. No ship will be leaving here for Europe until one arrives from England, and then only with the protection of a warship. Commissary General Day is expected here to inspect all the available provisions.

28 April - Ensign Reinerding returned and had arranged all the quarters for both companies according to His Excellence's last order.

29 April - I drafted the answer to Captain von Tunderfeldt's letter of 27 April. Nothing more can be done, except to have tents delivered from here in extreme emergency.

30 April - An express from Niagara brought the news that the fleet from Cork had arrived fortunately at Cork [sic], and at the same time 5,000 royalists there had declared for the King, and that 15,000 British troops and an equal number of Russians were expected there. It is also reported that Admiral [Augustus] Keppel has defeated the French fleet and captured numerous ships. The last bit needs confirmation because that news comes from the rebels. However, it is certain that Washington's Guard Regiment has been cut to mince-meat. It is also reported that Comte d'Estaing's fleet has been defeated. On 27 April the heavens fell, the good Captain Foy was taken from the world; a serious loss for our corps. Soon we may hope for the arrival of ships. During the present days, pilots from Quebec have gone to Bic. The court quartermaster, Lieutenant Barnes said in his reply that it is nearly impossible now for him to deliver batteaux. However, he will proceed with repairs to the damaged batteaux as quickly as possible.

May

1 May - A letter about the batteaux to Lieutenant Colonel von Barner. We dined this evening with him. Later a small disagreement about the dogs! Today I signed many supply requisitions.

2 May - Four deserters were reported again by Lieutenant Colonel von Barner, three jaegers and one servant from his company. Between 23 and 24 April four men from Captain Thomae's Company had deserted also. All of them took their weapons.

3 May - This was made known to the brigade and to all the local governments. During the evening two strong thunderstorms came from the west.

4 and 5 May - Nothing new.

6 May - Again, five deserters from Captain Thomae's Company, who deserted between 3 and 4 May. The captain's report states the first deserter, Hahne, claimed in the battalion, that it was easy to enlist in the Mountain Scots at Montreal where conditions were much better. Following such report, the appropriate punishment was carried out. A courier passing through here on his way to Quebec, who had come across Lake Champlain from New York, departed that place on 23 March and reportedly our situation there is quite good. His dispatches were kept secret. The rebel's scarcity of foodstuffs has kept them from undertaking any action against Canada this winter. The start of the repairs on the local batteaux.

Journal of Lieutenant Friedrich Julius von Papet

7 May - Lieutenant Colonel von Barner went to his battalion in order to inspect it and to determine the reasons for desertions therefrom.

8 May - Mons Guichi came here and had a mission to the brigadier from His Excellence. Later Captain von Zielberg will have charge of building new barracks and fortifications at Pointe du Lac. The captain therefore had on

9 May - received the order to march there with his entire company. Initially the workmen will have nothing to do other than cleaning the place for these buildings and fortifications. Many orders and letters to the brigade. We were notified today of two repeat deserters from Lieutenant Colonel von Barner's Battalion and his company. An article of instructions for Captain von Zielberg.

10 May - Captain Rosenberg visited the brigadier. Lieutenant Colonel von Barner is still at Riviere du Loup and is accompanied by Auditor Wolpers. Reportedly two deserters have been arrested at Montreal.

11 May - Lieutenant Colonel von Barner returned from his trip to Riviere du Loup. An investigation of the two deserters is now taking place. Some inhabitants have been implicated in this desertion. Colonel Carleton wrote that four more were arrested at Montreal. Captain Rosenberg is very displeased by the desertions from the von Barner Battalion. The company of Captain von Zielberg passed through here today en route to Pointe du Loup.

12 May - Captain Rosenberg's Company has a man who shot himself due to melancholy and homesickness. A deserter from Captain Thomae's Company turned himself in to the first company. Captain Rosenberg paid his respects to the brigadier this evening. The latter felt indisposed. I, better than anyone else, know the reason.

13 May - I answered several representations from Lieutenant Colonel von Barner today. An express courier brought the news that a three-masted ship, bringing molasses, coffee, sugar, and rum, had arrived at Quebec. This ship is reportedly one of the French ships which had been made a prize. A letter from Captain von Tunderfeldt contained the news that the four previously mentioned deserters had been captured on the Yamaska River on 11 May by some royalists. They had resisted and one of them, Friedrich John, was still at Yamaska seriously wounded, while the three others were in arrest at

Journal of Lieutenant Friedrich Julius von Papet

Montreal. The total losses from Lieutenant Colonel von Barner's Battalion due to desertions, missing, and death, now amounts to 21 men, of whom six were retaken, one found again, and one is dead. It is hoped that the others will be recovered. Toward evening an exchange of words developed between a newly arrived English Doctor Apitail and Lieutenant Colonel von Barner's host, Fraser. The first, who was drunk, shot the other in the left breast. On the complaint lodged by Colonel von Tonnecour on behalf of Fraser, the doctor on

14 May - was placed under arrest by the brigadier and the matter was referred to the justice of the peace of the district, Mons. Guichi. During the evening my servant caused me much vexation.

15 May - Three deserters of Lieutenant Colonel von Barner's Battalion, whom the Indians had caught at St. Francois, were brought from la Baye. The Indians received twelve piasters as a reward. There are still nine men missing from that battalion. These three plus the mentioned Englishman on

16 May - were taken, the three to Montreal and the Englishman to Riviere du Loup, by an escort of two non-commissioned officers and twelve men. Toward noon Colonel Carleton passed through with Lieutenant Colonel von Barner, at which time Seigneur le Nandiere paid his respects to the brigadier.

17 May - Nothing new.

18 May - News was received that two men of Captain Thomae's Company had joined the Mountain Scots at Montreal as officer's servants, whose masters were prisoners of the rebels. Lieutenant Wallmoden had learned this on his own and they have already been returned. Likewise, Lieutenant Colonel Praetorius reported that three deserters from the Hesse-[Hanau] Jaegers had been delivered to him and that he had sent them to the company of Captain Rosenberg at St. Culbert. Four men are still missing. The Hessian Jaegers have requested that the reward money which the government pays to the local residents and Indians, be paid to them. However, this would set a precedence. In Lieutenant Colonel Praetorius' letter something was included about which the brigadier was very annoyed. I requested written orders from the brigadier concerning a reply thereto.

19 May - Strong northeast wind with which we hopefully await an early arrival of ships from Europe. Many small ships pass here en route to Sorel from Quebec.

Journal of Lieutenant Friedrich Julius von Papet

20 May - Still a good northeast wind. An inquiry to His Excellence concerning charging and powder for the recruits and to request permission for the company to conduct target shooting exercises, also an explanation of the reward which is paid for each captured deserter by the government. There was another deserter from the von Barner Battalion returned to la Baye this afternoon. An inhabitant had provided the deserter with Canadian clothing in exchange for the deserter's jacket. This inhabitant will also be questioned by me. According to the statement of this deserter, de Triff, he had been kept first in Biberte and then in a nearby mill for some time. The miller had told him that recently four Indians and three Canadians had passed through en route to Quebec from the rebels with letters, and they were to return again in a few weeks, and, if he [the deserter] could wait so long, they would take him with them. The more far-reaching circumstances of this were sent to Colonel von Tonnecour, who will report them to His Excellence. We dined this evening with Lieutenant Colonel von Barner.

21 May - Lieutenant Colonel von Barner was notified in a letter from the English Major Noerden that two more deserters had been caught, who were trying to join the Scots. They were arrested and escorted to Riviere du Loup. Four piasters were requested for each man. His Excellence has said he will make it known in every parish that the inhabitants will be paid a reward of eight piasters for each deserter brought in. The von Barner Battalion still has one man, by the name of Busch, missing. There is still not the least news of any ships arriving from Europe nor from Halifax.

22 May - Many storms during the evening. The missing for sometime and previously Corporal Beckmann, returned today. He was half-starved, having eaten only berries for a long time, and he gave many signs that all was not right in his head.

23 May - With the Whitsuntide celebration today, much longing for my dear fatherland. Dinner this evening with Lieutenant Colonel von Barner.

24 May - The brigadier gave a dinner for all the officers here.

25 May - Still no ships. The reward of eight piasters for every deserter recaptured is to be paid to every Canadian and Indian, as well as to the troops. As to the first [recruits, their weapons] are not to be charged with powder; the shooting at targets is to be done in camp,

Journal of Lieutenant Friedrich Julius von Papet

but both must be held in abeyance until a new shipment of ammunition arrives.

26 May - Nothing new, but very hot.

27 May - Many orders and letters to the brigade, as well as reports and lists which must be sent out tomorrow. This afternoon an English officer courier en route to Quebec. He told the local postmaster a rare bit of news, namely that 4,000 rebels with 500 batteaux were marching against Niagara and the area above that. At the same time 2,000 men were to attack St. Francois and pay us a visit here. This news can apparently be considered with the other incorrect figures and reports.

28 May - Nothing new

29 May - Many truths for someone - who failed to appear yesterday, as required by polite custom as well as for having overstepped decency. The result of this behavior, in this instance, for example, will lead to nothing more than the most contagious and finally the utmost degree of disrespect.

30 May - The brigadier departed at three o'clock this morning for Pointe du Lac and Little Michiche, in order to inspect the companies of Captains von Zielberg and von Schlagenteufel. The senior field cashier and I dined with Lieutenant Colonel von Barner. The brigadier returned here about six o'clock, having eaten at noon with Lieutenant von Sommerlatte.

31 May - Today the English Captain [Robert] Mathews, who came from Niagara, and is to be assigned as adjutant at St. Vincent, said that in the upper lands of this province everything is quiet. The rebels, with 1,500 men attacked Detroit, but because of a shortage of provisions, had to withdraw. He also said Detroit was well-fortified and with a garrison of 300 men could defend itself against an attack by 3,000 men.

[The next twelve pages, from 31 May through 1 October 1779, were transcribed with difficulty, and it is only due to the assistance of Mr. and Mrs. Henry Retzer of Hanover, Pennsylvania, that enough of the nearly illegible handwriting was transcribed so that a translation could be made. The translation should be used with extreme caution however, as many words could not be deciphered with confidence, and many could not be deciphered at all. Also, from the content of the diary it appears that this portion of the diary may have been written by someone other than von Papet.]

Journal of Lieutenant Friedrich Julius von Papet

4 June - Captain Mathews, of the 8th Regiment, who until now has been in the garrison at Niagara, was named in a general order today as secretary in this province in place of the deceased Captain Foy.

7 June - Mister La Maistre passed through here this morning. He halted at Colonel von Tonnecour's, leaving the order that all the livestock should be driven from the local plain outside the city and allowed to pass to grazing areas, because 4,000 men were to camp there in the future. Reportedly he has many letters with him for St. Francois and hastened on to Sorel and Montreal.

8 June - Captain von Tunderfeldt wrote that Major [Samuel] Holland, Captains [Patrick] Sinclair, [Malcolm] Frasier, [Neil] MacLean, and [David] Grant had arrived in Halifax. The gentlemen made the trip on land and reportedly departed Halifax on 8 May. There is still no news of ships arriving from England. Many letters for the Germans are lying at Halifax. It is supposedly certain that all our Convention prisoners are to be exchanged and will come to Canada. Reportedly Colonel von Speth is now at Halifax.

12 June - There are once again many rumors that the rebels are approaching with 400 batteaux, by way of St. Charles, and that on their march from New England, they have already chopped a road for seventy-five miles through the forest.

15 June - On three different houses in the local city placards have been nailed up, dated in October at Boston, and signed by Comte d'Estaing. The content, directed at the Canadians, announced that they were to remember their French blood at all times and serve the interest of their former master rather than the present one. These placards were prepared on the order of the French king. Colonel von Tonnecour has fully investigated to determine if any inhabitants of this city had knowledge of the distribution of the placards and a number of residents had to swear an oath. However, nothing was discovered. All the suspicion is directed at a book publisher in Montreal, who already is in jail in Quebec for a number of suspicious activities. This suspicion is all the stronger because Comte d'Estaing had already departed from Boston in August 1778.

15 June [sic] - In a letter from Colonel Praetorius it was announced that on 19 June he had been notified by Lieutenant Colonel St. Leger to be alert because Captain Fraser, who commanded at St.

Hyacinth, had been informed by the Indians of 600 rebels marching on this province from the Connecticut River, and it was not known if more were following them. Upon receipt of this news Colonel Praetorius had established pickets on his flanks as well as along the east bank of the river, and worked diligently on defensive positions. On the 22nd a sergeant, from the rebels at Beloville, was captured by one of the patrols sent out, and taken to Sorel. The main patrols go as far as Hyatsville, a full ten miles from the quarters, through water and swamps, on a continuous basis, pending further orders from His Excellence, for the brigadier to have the companies of the regiment move closer together. It was reported from Quebec that 22 ships had arrived from Liverpool. The news which they brought consisted of the following: The fleet sailing to Quebec departed from England toward the end of April.

29 June - As to the report of the 25th of this month to His Excellence from Lieutenant Colonel von Praetorius, he believes the report from the Indians to be false, and therefore it is not necessary for the Prince Friedrich Regiment to draw together. If such occurs it will allow the reentering of their quarters. His Excellence has been aware for some time that the rebel Witcour (whom Brigadier Gordon had discovered) was lurking in the woods with some troops near St. Jean, waiting to carry out some type of undertaking. Also, at this time of year it has been customary for the rebels, in order to advise their troops, to try to determine if the fleet has arrived, what it has brought with it, and what can be learned here. It is also good if at the same time the spies can be captured. If a march is toward Berthier, His Excellence can advise the brigadier whether the von Barner Battalion posts at St. Francois, Nicolet, and Vondrville are to draw together; which will apparently occur.

16 July - Fortunately for us, the fourteenth and fifteenth ships with provisions from Ireland have arrived at Quebec.

They sailed from Cork on 17 April. The fleet from England was to follow fourteen days later, and therefore can not be here before the end of this month. Tomorrow the remaining thirteen ships are expected at Quebec. Reportedly 2,000 men are coming here. As there has been a shortage of provisions previously, and such have now arrived here, it can be assumed that the order to march to Berthier will soon follow, as soon as the magazines are established there.

Journal of Lieutenant Friedrich Julius von Papet

19 July - At noon an express arrived with the news that Colonel von Speth and Ensign Haeberlin have arrived at Quebec on the transport *Eagle*. Two more ships with the other exchanged prisoners are expected from Halifax. The ten remaining ships with provisions from Ireland have arrived.

25 July - At midday the exchanged prisoners arrived here under Captain von Gleissenberg and Count Graefe. They had been armed at Halifax with 25 muskets and cartridges, and had brought three batteaux with their baggage from Quebec. In one of the batteau was a part of Colonel von Speth's baggage, as well as a black female slave, who together with some other slaves owned by a local resident named Despuis had accompanied Lieutenant Colonel Barner's Battalion during the army's march in 1777. Upon the return of Colonel von Barner to Canada the female slave took employment with Colonel von Speth and now has again returned here. Because of this a far-reaching legal case, conducted by the government, has been brought against Lieutenant Colonel von Barner. The troops all have French uniforms, blue coats with red facings. The French had shipped the uniforms to the rebels, but the ship was captured and taken into Halifax. The troops had to pay for the coats with their own money. Officers as well as privates were glad to be here again. None of them were satisfied with the living conditions in the colonies, although they describe the land as a paradise compared with Canada. The Loyalists primarily wish to shoot the rebels.

26 July - The exchanged prisoners were assigned to the brigadier's battalion. Today two exchanged English officers and 65 English soldiers also arrived here.

30 July - A man from the Company of Captain von Schlagenteufel's Rhetz Regiment reported here after having ransomed himself from his captivity, which had commenced on 7 October 1777. Corporal Pfeifer and a man from the Grenadier Battalion returned with him. Those two remained behind with Captain von Hambach. The previously noted Musketeer Hencke provided the following description of his captivity and release. About 44 men had been captured at the post and taken to Albany on 7 October 1777. Some of those who remained in captivity were then divided among farmers in the countryside and had to work for their provisions for ten months. When the harvest was finished, they had been asked if they wished to desert, but almost as one, they had refused. Therefore they were put in the jail at Albany. A commissary for the rebels, who was a German, took them out and provided them with passes so they could go wherever they desired. Shortly thereafter they met a lieutenant from Colonel [John] Butler's Corps, who covertly recruited all royally inclined for that corps. Several of the captives had enlisted with him and went to the corps at Kanazego. They had been encouraged to take that service, as it was immaterial where they served the King. Eight men remained there. However, the non-commissioned officer, a grenadier, and himself, wished to return to their own troops. They were then directed to Niagara with four Englanders, and from there to Duck Island and then on to Montreal. Colonel Butler's Corps consisted of about 250 regular troops and several thousand Indians, all of whom did great damage to the rebels.

31 July - The slaves, formerly the property of Despuis, deceased, brought here by Lieutenant Colonel von Speth, were taken by four armed Canadians, and from what we hear, they were returned to St. Francois.

1 August 1779 - Nothing new except many wishes for a long and happy life for the truest Father of our Land.

17 August - It was reported at Quebec that the fleet had finally arrived at Bic. Some ships of the fleet had already arrived at Quebec. When the fleet set sail our recruits had still not arrived at Portsmouth. Several letters for us Germans arrived with the fleet. A company of jaegers for Lieutenant Colonel von Creuzbourg's Corps arrived.[41] Because their ship is so large His Excellency will allow that company to land at Beauport, where the men can rest from the voyage and recover their health. Then they will be sent here. At the same time many uniform items for Captain von Schoell's Hesse-Hanau Detachment have been sent with them.

19 August - Thirty-six more ships have now arrived at Quebec, including a frigate with 60,000 guineas; a second frigate with 10,000 guineas is awaited. This money shipment is necessary in the province as there have been many occasions and times when there has been a shortage of cash.

20 August - According to the local newspapers this fleet sailed on 1 May from Spithead and 23 May from Torbay, under the escort of the

Journal of Lieutenant Friedrich Julius von Papet

warship *Defiance*, of 64 cannons, and the frigates *Quadalope* and *Brilliant*. Our recruits are to be expected with the second division.

22 August - Lieutenant Colonel von Speth was assigned command. The general's headquarters had named His Excellency a brigadier instead of Brigadier von Ehrenkrook, and arranged for the other to resume his duty in the army as a lieutenant colonel. (Although Ehrenkrook was junior to Speth, still it created for the first, who is a passionate, sensitive man, a furious scene, when the degrading action was announced. Papet wrote, "I will not comment on the scene at the parting of the two commanders.")

Concerning Holland, Papet wrote, "He is a large, pleasant man, who has served for a long time, and accepted and solved the problems of this province for fifteen years, and owns a beautiful estate (Holland House) at Quebec."

The troops were mustered on orders of Haldimand. Major Holland was designated as commissary.

At that time the troops of Captain von Plessen's Company were at Cape Madeleine, with some at Trois Rivieres; von Schlagenteufel's Company at Trois Rivieres, von Zielberg's Company was at Point du Lac and Machiche; Lieutenant Colonel von Ehrenkrook's Company at Trois Rivieres; Lieutenant Colonel von Barner's Company at Prairie du Loup; Captain Thomae's Company at Maskinonge; and Captain von Rosenberg's Company at St. Colbert. Lieutenant Colonel von Creuzbourg's Hesse-Hanau Jaeger Corps was at L'Assomption with Captain von Castendyck's Jaeger Company in the parish of Repentigny, Major von Francken's Company in Lachenay, and Count Wittgenstein's Company in Terre Bonne. Papet says, "This Jaeger Corps is certainly one of the best, all beautiful young people, well-dressed, and excellent marksmen."

Brigadier Speth showed his great displeasure with many companies. Ehrenkrook had allowed the troops to become slovenly. Holland noted many had grown old and said they must have already made many campaigns. A list with three columns was immediately prepared, one for those who were fit, another for those fit only for garrison duty, and the third for invalids.

Captain von Schoell's Detachment is on LaRoche Island; Captain Hambach's Corps at Vaudreville; the Hessian Battalion in St. Jean, Captain Dietrich's Company of Praetorius' Regiment in Vercheres, and

Journal of Lieutenant Friedrich Julius von Papet

the other three companies of that regiment in and near St. Charles. Lieutenant Colonel von Hille is at St. Antoine, Lieutenant Colonel St. Leger in Sorel, and the headquarters and staff are at Trois Rivieres. At the moment none have entered camps.

8 September - Again there are rumors that 7,000 rebels are on the move against Niagara. This much is certain, 800 men have been sent to that post.

10 September - His Excellence continually speaks of camping, but nothing is decided. -- According to reports which several ships have brought, war has broken out with Spain. Fifteen ships-of-the-line from Denmark and twenty from Russia are awaited at Portsmouth.

11 September 1779 - An order (15 September) has been circulated to frighten deserters, that the Indians have received orders from His Excellence to scalp all deserters encountered on their way to the rebels.

17 September - General [Francis] MacLean has made an attack toward the Connecticut River from Halifax with 1,000 men. Unfortunately this did not meet with the greatest success. The area is surrounded by water where few warships can travel, so that things do not look good for him. Recently Brigadier von Rauschenplat has had six deserters. On orders of His Excellence, Captain Hugget's Jaeger Company is to march from Beauport to Sorel on 18 September.

20 September - Today tents and field equipment were issued to both battalions.

21 September - I completed an order that all units in barracks were to camp so that the barracks could be thoroughly deloused and cleaned. (The tents were set up near the barracks.)

1 October - On orders of His Excellence, Captain von Hambach, with his company, is to begin the march to Montreal on 7 October, where it is to remain for the time being in garrison. Also, if possible, Lieutenant Colonel von Creuzbourg, with three companies of Jaegers, is to move out toward LaPrairie, leaving one jaeger company at Sorel.

JOURNAL

of the sea voyage to North America
and also the campaign conducted there
5 October 1779 to 10 October 1783

as actually experienced and recorded by

Friedrich Julius von Papet, Jr.
1st Lieutenant in Major General von Rhetz
Regiment
and
since 20 November 1777
Brigade Major with the German troops in
Canada

2nd Part

Journal of Lieutenant Friedrich Julius von Papet

October

5 October - The news arrived with the mail today that our recruits have finally arrived at Bic. According to the list sent on ahead, they consist of one officer, one staff surgeon, one company surgeon's mate, eight non-commissioned officers, two drummers, and 261 privates, and were escorted here by three captains.

His Excellence will send them here as soon as possible. Captain von Plessen will come here and today has received the order to proceed at once to Quebec. Reportedly war has been declared between Spain and England. If so, then there is also an alliance among England, Russia, Denmark, and Holland. A list of all the craftsmen in the regiments has been requested. For this purpose all the lists are to be submitted in duplicate and His Excellence desires they all be assigned to various ships. It is assumed that the von Barner Battalion will be assigned quarters in Montreal this winter.

[**6 October**] - This evening a serious complaint against Captain von Zielberg was received by the brigadier from Lieutenant Wolgast. According to this complaint the captain is guilty of making several derogatory remarks about Lieutenant Colonel von Barner and Lieutenant Wolgast. The brigadier sent this complaint to Lieutenant Colonel von Ehrenkrook who is to have it investigated by the auditor.

7 October - We received, from an express, a large bundle of letters from London, which arrived in an English ship. Captain von Tunderfeldt reported that the three captains and our recruits are now at Quebec, and possibly, with the present favorable winds, will soon come to us. The conduct of Captains Thomae and Wechsel has not been the best. The first has supposedly made improper comments and the latter was drunk in His Excellence's presence. As much praise as Captain Raabe has earned, an equal damage has been done to us by the other two.

8 October - Lieutenant Colonel Praetorius was requested to come here with his adjutant, as soon as possible. It was mentioned to Lieutenant Colonel von Creuzbourg by us in conjunction with the march of his three companies to La Prairie that he should hasten the movement of the invalids and laborers.

Journal of Lieutenant Friedrich Julius von Papet

With today's mail we received dispatches from Germany, according to which the recruits were to be divided among the regiments so that they would be of equal strength. Under the above orders, one was received that no more money, except as previously authorized from Germany, could be spent. Sharply increased regimental costs were to be delivered to the senior field cashier. An order to return the invalids to Germany.

The uniforms for the von Barner Battalion arrived, and for the others according to the number in the old regiments, 120 pieces per regiment. We are also to help ourselves as best possible. The tents, because of the limited time are not yet ready to be sent over and can be expected only next year. Today I suggested how the recruits should be divided among the regiments. Some of the dispatches were addressed to Brigadier von Speth. Two of the ships with the recruits sailed today with the continuing favorable winds. One, with the uniform items and Captain Weiss, has arrived at Quebec because the items for the Anhalt-Zerbsters must first be unloaded.

10 October - Lieutenant Bodemeyer with the requested laborers and the invalids left our corps for Quebec. The latter consist of three non-commissioned officers and twenty men; the laborers of three non-commissioned officers and 31 men - one non-commissioned officer and eighteen men are Hessians. This morning the recruits were sent with four batteaux toward Feinds Heebertin, to debark there, and then they are to march overland.

11 October - The brigadier and Lieutenant Colonel von Barner decided to go to meet the recruits. They traveled in a batteau and plan to return here tomorrow. Prior to their departure an incident developed between Captain von Zielberg and the auditor. The first had stated that he did not want to be questioned. Therefore, according to the regulations which are in effect, it must be sent to Germany.

12 October - His Excellency made a gift to all the troops. For every non-commissioned officer, drummer, private, and recruit, one pair of long breeches, one pair of mittens, one pair of shoes, and one blanket. The list of men is to be submitted at once. Also today, I ordered several items for the local work which order must be sent to Germany.

13 October - The arrival of the recruits and many items from Germany. The brigadier was dissatisfied about the poor quality of the

Journal of Lieutenant Friedrich Julius von Papet

uniforms of the recruits and the uneven distribution of such. Most of the recruits have badly worn jackets and some of the uniforms have been worn already one and one-half years in Brunswick, and yet they are passed off on us here as new. A great dinner at the brigadier's. Indiscreet behavior by Captain Thomae in his quarters.

14 October - The distribution of recruits among the regiments according to my plan. Dinner like yesterday.

15 October - Captain von Tunderfeldt wrote that Lieutenant Bodemeyer has arrived at Quebec. All the ships are to depart on the 20th and the last frigate on the 25th. Today I closed the letter to my dear sister.

16 October - The copy of the letter of the 21st to the Duke, as well as one to the Hereditary Prince. The arrival of the ship *Oegel*, on which was the new chaplain and other things for the recruits. Now only Captain Weiss with the baggage and uniform items is missing.

19 October - Captain von Tunderfeldt reported to us how Mons. Collier, a commodore, had caused the rebels to suffer a severe loss and destroyed almost all of their privateers. A large part of them had been shut in the Penobscot River by MacLean's Brigade. By chance Mons. Collier arrived there with four ships-of-the-line, captured three frigates, burned fourteen frigates of 16 to 32 cannons, captured 24 transport ships, and from them 322 cannons. The rebels lost 300 men and the entire loss on the King's side consisted of 77 men. A letter to privy councillor von Praun [or Braun].

20 October - Everything packed, even my small present for Germany. I gave this and the first part of my journal, as well as the letters, to Captain Raabe to deliver.

21 October - The officers departed for Quebec in batteaux. A gruesome murder was committed at Pointe du Lac yesterday evening between eight and nine o'clock. Ensign Graefe, who has his quarters two houses distance from the scene, found his host, by the name of Portiers, and his wife, a daughter of ten years of age, a woman who worked on the river, and the Dragoon Wolte at eleven o'clock in the evening. The brigadier ordered a thorough investigation and that a record be made of everything. We went there also, and I must confess, I have never seen a more gruesome sight. The militia in every parish on both sides of the river were asked to find the perpetrators. Notice of this terrible deed was sent to every settlement. As three men had been seen in a canoe near Becancour early this morning, one non-commissioned officer and seven of our men were immediately sent out with an officer of the militia and Chevalier de Tonnecour and some armed Canadians, and it is hoped they will not be able to escape.

22 October - Two murderers were caught. The principal participant escaped into the woods. At eleven o'clock they were brought here. These two Englishmen from the 29th Regiment had arrived from England as recruits this year, and had deserted. They were questioned and stated that the murders were committed by the escapee, and they had only been present at the time. The escapee is still free. The report concerning this band was sent to His Excellence. There has never been an example of such a murder here. The five victims were brought here today for burial. The order came today for Captain von Schoell's detachment to march to Quebec. Therefore Lieutenant Colonel von Creuzbourg received the order. At the same time we received the assignments for winter quarters. Accordingly, we and the von Ehrenkrook Battalion are assigned in Berthier, the von Barner Battalion in Montreal, and the Prince Friedrich Regiment and Lieutenant von Creuzbourg remain at Prairie, Longuille, Boucherville, and Varennes, and one company of the corps at Yamaska and St. Francois, the 31st Regiment and Captain von Schoell's detachment at Quebec, the 34th and 53rd Regiments at Sorel, the 29th Regiment and a detachment of the Prince Friedrich Regiment at St. Jean, Ile aux Noix, and Pointe au Fer, the 84th Regiment and Sir Johnson's Corps above Montreal, and the Emigrants Battalion at Pointe du Lac and Nicolet. Two sailors who had deserted from a transport ship were arrested today. They and an English deserter, who has been held here for a long time, are to go aboard a ship sailing for Quebec. This evening another sailor, who deserted, was brought here from Becancour in arrest.

23 October - Musketeer Heinemann, who is on leave, took a representation for His Excellence to Quebec concerning the baggage left here. Also one to the quartermaster general, Mr. Carleton concerning the winter quarters for the von Ehrenkrook Battalion, because its parish is too small for the battalion and the general staff.

26 October - The officers from Germany sailed from Quebec yesterday, after embarking on the ship *Present Succession*. Our dispatches in chest number one arrived aboard a frigate and are to be returned to the officers at Portsmouth. The officers have chest number two with them. The local governmental jurisdiction is so extensive that it extends to postage on letters. I received correspondence that His Excellency has written that no costs be spared in the effort to catch the third scoundrel. Much correspondence is received from Lieutenant Colonel von Creuzbourg. Lieutenant Knesebeck departed today with his belongings. The grand vicar has allowed religious services to be held in the local church. On 1 November the small frigate *Viper* sails for England.

30 October - The entire detachment of Captain von Schoell has arrived here, close to the city, and been quartered in the parish. A deserter from the 84th Regiment at Pointe du Lac was delivered here. An English officer will take this deserter to Sorel, along with twelve invalids from Quebec. I have the unpleasant task of sharply replying, in the name of the brigadier, to the last letter from Captain von Tunderfeldt.

31 October - Captain von Schoell's detachment departed for Quebec after all the officers had dined with the brigadier, and all their baggage had been loaded. I must admit that those people looked very good in their new uniforms and that by comparison ours were shabby. A detachment of 200 English from the 31st Regiment passed through here en route to Quebec.

November

1 November - Sentence was carried out against the dragoon deserter Lange. As he did not want to run the gauntlet, he was fastened to a pillory at the barracks place and beat with a lash [feder = feather?]. This created a great sensation among the Canadians. I have not been well for the last few days. Four more men came from Niagara, who have ransomed themselves; three men from the von Barner Battalion, one man from the von Ehrenkrook Battalion.

2 November - That was reported to Quebec today. Colonel Butler had a man at Niagara arrested because he wished to return to his corps here and the others were sent to Fort Stanwix on reconnaissance. An order to the brigade concerning the overcoats and the proferred presents. Today the order finally arrived for the troops to enter winter quarters. The Prince Friedrich Regiment is now to occupy St. Ours parish, and is to detach a company to St. Jean. Lieutenant Colonel von Creuzbourg is to send one officer, the necessary non-commissioned officers, and fifty jaegers to Ile aux Noix, which are to be used for patrolling there. The von Ehrenkrook and von Barner Battalions thereafter will march on 5 November, and I finished all the orders for that today. Before the march order arrived, Lieutenant Colonel von Barner showed a march order received from Brigadier MacLean that he should have a company march at once. Brigadier von Speth was very annoyed about MacLean issuing an order to his brigade as it was not under MacLean's command. Brigadier von Speth therefore ordered Lieutenant Colonel von Barner to write to Brigadier MacLean that after showing MacLean's order to Brigadier von Speth, he had received the order not to have any men march until he had received orders from Quebec. A copy of Brigadier MacLean's order, as well as this order, was sent to His Excellency.

3 November - Ensign Reinerding of the battalion and Ensign Haeberlin from our side were sent ahead to arrange quarters at Berthier. An instruction for Lieutenant Hertel and an order to Lieutenant Colonel von Ehrenkrook concerning the guards in the new quarters situation and the list of quarters.

4 November - The announcement from His Excellency concerning our departure. An order to Lieutenant Colonels Praetorius and von Creuzbourg concerning the quarters lists. We dined at Commissary Sills. The arrival of Captain von Plessen's Company. With it a complaint concerning the escaped murderer. A letter from Mons. Guichi about Captain von Zielberg. I answered it, and Lieutenant Colonel von Ehrenkrook received the order to leave it, as well as the craftsmen, in Pointe du Lac. Many departure visits including visits to Canadians, who were greatly surprised. They did not wish to have us leave, and wish the English doctors all possible misfortune. I sent my baggage ahead in two rented vehicles. The rest went in batteaux. Because it had already frozen hard, it could only be wished that those batteaux would sail well on Lake St. Pierre.

8 November - The von Ehrenkrook Battalion is to enter quarters. The companies of Captain von Plessen, Captain von Zielberg, and von Ehrenkrook are first to be inspected by the brigadier at the ford. Lieutenant Colonel von Ehrenkrook had forgotten to tell the brigadier about the arrival of his company which drew a reprimand from him.

Journal of Lieutenant Friedrich Julius von Papet

The quarters for the companies were arranged by [Hesse-Cassel Colonel Johann August] Loos, [possibly] with the general staff at Petite Riviere Berthier, the battalion staff and the company of Lieutenant Colonel Ehrenkrook on the main river at Berthier, the company of Captain von Schlagenteufel at St. Culbert, that of von Zielberg at la Norvit and LaValtrie, and of von Plessen at St. Sulpice. The brigadier and I visited the local seigneur Mons. Colbert today. He is a Scot by birth and previously served in Germany as an English grenadier captain. After the peace, he came here, sold his commission for 24,000 livres and bought the local lordship, which is six kilometers wide and 24 kilometers deep, for 6,600 livres. It is one of the best in the land and due to the improvements which he has made, now has a yearly revenue of 40,000 livres. The murderers were escorted to Montreal today. A visit from the local parish priest and the militia captain of the large river Olivier.

10 November - Captain von Tunderfeldt wrote that the 2,000 men had not yet arrived at Quebec. Therefore, His Excellency sent the necessary pilots from Quebec to Bic. The complaint by the brigadier against Brigadier MacLean was answered by His Excellency. He agreed with the brigadier that the previous order from Brigadier MacLean broke all the rules of service and therefore wrote the same to Brigadier MacLean. An order to Lieutenant Colonel von Ehrenkrook. This afternoon the senior field cashier surprised us with a visit. We then accompanied him back home. In his quarters the brigadier summoned Ensign Reinerding and spoke very plainly to him.

12 November - Lieutenant Colonel von Barner wrote that Captain Rosenberg's Company and 75 men of Captain Thomae's Company were to move into the barracks at Montreal on the ninth. The rest of the battalion was to camp in the country near Longe Pointe because the barracks were not yet finished. He described the conduct of Brigadier MacLean as especially polite and obliging. Quarters for the subaltern officers were unavailable for less than eight piasters a month (the King's allowance was two and one-half piasters a month), and the officers had to pay the host the remaining portion. Brigadier MacLean had therefore written to His Excellency on behalf of the officers. Another jaeger, who ransomed himself, has arrived from Niagara. A deserter from Captain Thomae's Company in 1778 was captured by the inhabitants of LaValtrie, when he reported to them. He was then sent here from that place. This afternoon we walked for pleasure along the great river and toward evening visited the local militia captain and the parish priest. We then continued on to the senior field cashier's and to Lieutenant Colonel von Ehrenkrook's. Therefore the brigadier, as well as the lieutenant colonel and Ensign Reinerding, jointly complained about the provisions. Upon our return home we found that the troops on work detail had received no provisions for three days. They were so angry about the neglect that they had planned to clearly state their situation tomorrow and that they had to be better cared for.

13 November - A general order concerning the provisions. There is not the best news from Quebec concerning the 2,000 men who are awaited. It is reported that they were separated from one another by a storm and it is doubtful that they can now arrive at such a late date in the season, and might now be forced to go to Halifax. We have no previous information concerning the composition of those troops.

22 November - A frigate has arrived at Bic, seven weeks out of Portsmouth. It brought the news that the French and Spanish fleet was at Brest, and the English fleet at Portsmouth. Twenty ships of the Russian Empress [Katherine the Great] were also expected there daily. In a letter to me, I was made to understand that His Excellence was very dissatisfied with the frequent German requests and especially those of Lieutenant Colonels von Creuzbourg and von Barner. His Excellence wished to be rid of us, and the situation could easily arise whereby we would be sent to the West Indies. Unless confirmed, I am not in a position to evaluate the situation. A detachment of English, consisting of one officer and thirty men, arrived at Trois Rivieres, and therefore our command of twenty men at that place must soon be reduced.

The Journal of Lieutenant Friedrich Julius von Papet
January 1780

1 January - And so one year of one's life after the other passes! Four sad years, sad in every respect considering my absence from my dear beloved fatherland and the best years of my life have been wasted! --But what all have I learned? I have gotten to know people from a different viewpoint and my longings to be home increase each day and how much more will they increase with the coming year! A large social gathering at the brigadier's as they have come to extend their congratulations.

6 January - We were invited to a wedding today, as tomorrow a dragoon is to be married to a Canadian. The wedding is to take place in Cornet Graefe's quarters and everyone from the brigadier's suite is invited.

7 January - The entire suite went to the wedding. Shortly thereafter this pair was married by the chaplain of the Prince Friedrich Regiment. The bride received many presents. After the wedding all the officers returned to the brigadier's for dinner. Finally an answer from Lieutenant Colonel von Creuzbourg, which after looking over the report did not give clear satisfaction. He promised in writing to appear at the brigadier's on the evening of the tenth.

12 January - Captain von Tunderfeldt wrote that for some time a person has not been safe from being attacked and robbed during the evening in Quebec. Anything can happen at night. Even the ship's captain Steel, of the Treasury brig *Polly*, was wounded a few days ago and died two days later. The perpetrators were English. Today all the reports, seniority lists, and lists of professions for our corps were sent to Quebec.

21 January - The brigadier and I went to visit the Prince Friedrich Regiment at St. Dennis. We departed at nine o'clock, halted at ten o'clock at Lieutenant Barnes' at Sorel, and arrived at Lieutenant Colonel Praetorius' at three o'clock. After being taken to Lieutenant Colonel von Hille's quarters, and meeting him there, all the officers went to dinner together. We were very well-treated. Lieutenant Colonel von Hille explained the health situation to the brigadier and spoke plainly. We remained together until two o'clock. We were then quartered on the rich merchant Jacobs, who had been born in Hamburg and had established himself in St. Dennis fifteen years ago. At our

The Journal of Lieutenant Friedrich Julius von Papet

quarters we met Commissary General Day, who also had quarters there. It pleased the brigadier to meet this worthy gentleman. In his face he strongly resembled our privy councilor Dyon. We did not get to bed until three o'clock. I could not sleep.

24 January - We left St. Dennis at eight o'clock in the morning and by twelve o'clock were already back in Berthier. We changed our clothing and then departed with Cornet Graefe and Haeberlin for dinner in Sorel with Captain Twiss and Lieutenant Barnes. The meal consisted of eighteen covers and there was considerable drinking. At the same time, there was a ball in Sorel, which we were invited to attend as special guests. The brigadier and I danced only a minuet. We then took our departure and returned to Berthier. The two other gentlemen remained there.

29 January - Lieutenant Colonel von Creuzbourg and his adjutant went to St. Francois in order to inspect the company of Major [Herman Albrecht] von Franken of his [Hesse-Hanau Jaeger] corps. They are to return here tomorrow.

This afternoon Captain von Plessen visited the brigadier. The English Captain [Fane] Edge of the 53rd Regiment visited the brigadier this afternoon and invited Ensign Haeberlin to dinner tomorrow. An officer of Sir Johnson's corps, who had come down the Mohawk River, passed through Sorel, and brought confirmation of the defeat of d'Estaing's [French] fleet. According to the reports, the French lost four ships-of-the-line and seventy transport ships. The affair took place in mid-November.

February

12 February - His Excellency will be very pleased when the inhabitants, who have recently exchanged the uniforms of a few deserting soldiers, have been exposed. He wishes, above all, to severely punish every inhabitant who has given shelter to a deserter.

15 February - The savages commit many excesses in Montreal, even attacking the guards, and it takes great restraint to control their attacks when they are drunk. Still no deserters have been made to understand that the inhabitants must be advised that they can not provide shelter or clothing without being punished.

The Journal of Lieutenant Friedrich Julius von Papet

16 February - Lieutenant Colonel Praetorius and Captain Sander returned to St. Dennis. They were accompanied by the brigadier as far as the church on the Isle de Bic.

23 February - There was such a terrible storm here as I have never previously seen. The wind had so completely covered the road with snow that I needed two men with snow shovels to clear the path so that I could get to the brigadier's quarters. The brigadier, as well as Lieutenant Colonel von Hille, found it necessary to postpone their trip today, and everyone who went outdoors risked being lost in the snow. Nevertheless, I had to go out toward evening to return to my quarters.

24 February - The strong winds continued today but only from another direction. I went to the brigadier's on snowshoes this morning, and therefore was prepared to proceed over mountains of snow. At evening, however, on the way back to my quarters during the darkness of the night, I did not fare so well. I fell in a hole and the strap, which held the snowshoe on the foot, broke off one foot.

March

28 March - It stormed so much during the past night that I thought at any minute the house would collapse about my head. About two o'clock Lieutenant Barnes came from Sorel with a message for the brigadier from Lieutenant Colonel St. Leger concerning the detachment of one officer and forty men. Mons. Barnes sought to have the brigadier order militia Captain Oliver to have the detachment quartered as best possible on the great river. I prepared the necessary orders today concerning this to Lieutenant Colonel von Ehrenkrook and the militia captain. Lieutenant Barnes dined with us. Lieutenant Colonel von Barner reported that Mons. Hildel of Captain Thomae's Company deserted on 21 March.

29 March - Concerning the departure of His Excellency from Quebec, it is now quiet again. In Quebec many new things happening which must come from Halifax.

30 March - The monthly reports, including the submission of the half-yearly accounts, were sent to Lieutenant Colonel Carleton.

The Journal of Lieutenant Friedrich Julius von Papet
April

5 April - During the past night various persons, including some important ones, were hurriedly escorted to Quebec, in arrest. It is thought that they were arrested for a suspicious exchange of letters. The council is to meet. Toward ten o'clock news arrived from Halifax. According to that news more than 120 transport ships have been captured from the French. The contingent accounts have been returned because those of the deserters and those of the guard lists must be separated. Today it rained hard and the rivers are already full of water.

9 April - The Quebec newspaper carried the King's December 1779 address to Parliament. That speech, as well as the consent agreement of the Parliament, declares a vigorous prosecution of the war, without any doubt. Rain all day and although the rivers already have much water on top of the ice, the Canadians still drive their carriages on them.

10 April - A letter to Lieutenant Colonel von Ehrenkrook. To make it easier for the posting and relief of the local guards of his own company, due to the bad weather, bad roads, and the distance from the company, the brigadier has authorized having the watch consist of not more than one non-commissioned officer and six men.

19 April - The mail arrived very late today. The letter from Captain von Tunderfeldt mentioned that a ship with returning captive Brunswickers was to have arrived at Quebec, but because of the hindrance of a storm, this ship had to spend the winter at the Island of St. John in the Gulf of St. Lawrence. General MacLean had sent provisions there from Halifax in case they could not be supported at that place. However, a letter from Captain [Jacob Wilhelm] Bode of the Hessian [Seitz] regiment lying at Halifax to the brigadier identified the troops more exactly and mentioned that the men were from both the [Hesse-Cassel] von Lossberg and von Knyphausen Regiments. A ship with those men had spent the winter at St. John and one with Colonel Loos had returned to New York. That letter also mentioned the affair of Mons. [Admiral Sir George] Collier at the Penobscot River, and also the defeat of Comte d'Estaing's fleet at Savannah, during which he lost fourteen ships-of-the-line and 1,600 men, and was himself wounded three times. Reportedly the rebels lost 321 officers, and privates in proportion. Furthermore, at the end of October, General MacLean returned from the expedition to Penobscot, leaving Colonel [John] Campbell of the 74th Regiment in command at that river, and that he was in condition to resist all rebel efforts against him.

News at Halifax is to the effect that the Prince of Mecklenberg will take over command of all the Hessian forces. The famous Captain [James] Cook, who sailed from England four years ago on a voyage of discovery, has reappeared according to a Chinese newspaper. The Dragoon Wuelner, who lay at Batiscan for a time, has found a source of salt from which good white salt is obtained. This dragoon therefore sent a notice to His Excellence requesting employment by the government at a salt works. His Excellence is in agreement in this situation in so far as having a salt work established there. The brigadier was very annoyed that the notice was submitted without his consent.

29 April - Cornet Graefe and Ensign Haeberlin went to Sorel today in batteaux. The latter has various things to do concerning the batteaux, the fords, and some trenching tools for our gardens, and is to try to obtain them. They returned toward evening and had been successful. They brought the news from Sorel that the English Captain [Alexander] Scott of the 53rd Regiment (an excellent officer), with a detachment of five officers and 120 men is to leave tomorrow on an expedition beyond Lake Champlain. The 34th, 53rd, and 29th Regiments and Lieutenant Colonel von Creuzbourg are each to provide an officer and thirty men. Ten ships are to depart from Quebec and cruise in the Gulf.

30 April - Several letters to the Prince Friedrich Regiment, as well as an order to put the winter caps away and to change out of the winter clothing on 15 May, and to store them. Mons. la Valtrie invited us to his fishery today. However, because of the brigadier's indisposition no one could accept, except Cornet Graefe and Ensign Haeberlin. Toward noon Captain von Schlagenteufel and Ensign Fromme came for a visit. This afternoon I visited Lieutenant Colonel von Ehrenkrook and the senior field cashier. Nevertheless, I know that when I am not present, the first does not speak well of me, but I am assured that he absent-mindedly is the only one who sides with me. This evening the brigadier felt really bad. We received many seeds from Montreal and now have a surplus of all kinds.

The Journal of Lieutenant Friedrich Julius von Papet

May

2 May - It is reported that the rebels are assembling at Ticonderoga in order to obtain revenge against the attack on Tohneeborough's house. Captain Scott with his detachment will try to verify this.

3 May - The order arrived from Quebec that a new detachment of workers, consisting of three non-commissioned officers and 44 men, was to be provided for Quebec. The Prince Friedrich Regiment is to provide one non-commissioned officer and 22 men and the von Ehrenkrook two non-commissioned officers and 22 men. In addition, a similar detachment is to be supplied to Couteau de Lac. It will be provided only from the von Barner Battalion and will consist of one non-commissioned officer and seven men and some handymen. Captain Laros will be in charge. All told this amounts to four non-commissioned officers and 58 men from the Germans. I completed the orders for this today and they are all to assemble here in Berthier on the tenth.

10 May - The work detachment from the Prince Friedrich Regiment, consisting of one non-commissioned officer and 22 men, arrived here, as did the auditor. The latter arrived here already yesterday evening and because he forgot to report to the brigadier and the lieutenant colonel, and only did so this afternoon, the brigadier was annoyed by his negligence. The brigadier ordered the lieutenant colonel to place the auditor under arrest at the staff watch, after the auditor completed his investigation, and early this morning, after paying the travel expenses, to demote him in the regiment. Because all the batteaux have been taken to the great river, I had to deliver this order to the senior field cashier's quarters. During the time the brigadier and the lieutenant colonel were gone, in order to have something to say about the delay in the investigation, I remained with the senior field cashier. We were joined by Captain von Zielberg and Cornet Graefe, who will go in batteaux tomorrow, the first to Pointe du Lac, and the latter to Trois Rivieres, with us. Upon our return home we paid our respects to militia Captain Olivier, because he had not refused giving quarters in his house to twelve men of the work detail, when the notary public, who had a simple exemption, would not

The Journal of Lieutenant Friedrich Julius von Papet

take them. I had to talk very plainly to the latter, and the brigadier ordered his house to be occupied by twelve men this evening, due to the necessity of the march, and no one is exempted from quartering men for one night. Afterward we visited Mons. Cuthbert and Captain von Zielberg, and Cornet Graefe dined with the brigadier.

11 May - The brigadier, I, and Ensign Haeberlin departed at five o'clock this morning in two carriages, Captain von Zielberg and Cornet Graefe went in our batteaux with three others, to where our workers were. We arrived at Trois Rivieres at two o'clock and the batteaux arrived at five o'clock. It had been very rough on Lac St. Pierre due to contrary wind. Once when they raised the sails, the mast broke and one batteau quickly sank. We stopped at Commissary Sill's in Trois Rivieres. He acted very strange and had given his post over to another. Therefore we had to take lodgings in the posthouse. We ate a bit on the hills to the south, inspected the barracks, and conducted a small business transaction. The brigadier himself took some yellow cloth and lining for Captain von Schlagenteufel and Captain von Zielberg from the baggage that was there. Thereafter we made several visits. A local inhabitant, MacBean, made a request concerning a batteau damaged in the previous year, and was promised that the repair would be discussed with Mons. Barnes at Sorel.

12 May - We departed in batteaux at six o'clock and landed at a house in Batiscan. This was necessary because it was impossible to arrange the hire of a carriage by any means. From Batiscan the brigadier rode in a carriage with Ensign Haeberlin and I traveled in a batteau to Grondine and landed near my former quarters. I met the brigadier, who was waiting for me, and was exceptionally well received by him.

13 May - We departed at five o'clock in the morning in two coaches. Near the church at Grondine we could clearly see our batteaux ahead of us. At four-thirty in the afternoon we arrived at Quebec. We visited Major Holland. Lieutenant Bodemeyer came out of the city of Quebec to meet us and informed us about our quarters. The brigadier and Ensign Haeberlin were quartered in a very good house, directly opposite Lieutenant Bodemeyer's quarters. I stayed with the latter. Captain Schoell and his officers paid a visit to the brigadier. We then went to the castle and spoke with His Excellency in the garden, where he received us most pleasantly. Captain von

Tunderfeldt entertained us for dinner and at twelve o'clock we returned to our quarters.

14 May - Together with Captain von Tunderfeldt we visited Lieutenant Colonel [Allen] MacLean, commandant of Quebec, Lieutenant Colonel Carleton, Brigadier Powell, and Lieutenant Governor Cramahe, and then went to the levee where many were in attendance. Afterward we visited at Lieutenant Bodemeyer's until three o'clock. Lots of conversation during dinner, twenty covers, supper with Captain Schoell, and home at eleven o'clock.

15 May - Numerous morning visits, inspection of the laborers of von Schoell's detachment and at the barracks. We dined today with Captain von Schoell. A walk this afternoon to inspect the work at the new defenses, which are very extensive, and built entirely into the cliffs. Supper at Captain von Tundefeldt's. His Excellence and Brigadier Powell were also present and the meal consisted of twelve covers. Conversation at dinner - - I played chess.

16 May - I completed writing proposals to His Excellence. We dined with His Excellence and I must say that we ate well by German standards. Entertained by dogs after dinner. After dinner the brigadier and Ensign Haeberlin drove to Major Holland's country home, and I and Lieutenant Bodemeyer visited the lower city during that time, and also viewed the area where the rocks had previously fallen at Cape Diamond, which was very frightening to see. I then ate supper with Captain von Schoell.

17 May - Inspection of Captain von Schoell's detachment and then drill which earned the highest praise, and I must admit that it was better than any of us expected. We ate breakfast in a tent. At ten o'clock we went to Lieutenant Colonel Carleton's and showed him the draft proposals to His Excellence. At twelve o'clock two two-masted ships arrived, the first this year. From all appearances, when they come from the West Indies, they bring much news with them. We dined today with Lieutenant Colonel MacLean, the present commandant in Quebec. There was much drinking. I and the others, except for the brigadier, were forced to stay there that evening. The hautboists of the Prince Friedrich Regiment were brought in, there was dancing, and supper at eleven o'clock. About nine o'clock I found the opportunity to depart and it was fortunate that I left there sober, although I had a severe headache. The two ships brought the following news: That Admiral [George Brydes] Rodney had captured eleven ships-of-the-line from a Spanish admiral off the coast of Portugal. The ships were loaded with rum and molasses and had departed from Surinam in the month of March. During the passage through the West Indian islands they saw nothing but English ships, and during the trip coming here, no enemy ships were encountered. That a packet boat from Martinique was captured and all the dispatches sent immediately to England. From these it was discernible that there was a shortage of almost everything on Martinique. Therefore the English fleet in the West Indies was noticeably strengthened and Admiral [Peter] Parker captured the entire French transport fleet sent there, and it can certainly be hoped that by now Martinique has been captured.

18 May - The brigadier delivered the draft proposals to His Excellence in the garden. Therein it was proposed that the Prince Friedrich Regiment and the von Ehrenkrook Battalion be permitted to unite at Berthier. A general order to the brigade concerning the batteaux. It was written to Lieutenant Colonel Praetorius that he was to use a detachment from his regiment to seek some rebels who try to sneak through the hills near Chambly every spring in order to learn what had been brought here by the fleet. His Excellence promised to pay ten guineas for every rebel brought in, but this was to be carried out as carefully and as secretly as possible. Dinner with His Excellence and relaxation during the evening.

19 May - An auction of possessions of the Englanders who were captured with Burgoyne. The sale of the items did not go especially well. The brigadier bought three officer's tents for a good price. We dined with Captain Twiss, and Captain von Tunderfeldt drew a reproach upon himself from the brigadier. His Excellence went to the levee with Major Holland and apparently will not dine with us.

20 May - Brigadier Powell, Lieutenant Colonel Carleton, and I dined with Dr. MacBean, a short hour from Quebec, close to the St. Lawrence River, a very pleasant location. I went there with the latter, on foot, and returned the same way. This doctor is a passionate chess player, but because I was a better player, I gave him a few lessons. The news arrived today that a German merchant at St. Jean and the small fort there suffered a fire during which much powder exploded. It was also reported therein that opposite la Norvit, the royal wood for construction caught fire, and much has already been burned. Supper in the evening with Captain von Tunderfeldt and Captain Mathew. On our return home, a stretch which was unfamiliar to me. Due to a request by Lieutenant Colonel von Hille a letter from the brigadier was delivered to Lieutenant Colonel Carleton. The arrival of Captain Hugget as deputy engineer and the departure of Captain Twiss to St. Jean and Carleton Island.

21 May - The brigadier, Captain von Tunderfeldt, I, and Haeberlin dined at the country estate of Dr. MacBean. The dinner consisted of fourteen covers. I and Haeberlin drove there in a coach and by seven o'clock we were back home.

22 May - Brigadier von Rauschenplat and Brigade Major Picquet arrived. They reported to my brigadier at once. We then made a counter-visit and all dined together with His Excellence. The brigadier wished to take his leave today so that he could depart tomorrow, but His Excellence requested that he remain here for a few days as he was still waiting for information about the assembling of troops at Sorel. We were allowed to assign the entire command at Trois Rivieres from our brigade and the English officer with his troops was to be relieved when our troops arrived there. The designated fleet went today to cruise from here along the Gulf, but returned at once because of contrary wind. This evening a whist party at Brigadier von Speth's. Received money for the lights [candles] from Barracks Master Murray amounting to nine pounds, thirteen shillings, six pence.

23 May - We dined again with His Excellence. Brigadier von Rauschenplat apologized for his negligence. After dinner we strolled in the city and during the evening I and Lieutenant Bodemeyer ate at Captain von Schoell's. His Excellence received confirmation today, from officers returning from a reconnaissance, of news concerning Spanish losses which had been brought here by ship, as it had also appeared in the rebel newspapers.

24 May - During the previous night an express arrived from Niagara with letters from General [Henry] Clinton. In those dispatches the news is contained of how Admirals Ross and Rodney defeated a Spanish fleet of eleven ships-of-the-line, the smallest of which had seventy cannons, near Cadiz. Six ships-of-the-line with the Spanish Admiral [Don Juan de] Langara [y Huarte] were taken into Gibralter, two ran aground, one blew up, and two, which were heavily damaged, sought refuge in the harbor at Cadiz. As a result of this affair, the two admirals captured a transport fleet of 23 ships. After the battle, which did not last very long, the Spaniards immediately raised the siege of Gibralter. Also in the dispatches there was information that General Clinton had captured the city of Charleston in the Carolinas. The loss for the Spaniards is said to amount to ten million pounds sterling. In a few days a *feu de joie* will be fired here celebrating this good news. The report concerning the fire at St. Jean on 17 April from Lieutenant Colonel Praetorius. Lieutenant Colonel von Barner reported many sick in his battalion and requested fresh provisions and vinegar for them, which the brigadier authorized being issued by Commissary Day. To supper at Captain Mateus' with Brigadier Powell.

25 May - A notification to Lieutenant Colonel Praetorius concerning the assembling of the troops. Today's Ascension celebration was very simple, except that the local bishop carried the monstrance. The good news was printed in today's newspaper. We dined at His Excellence's and during the evening I and Lieutenant Bodemeyer ate supper at Captain von Schoell's. From all indications we will leave Quebec in a few days.

26 May - Le Maitre announced that tomorrow the order will be issued for the von Ehrenkrook Battalion to assemble together in the barns at Berthier. The Prince Friedrich Regiment is to remain where it is until receipt of further orders. The brigadier dined with us, Captain von Schoell, and Lieutenant Bodemeyer in an auberge [inn] and during the evening we ate at Captain von Tunderfeldt's. The locally outfitted fleet finally set sail into the Gulf this morning. To conserve powder, the *feu de joie* was not executed today. We had our first electric storm here.

27 May - Dined at Mons. Cerheran's. Because of the heavy drinking, on which a person can over-indulge, I do not feel at my best and wish from the bottom of my heart to be back in my quarters.

28 May - A request for powder for firing. We dined today at Doctor General Kennedy's. Preparations for tomorrow's departure.

29 May - In the morning we paid our respects to His Excellence. He answered all the brigadier's draft proposals orally and approved of the assembling together of the von Ehrenkrook Battalion. The Prince Friedrich Regiment, however, should not remain where it now is, but it is his intention to have it camp at St. Jean. Powder is to be issued to us at Sorel for firing. Because of a shortage of provisions, he can not consent to a ration for the wives and children. A guard is to be assigned to the batteaux bridge at Berthier. The von Creuzbourg detachment at Carleton Island is to be relieved. We ate a light breakfast at Captain von Schoell's, where he gave me a medical chest for the regimental surgeon of Lieutenant Colonel von Creuzbourg. At ten o'clock we departed from Quebec in batteaux. We stopped at a mill at St. Augustine, ten miles from Quebec, because of the ebb tide, and remained there overnight.

30 May - We departed at four o'clock in the morning and arrived at Deschambeau at six o'clock in the evening, where we spent the night. Underway we fished. We covered thirty miles today.

31 May - Our journey continued to Cape Madeleine, where we spent the night in the local posthouse. If it had not been possible to pull the batteaux from St. Marie to this place, it would have been impossible to have traveled 35 miles against the current, nor to go so far.

June

1 June - We crossed the Genonse River with a good wind at seven o'clock and arrived at Trois Rivieres at eight o'clock. After our arrival and after disposing of various things and arrangements at the detachment there, we took the post [coach] and departed therefrom at eleven o'clock. We had conversations with Mons. Guichi and Captain von Schlagenteufel and arrived at Berthier at seven o'clock. We were greatly surprised when we saw our well-laid-out gardens. The Dragoon Senff had prepared a large vegetable garden for the brigadier and its beauty was certainly appreciated. Work on the new batteaux bridge was already well underway.

2 June - We drove on to the great river and made several visits. From there we took the senior field cashier back with us for dinner and supper. A notification from Mons. la Maitre to the brigadier that His Excellency had given Lieutenant Colonel von Ehrenkrook the order to march with his entire corps to Isle la Motte and to camp there. That island lies in the middle of Lake Champlain, is reportedly uninhabited, and is not healthy. It defines the border of Canada from this side.

The Journal of Lieutenant Friedrich Julius von Papet

During the first years part of our corps was thereon and at that time was not in the best of condition. The tents are to be delivered and the provisions received at St. Jean. An order from Lieutenant Colonel von Ehrenkrook concerning the eighteen men from Trois Rivieres and even more workers to Quebec as well as notification to the companies of the battalion that in the future the guards are to move into cantonments, or more likely, barns here.

3 June - The list of losses from the fire at St. Jean arrived from the company of Lieutenant Colonel Praetorius. They were, as had previously been expected, very great. They are to be sent to Quebec with the next post. A general order from headquarters setting forth the particulars of the forage money for 165 days during 1779 was sent to Lieutenant Colonel Carleton. A visit to the brigadier by Captain von Zielberg, Lieutenant Sommerlatte, and Cornet Graefe. They remained overnight with us.

4 June - Cornet Graefe and Ensign Haeberlin were sent to Sorel. Yesterday we were invited for dinner at Mons. Cuthbert's. The brigadier however, had to refuse. Most of the fruits of our garden froze this night, only a few remain eatable. After dinner the brigadier and I drove to Cuthbert to Captain von Schlagenteufel's and ate supper with him. When passing through the woods it was unpleasant to see what damage the frost had done therein during the previous night. Today was exceptionally cold with a northeast wind. The ensign returned from Sorel this evening at about ten o'clock. The King's birthday had been celebrated there. Both the artillery and the infantry had fired and they dined with Lieutenant Colonel St. Leger. The latter planned to visit the brigadier here tomorrow.

5 June - The courier continued from here to St. Jean to give the order to Lieutenant Colonel von Creuzbourg from His Excellency to proceed to Quebec with his entire corps in two ships and batteaux. A detachment therefrom is to remain at Ile aux Noix and an officer and fifty men at Carleton Island. The brigadier was greatly offended that this march order had not been sent to him first.

6 June - An order to Lieutenant Colonel von Ehrenkrook to have his company of the battalion move into barns here on the ninth. A visit to the brigadier by Mons. la Valtrie, Mons. Estimonville, and Lieutenant von Sommerlatte. They remained for dinner, supper, and slept at our quarters. The detachment of Sir Johnson has returned back over Lake Champlain, and have made many prisoners, whom they again released. The rebel Colonel Fischer was scalped by the Indians during this expedition. Colonel Sir Johnson at this opportunity recovered buried silver items with a value of 900 pounds sterling and brought them with him. A militia captain from that region came over to us with his entire company of 150 men and took service with Sir Johnson's corps. This corps, because of the wood-cutters, had a very difficult route and supposedly the rebels are in a very miserable condition. Today the brigadier inspected the detachment which is to go to Trois Rivieres, as well as the laborers for Quebec. This morning discipline was administered at the von Ehrenkrook Battalion on four wagoners, who had recently committed theft.

7 June - The departure of the detachment to Trois Rivieres and the laborers to Quebec. The brigadier went to see the administration of discipline again today and Mons. la Valtrie went with him. Afterward the brigadier inspected the barns and the exercise place. Later I figured the costs of the trip to Quebec, including items purchased there, at 160 Reichsthaler.

8 June - An order concerning drill and the permission for each company to have a sutler on the direct orders of the brigadier.

10 June - An announcement from Quebec that His Excellency desires the von Ehrenkrook Battalion to move to Quebec in the next few days and for it to camp there. He will deliver the tents for it and expects the responsibility therefore to come from our country. The requests therefore are to be submitted at once. A march order for Lieutenant Colonel von Creuzbourg on the south side of the St. Lawrence River to march on land to Pointe du Levi, in case the ships at Sorel are not yet ready and Lieutenant Barnes is to provide two batteaux per company for the transportation of baggage. An order to Lieutenant Colonel von Ehrenkrook to submit his request at once for the necessary tents for camping. The brigadier decided to go to Montreal yet today and at ten o'clock departed for that place with Ensign Haeberlin. His Excellency has spoken as if he does not wish to regain anything lost by the fire at St. Jean. At noon Captain von Schlagenteufel and his officers dined with me, the senior field cashier, and Ensign Reinerding. The officers are to judge the latter's drill, etc.

14 June - Tomorrow, the fifteenth, Lieutenant Colonel von Creuzbourg will depart for Quebec. At nine o'clock the entire group separated. The heavy artillery park has also left for Quebec. It is said that the desire of General Haldimand is to assemble all the troops at Quebec, and to set them in motion, because it has been learned that two French fleets have put to sea, the whereabouts of one is unknown, as are its intentions, and where it is to go. The last ships which arrived here reportedly sighted eighty ships sailing together.

15 June - A letter from Lieutenant Colonel Praetorius, if it were the brigadier's desire to inspect both companies at St. Charles on 16 June. This morning the brigadier with Ensign Haeberlin went to the great river. Primarily the uniform items and the accoutrements of this battalion were very pleasing to the brigadier and he therefore complimented Lieutenant Colonel von Ehrenkrook this evening. He determined that the company of Captain von Plessen conducted drill the best. Several of the junior officers of the von Ehrenkrook Battalion dined with the brigadier. We accompanied them to their batteaux and returned with the horses of Lieutenant Colonel von Creuzbourg, who will go from Sorel to Quebec on land, on this side, back to our quarters. Lieutenant Colonel von Creuzbourg's corps embarked this afternoon at five o'clock on two large ships at Sorel in order to go to Quebec. Lieutenant Colonel Praetorius awaits the brigadier tomorrow at St. Charles.

28 June - Numerous dispatches came from Major General von Riedesel for the brigadier and many letters for the corps. These were brought in two ships which brought the Hesse-[Cassel] von Lossberg Regiment and the 44th Regiment. Many troops from both of these regiments were lost in a storm last year; from the first two whole companies under Major [Ludwig August] von Hanstein. The regiment commanded by Colonel Loos landed at Quebec. All other news which these ships brought is generally favorable for us. Because of much work I will say nothing about that. Major General von Riedesel is still at New York awaiting the return of Lieutenant Cleve, whom he sent to Brunswick to learn if it is his ruler's desire that he remain with the captives or remain with the local troops. For my part, I was finally fortunate enough to receive a letter from my dear brother, which was dated 24 March 1779 at Staunton, Virginia, and wherein he described his health to my satisfaction. Lieutenant Dove had arrived in Virginia with the baggage on 8 February 1780. With the transport from New York there was also a shipment of exchanged prisoners, 77 men,

The Journal of Lieutenant Friedrich Julius von Papet

which arrived here under Captain Schlagenteufel of the Specht Regiment. At the request of Major General von Riedesel all the baggage and various items for the officers will be shipped to New York. Therefore all necessary preparations have been made here for their transportation from Trois Rivieres to Quebec, and Lieutenant Barnes is to deliver the necessary ships. Count von Wittgenstein and two officers passed today with their detachment of 100 jaegers, who have previously been stationed at Carleton Island and had spent the night here. The officers ate their evening meal with the brigadier.

29 June - The brigadier went to Sorel and I remained at home in order to prepare the dispatches, on which I have had to work day and night with a copyist, to Major General von Riedesel. The brigadier returned about two o'clock and brought the news that a ship had already gone from Sorel to Trois Rivieres today so it could load the things at Quebec. The regiments are to send their letters to the general.

July

4 July - This evening the brigadier and I took our departure for Quebec. It had been decided to leave for Quebec at twelve o'clock on this night, because of the heat of the day, if the letters from Quebec contained nothing new.

The letters arrived from Quebec and His Excellency wished to see the brigadier. They contained few references that the Ehrenkrook Battalion was still to go to Quebec. Therefore, we, the brigadier and I, went in a coach with post horses at twelve o'clock, and the batteaux were ordered to follow with our and the above noted items to Trois Rivieres.

5 July - We arrived at Trois Rivieres at eight o'clock. We found all the items to be sent to New York in the best of order and prepared for transportation. We dined with the Jew Hard. At one o'clock all items were loaded on a single-masted ship and because of the favorable wind, the brigadier decided to go aboard the ship with me and Cornet Graefe, and to sail to Quebec thereon. We set sail at three o'clock and the batteaux had to follow and stay near us. Near Batiscan the wind became contrary and the ship anchored. The night, which I was forced to spend on this filthy ship, had much similarity with that of ... and it will remain unforgetably with me also.

6 July - There was a complete calm during the morning, and we finally entered the batteaux, as did Cornet Graefe, a thing I had wanted to do for some time. Cornet Graefe was to deliver the items for New York at Quebec. Off Cape Diamond, not far from Quebec, we found the English Artillery camped close to the bank of the river. An hour from Quebec we left the batteaux, which could not advance much, and proceeded on foot. On the way a severe storm struck us and we were thoroughly soaked. The brigadier and Cornet Graefe took shelter in the lower city and I went, or more correctly ran, to the upper city, tiring myself greatly, in order to get a carriage for the brigadier. Within half an hour I obtained Captain von Tunderfeldt's carriage and everyone alighted at Lieutenant Bodemeyer's house. Our quarters were arranged as before. We ate at Captain von Schoell's.

7 July - We visited Brigadier Loos and then all went to dinner together. Afterward the brigadier inspected the assembled troops of Captain von Schlagenteufel, Jr. According to a general order some companies of the recently arrived troops are to march to camp in order to work on the defenses. This general order also specifies that all the officers are to be provided with tents. Later we dined with His Excellence, which was followed by a very earnest discussion between His Excellence and my brigadier, the cause of which was the relief of Captain von Schlagenteufel's detachment. I can only guess that the entire discussion was created by the senior field cashier. We dined magnificently at Captain von Tunderfeldt's and also drank seriously. The table contained sixteen covers and we had six sorts of wine.

8 July - We dined with Brigadier Loos. He provided many comical stories of the former campaign in Germany. During the afternoon the exchanged prisoners were divided among the various units and we spent several hours during the evening in Captain von Schlagenteufel's quarters. His Excellence promised to allow the ships to sail to New York soon.

9 July - Almost all the commanders of corps and regiments were in Quebec and dined with His Excellence. I had a group to dinner with me at an inn, for which I had to pay dearly. A letter from Lieutenant Colonel Praetorius concerning two masons and also a letter to Colonel von Frohenhausen. According to rumor, much planning is underway for an expedition to the upper country.

10 July - The brigadier took his departure from His Excellence, in order to leave on the twelfth, and to arrange for the items to remain as already planned. That is, Captain von Schlagenteufel is to travel with us and therefore Cornet Graefe remains behind. Toward eleven o'clock those plans were changed by His Excellence and the entire detachment is to go with us in four batteaux to the Rytre [?]. At twelve o'clock everything was changed again and the order arrived that instead of this detachment, two companies of the von Ehrenkrook Battalion were to march down to Quebec, for which purpose twelve batteaux came down to Quebec for the use of the detachment.

Finally today all the dispatches were completed which are to be sent to Major General von Riedesel at New York and it was suggested that he give the best possible care to the [Hesse-Hanau] Fitsch Free Corps. This last one is to bring all the baggage as well as the Musy [?] Wilhelm von Riedesel to New York again. Lieutenant Colonel von Ehrenkrook was informed by post concerning the march of the two companies to Quebec. At nine o'clock this evening the brigadier and I departed from Quebec in a carriage. We left all our belongings in the batteaux which are to depart tomorrow morning. At the city's exit gate we were met by His Excellence and Captain von Tunderfeldt in their coach. They halted and we exchanged courtesies once more. We dismounted again at the house of Major Holland and paid a brief visit to him and his family. As we changed horses at the fourth posthouse, a Canadian swindled twenty bottles of wine from me in a special manner. I had brought them from Quebec for my journey.

11 July - We arrived at Trois Rivieres at four-thirty. After eating a bite at the local posthouse, we again departed at eight o'clock and arrived on

12 July - at two o'clock in the morning at Berthier. I immediately wrote to Lieutenant Colonel von Ehrenkrook that he was to report in person to the brigadier at ten o'clock. The four companies of the von Ehrenkrook Battalion were relieved today because the two companies of Captains von Schlagenteufel and Zielberg were to march to Quebec. Ensign Haeberlin was sent to Sorel to make the necessary arrangements with Mons. Barnes for the necessary batteaux, which will include the seven cannon-batteaux, also called ratteaux, each of which can carry fifty men, and are to be put at our service.

14 July - The order came from Quebec that the German troops were to be mustered in twelve days. The completion of the muster rolls was to be extended six months from six months. On 17 July the Commissary of Muster Major Holland was to begin with the Hesse-Cassel, the Hesse-Hanau, and the Anhalt-Zerbst troops. The list of the things sent to New York was delivered to the brigadier. On orders of His Excellence, Cornet Graefe is to remain for a time in Quebec. The cornet had Major Holland to thank for this, and I well know why. The terms of the surrender of Charleston have now appeared in the rebel newspapers. Reportedly General [Wilhelm] von Knyphausen has attacked and scattered a force of 1,500 rebels in the Jerseys.

15 July - The order concerning the muster was completed and sent by express with the order to the von Barner Battalion, and the ordnance private took the same to the Prince Friedrich Regiment.

19 July - Both companies marched off in seven ratteaux and six batteaux. Captain von Tunderfeldt wrote that the quartermaster sergeants and their guards had arrived in Quebec, and that Captain Twiss had already designated the camp sites for both companies. The warrants for forage money for 1779 have already been signed and sent to Herr [Mr.] Jordan. A copy of a letter to the Prince containing the report of the corps up to 30 April 1780.

23 July - At six o'clock in the morning the general staff and both companies of the von Ehrenkrook Battalion and the von Plessen Company were mustered by Major Holland at Grand Berthier. The brigadier was greatly annoyed by the long absence of the senior field cashier, so I was sent to get him, and if he did not wish to come, to threaten him with arrest. As he came to meet me, I kept the last resort to myself in order to spare such an insult to an honorable man. After the muster a very good breakfast was enjoyed with Lieutenant Colonel von Ehrenkrook and at eight o'clock Major Holland and his son left for Montreal, in order to muster the von Barner Battalion tomorrow.

24 July - The von Barner Battalion was mustered. A letter to Lieutenant Colonel von Ehrenkrook concerning the muster of the two companies at Quebec. I forwarded to Captain von Tunderfeldt the original pay records of the prisoners at Niagara who had ransomed themselves. During the afternoon a stroll to the island of Cheneville du Nord, although my similar strolls were ever more unpleasant due to various reasons. I wrote to Lieutenant du Roi that it was necessary to send others to replace the dead men at Sorel.

25 July - The Prince Friedrich Regiment was mustered. From the von Barner Battalion, according to the most recent list, four men have drowned during this month. A letter to Lieutenant Colonel von Ehrenkrook concerning how punishment was to be administered to those arrested from New York. Major Holland is expected here this evening.

26 July - Finally an order arrived from Quebec that according to determined specifications, powder and balls were to be received from the closest magazines. This general order was accompanied by a brigade order, and because the von Barner Battalion is short the most cartridges and also has the most recruits, it was determined by the brigadier that the Prince Friedrich Regiment would give two barrels of powder and 8,000 balls and the von Ehrenkrook Battalion one barrel of powder and 4,000 balls to the von Barner Battalion, or receive less. The two companies from here arrived at Quebec on 23 July. As tents for their use were already set up, they immediately moved into camp and on the following day had to provide sixty men for a work detail. On orders of His Excellence the non-commissioned officer and three men at Machiche rejoined Lieutenant Hertel at Trois Rivieres. The money for the candles used by the guard was paid to Captain von Tunderfeldt and I so informed the senior cashier today.

29 July - This morning, thinking it was already day (it was between two and three o'clock), I arose and saw on the horizon a very bright northern light, brighter than I have previously seen here. It appeared to be directly over my quarters and formed a sheet of light of nearly four square feet, which spread about in a circle of very white light rays, and changed colors moment to moment. This sheet was itself nearly red, white, violet, and was for the most part so made and of such appearance, as if sulphur burned. At the same time, the air had the smell of what is called by us Leyden smoke. When I asked among the Canadians if they had seen this same aerial display, they answered no, but a short time previous, when England conquered Canada, a similar one had been noticed. As I saw that explanations on natural grounds were unattainable from them, I left them to their day-dreams. A general order specified the amount of powder and four flints for each man in the company. According to Captain von Schlagenteufel both companies moved our of camp on 23 July. Neither straw nor blankets were delivered to the camp. Captain von Schlagenteufel complained therefore about Captain von Tunderfeldt not having looked out for the corps' best interest at Quebec. The entire companies have been desired for work every day, but he has not provided more than he could spare from the camp.

The Canadian pilots taken along were of little or no help on the trip. The small, armed ship *Merkur* has been captured by the rebels in the Gulf and retaken again by the armed ship *Wolf*. This afternoon the brigadier went to Sorel with Ensign Haeberlin and they spent the night there with Lieutenant Colonel St. Leger. Tomorrow I will cross over with Captain Plessen and Captain von Schlagenteufel, Jr. to dine. Militia Captain Olivier stopped today at the brigadier's and requested that his company might be moved out of the barns and lodged again in quarters as a harvest will soon be gathered in and the inhabitants must make preparations therefore.

August

2 August - The letter from Quebec did not contain the best news. Reportedly the savages have brought the news that the French have captured Halifax. An order to Lieutenant Colonel von Ehrenkrook concerning a halt to drill because of the great heat, and that all powder, after the previously designated use, be preserved and a list of that remaining be submitted.

5 August - Captain von Tunderfeldt wrote that His Excellency has ordered Captain Barnes to give eight cartridge boxes each to the von Ehrenkrook and von Barner Battalions, as well as some to the Prince Friedrich Regiment. On 3 August a ship of the English fleet, which sailed from Torbay on 30 May with 48 vessels, had arrived at Quebec. On its voyage this ship had met neither French nor Spanish ships. It had been attacked by a rebel privateer, which it had repulsed, in the Gulf. The ship's master said that the fleet was attacked later by the French. There is doubt as to the truth of this story, because it is assumed, as this is the first ship from England, that it will provide the man with a better price for his wares. Five ships with troops are in the fleet and many store ships for the various departments. No mail has arrived from Europe; such is all on the frigate *Sanoe*. That frigate and the *Plantora* [*Pandora* ?] have convoyed the fleet. Both frigates, after delivering the convoy, are to cruise in the Gulf. After delivering the deserters from the 29th Regiment Lieutenant Hertel is to wait here until two more of the same arrive from Quebec. His Excellence will soon announce the removal of the troops from the barns, but until then the situation remains as is. Captain von Zielberg has been designated as an engineer under Captain Twiss and Cornet Graefe, with one non-commissioned officer and twelve men, has joined the detachment of Lieutenant Bodemeyer. Notice of the death of our beloved Prince of the Land and Duke has supposedly been reported in an English newspaper.

12 August - His Excellence has ordered the two companies of the von Ehrenkrook Battalion here to camp at Berthier. The tents necessary for them are to be delivered by Captain Barnes against receipts. Lieutenant Colonel von Ehrenkrook was so informed and Ensign Haeberlin sent to Sorel concerning the transaction. Captain von Tunderfeldt wrote how a privateer of fourteen cannons was captured by the frigate *Hind* and another by Mons. Greefes. The two privateers reportedly had captured five transport ships from us in the Gulf; other reports even mention fourteen ships that we have recently lost in the Gulf, and one of which had a value estimated at 60,000 pounds. The alertness of the English fleet certainly does not merit praise. A few days ago a ship, coming from Boston, entered Quebec without having been stopped for any reason. Therefore seven batteaux have come to Quebec, each armed with two six pound cannons, and were then sent to posts at Bic Island. It is said that we can expect no recruits with the fleet. The provisions fleet sailed from England on 6 May and sailed around Scotland. Forty tents were received from Sorel today. However, because each is capable of housing at most five men, another 33 have been ordered. An electric storm accompanied by such strong winds that several barns were blown over the houses. My own host lost two.

13 August - I wrote numerous letters to Quebec. This afternoon Captain Barnes dined with the brigadier and everything concerning the two companies here taken care of. Captain Barnes delivered, all told, 33 tents, eight pavilion shelters, and eight extras. The records of the court-martial held for the deserter Gelbke were sent to the brigadier by the Prince Friedrich Regiment.

14 August - The two companies here moved into camp. The tents were set up in the camp. Today I received my forage money for 165 days in 1779. Lieutenant Colonel St. Leger and Lieutenant Thomas dined with the brigadier. This evening we made an inspection in the camp. The appearance because of a cradle...!

23 August - From Quebec the report of how an Anhalt-Zerbst detachment had recaptured eleven deserters from our corps at Latigan. The others of the fifteen have escaped. They defended themselves; two were wounded and had to be taken to the hospital. His Excellence had them chained two by two and ordered them brought here by an officer and twenty men for questioning. Nineteen ships have arrived at Quebec. It is believed that if our recruits do not arrive soon, that they must remain in Portsmouth for this year, because it would be difficult for a fleet to sail from there without a strong escort. His Excellence is very annoyed about the loss of the many captured ships and that a Spanish fleet has appeared in the West Indies. The frigate *Hind*, commanded by Captain Young, recaptured the five transport ships seized by a privateer and has taken them and the privateer to New York. That our Serene Highness the Duke died in April has been confirmed from England. His Excellence considers it necessary to make an example of the deserters. The munitions chests were sent to Sorel. Among the nineteen ships are two with provisions.

30 August - The order came from Quebec that the two companies of the Prince Friedrich Regiment which are in camp at St. Charles are to enter Fort Chambly. Therefore the order was forwarded yet today with the ordnance private who at the same time is also taking the last deserter, Huttinger, and our dispatches.

September

2 September - An order to the Prince Friedrich Regiment to provide one non-commissioned officer and fifteen men to the hospital at Trois Rivieres, and also the same to the camp, similar to the one of the von Ehrenkrook Battalion. The blankets for last year's recruits are to be issued in the next few days.

The Journal of Lieutenant Friedrich Julius von Papet

6 September - On 1 and 2 September five ships with provisions arrived at Quebec. They sailed from England on 6 May and passed the narrow passage by Beloeil. These ships encountered an unimaginable number of ice islands [icebergs] which were higher than their masts. A ship and a war sloop were lost in that region. In mid-June another fleet supposedly sailed for Canada.

10 September - Captain Barnes came from Quebec in the afternoon with the order for both companies of the von Ehrenkrook Battalion here at Berthier to march into camp at Sorel, because these companies are needed for a short time to work on improving the defenses there. His Excellency believed the brigadier, because of their nearness, would not have to change his location and could therefore remain with the staff in Berthier awaiting further orders. The brigadier was nonetheless very annoyed and believed that in this situation much could go wrong. Toward evening the Prince Friedrich Regiment non-commissioned officer with the fifteen-man detachment reported at Trois Rivieres. An unpleasant compliment from militia Captain Schmidt concerning neglected payment for a carriage by a garrison officer on command from the von Ehrenkrook Battalion was passed to the lieutenant colonel.

11 September - A petition to His Excellency concerning the march of the two companies to Sorel as directed.

Lieutenant Bielstein received an order to go to Trois Rivieres with one non-commissioned officer and fifteen men of the Prince Friedrich Regiment to relieve Lieutenant Hertel. Whose orders!... A list to Colonel Carleton was submitted by Lieutenant Colonel Practorius for seventy blankets, etc., which were lost in the fire at St. Jean, also an order concerning acquisition of missing wood for cooking for the camping company, was requested. During the afternoon Major [Alexander] Dundas came from Quebec and brought the brigadier a letter from Major General von Riedesel, which had come from Halifax with an express. This letter was dated 2 July 1780 at New York and accompanied by the duplicates from the months of April and May 1780. In the newer one the general let the brigadier know he had been informed by a letter of 24 March from Privy Councilor von Feronee that His Serene Highness, the Duke, before his death, had promoted the brigadier to colonel. At the same time, His Majesty the King had sent General Clinton a letter to have the general exchanged and sent to

Canada. Because the negotiations were underway concerning the exchange of the Convention prisoners, they will initially wait, but as soon as such appear fruitless as were the previous offers, they will be terminated. However, it appears almost certain that by the end of the autumn 300 or 400 men will be exchanged from among the Convention prisoners. That created such joy for the brigadier and us that we have completely forgotten the unpleasant hours we experienced yesterday.

16 September - His Excellence has approved the brigadier's presentation in light of the two companies marching to Sorel and everything is to remain as it was previously. Captain von Tunderfeldt wrote that two ships had arrived at Bic, but it is still not known where they came from. The arrival of a batteau from Trois Rivieres with some men from the detachment traveling to Sorel for an investigation. In Quebec it is generally accepted that our losses at sea are greater than are yet known. Six hundred men are now working daily on the newly laid-out fortifications at Quebec. Colonel Carleton with the English Light Infantry and a company of Hessian Jaegers have gone to reconnoiter the route which Mons. Arnold took when he marched on Quebec. The express which arrived here recently from New York has already departed. He has taken nothing with him except a letter from His Excellence and was ordered by His Excellence to take nothing from anyone else.

20 September - His Excellence is very concerned that Major General von Riedesel, would depart from New York so late in the season when much danger is to be expected, because the month of October seldom passes without storms. A ship has arrived from Glasgow, but it brought no news. A provisions ship is also reported in the river. The Duke of Cumberland and Gloucester has again made his peace with the King and according to everyone is again serving his duty in London.

24 September - A few rumors such as - when the English garrison at Sorel marches farther up the river, we are to move into their place at Sorel.

25 September - This rumor is now confirmed because 100 men of the 53rd Regiment and 100 men of the 34th Regiment have marched to St. Jean. Currently three expeditions are in progress. The first, commanded by Lieutenant Colonel Carleton is along the route below

The Journal of Lieutenant Friedrich Julius von Papet

Quebec on which Mons. Arnold came here in 1775. The second is across Lake Champlain toward Albany and is commanded by Major Carleton. The third, toward Oswego, is commanded by Sir Johnson. No one knows yet with certainty where these expeditions are to go.

30 September - A letter desired on my behalf concerning the deserter Drummer Tonnies, to Lieutenant Colonel von Ehrenkrook. Lieutenant Colonel Carleton returned from his reconnaissance on the 27th. All the officers carried their own provisions on their back and had to sleep in the forest. The ship with which Captain Aplain took the baggage from here to New York, reportedly has arrived there safely. This news came with a ship from Halifax which is now in the river. Also, the entire French fleet has left the West Indies, taking many troops with it, apparently in order to conduct an attack. No one yet knows where it is bound. The English fleet is reportedly searching for it in two divisions. Today Captains Rosenberg and Gleisenberg traveled to Montreal.

October

11 October - We received the directive concerning winter quarters. Accordingly the von Ehrenkrook Battalion and our brigade and the general staff were assigned the villages of Kamouraska, Riviere Ouelle, Ste. Anne, and St. Rock. Therefore we will be eighty miles above Quebec, the advance posts toward the Gulf, a region that I have not yet seen. The whole army is, for the most part, assigned on the south side of the river. To proceed from here to our new quarters area we must move forty German miles [240 English miles], a very agreeable trip for us, and also for the troops as no uniforms and also no uniform assessories are available from Europe. In that region it is certainly three times colder than here. The brigadier has the privilege of settling where he wishes and where it is most convenient for him. He is considering going there soon, ahead of the others. According to the rebel newspapers General Cornwallis reportedly totally defeated General Gates not far from Charleston. The rebels admit having left 500 dead on the field. A very long letter from me concerning the reports and future correspondence to Captain von Tunderfeldt. The letter to my uncle is best written in triplicate.

The Journal of Lieutenant Friedrich Julius von Papet

12 October - The brigadier asked His Excellence to be allowed to first proceed to Quebec. I wrote to Lieutenant Bodemeyer regarding quarters for us in Quebec. The brigadier traveled to Sorel today, in part to determine the availability of batteaux. He checked that out with Lieutenant Colonel St. Leger and brought him back here where they dined, and the lieutenant colonel then returned to Sorel. We were invited to dine with him tomorrow if the weather allows. A visit from the senior field cashier who asked my advice about his future quarters. Corporal Mueller came today with two of the deserters involved with the conspiracy at Quebec and who had been detained in the hospital there because of their wounds. This evening my fourth letter to my sister.

13 October - The winter quarters assignments were announced. An order to Lieutenant Colonel von Ehrenkrook to pay the money for the capture of the eleven deserters at Quebec to Brigadier von Rauschenplat, whose last letter to the brigadier I had to answer. Both dispatch cases for Germany were closed today and delivered to Corporal Mueller, who is to deliver them on orders to Captain von Tunderfeldt's ship, as well as four packages for Lieutenant Bodemeyer. I wrote to Lieutenant Bielstein that he was to deliver an Englishman, who was in arrest, a sailor from Trois Rivieres, to Corporal Mueller to take to Quebec. As it rained heavily today and was exceptionally stormy, the trip to Sorel was postponed. Major rearrangements of the brigadier's quarters to insure the greatest economy.

14 October - It is written from Quebec that there is still nothing new concerning the second fleet. His Excellence made known a few days ago that if the uniforms for our corps did not arrive, he desired the brigadier to offer suggestions to him, in writing, that it caused the troops great suffering and that the troops could no longer serve without them. It is assumed that His Excellence will go to St. Jean during the coming days, but the specific day is not yet determined. His Excellence a few days ago said that he hoped to hear important news in fourteen days.

18 October - According to a general order of 15 October, His Excellence made known his satisfaction with the regiment which had worked for the engineer department, with a gift of winter clothing, consisting of a pair of winter breeches, a pair of shoes, a pair of shoe soles, and a pair of mittens for the non-commissioned officers, drummers, and privates, who had participated. The request by the brigadier to go to Quebec, has still not been answered. This answer is surely to be expected with the next mail. According to news from Quebec, Colonel Chevalier Johnson has returned from his expedition, as has Colonel Carleton. The first went to Fort Stanwix, and the latter to Albany. His Excellency has also sent a party of Indians on an expedition. A flag of truce of forty people has again arrived at St. Jean. On His Excellency's orders all invalids found in the corps are to be in Quebec on the 24th of this month with the necessary certification so as to be embarked for Europe. However, there is no means available at the corps for transporting them. It is reported that a ship from New York with an officer dressed in red and blue was in the river ten days ago, but it has since disappeared. The frigate *Pandora* [a sloop of 14 cannons], which is to convoy the fleet from here, has arrived at Quebec after nine days cruising in the Gulf. Because the Chasseurs [Jaegers] of Lieutenant Colonel von Creuzbourg have not given a day of work, they have also been excluded from receiving the gift. Captain von Tunderfeldt wrote that our new quarters were in the richest region of Canada. Very good houses should be found there. As regards the compensation for damages due to the fire at St. Jean, Captain von Tunderfeldt believes the general will approve nothing. Above all he is convinced that the companies made no effort to save the King's belongings. The English officers whose baggage was burned have had it paid for, because they lost everything trying to save the powder magazine, which they actually were able to do. The preparations for our trip were put aside. According to other letters the news that Cornwallis had defeated Gates was confirmed. A fleet of French and Spanish ships is reportedly blockaded at Newport and another in the West Indies has been defeated. The great fleet of the Duke de Chartres is shut in the harbor at Brest by the large English fleet under Admiral Hardy ... That is wonderful news! ... When the confirmation comes with the fleet, we will finally be able to hope that peace is near. This afternoon Lieutenant Colonel Carleton passed on his way to Sorel. He delivered a letter from His Excellency to the brigadier while passing, which was an answer to that of the 12th. According to this letter, the brigadier has been allowed to proceed to Quebec when it pleases him. The order for the necessary batteaux, for when the troops move out, has already been received from His

Excellence by Lieutenant Colonel Carleton. The brigadier therefore already today sent most of his, mine, and Ensign Haeberlin's baggage on ahead to Quebec in a batteau, accompanied by my scribe and my batman. The completion of the order to the brigade concerning the necessity of submitting the lists soon. An order to Lieutenant Colonel von Ehrenkrook that he was to depart Sorel in batteaux as soon as possible. Lieutenant Colonel Praetorius by a similar order was informed of the negative answer from His Excellence concerning the seventy blankets lost in the fire at St. Jean.

November

1 November - The Anhalt-Zerbst Regiment received marching orders. The regiment is to travel on the water in five ships to its quarters' location. There was a good wind for that today, but because of a shortage of provisions they could not embark. A report by Lieutenant Colonel von Ehrenkrook about two deserters and about obtaining two barks at Sorel for the transportation of baggage. Dined during the evening at Barracks Master Murray's. Brigadier Loos, whose double meaning discourse after dinner was carried on with me and the brigadier under four eyes [between us], was also present. His Excellence has requested the brigadier take the heavy cavalry swords from the dragoons because they are of no use here in this land. The brigadier agreed to this.

4 November - His Excellence was again asked if the regimental quartermaster could proceed to arrange quarters. His Excellence said however that it was still necessary to wait a few days as much concerning the quarters situation was to be changed. Today's general orders directed the barracks at the Schuitten Cloister to be ready this month so that they could be occupied by the 44th Regiment and the Knyphausen Regiment. The Lossberg Regiment was to be assigned to Beauport.

6 November - A general order directed the three regiments to march into their winter quarters tomorrow. There was still nothing mentioned for us. A letter from Lieutenant Colonel von Ehrenkrook concerning punishment for the guard who allowed [Gottlieb] Metzdorf to escape, and at the same time, if brick-layers were available in the Prince Friedrich Regiment and Ehrenkrook Battalion. The purchase of various items from the Jew French. He made certain remarks ... about the senior field cashier concerning which a certain captain was the cause.

7 November - The march of the three regiments. Much snow. Repeated hope for the fleet. This was strengthened yesterday from an arriving ship, which had seen such three weeks ago near Cape Race, etc. Reportedly the French have taken five East Indiamen ships of great value. Still no order to march today. A letter to His Serene Highness, the Duke. During the past night two to four feet of snow fell. The first order concerning our march into winter quarters at Kamouraska. According to the same our two companies were to embark at eleven o'clock, and it was already eleven o'clock when I received the order - and even later. There were no ships on which to embark. The situation was such that His Excellence had to assign small ships of 25 tons, on which barely thirty men could embark with their baggage. Nothing has been said about Captain von Schoell's detachment. When the impossibility of such an embarkation was finally understood, Captain Schenk was directed to make the necessary preparations.[42] Then the second order arrived - both companies of Captain von Schoell's detachment to be prepared to embark tomorrow; the tents and all other camp equipment, which had been used here, to be taken with the companies; and the embarkation of all the troops tomorrow at Drummond's Wharf, on the ships *Polly*, *Liberty*, and *Lark* - in writing and dated 8 November. I answered the senior field cashier's letter. Continued hoping for the fleet. Orders to Captains von Schlagenteufel and von Schoell.

9 November - Loading baggage on the ships *Polly* and *Lark*. The *Liberty* has not yet arrived. On the first Schoell's detachment and its baggage were loaded, and on the latter, after both companies were assigned ships, the baggage of Captain von Zielberg's Company, the rest of Captain von Schoell's detachment, which came to about 113 men, and then so many of Captain von Zielberg's men that the total amounted to 217 men. If everyone is on board, the ships are to sail at eight o'clock tomorrow morning, without waiting for the *Liberty*. Orders to this effect to Captain von Schlagenteufel.

10 November - Von Schoell's detachment and its baggage were loaded on *Polly* at nine o'clock this morning. On the *Lark* - the rest of the von Schoell detachment, most of Captain von Zielberg's Company, and all its baggage. Added thereto are the troops from Lieutenant Bodemeyer and the quartermaster sergeants and quartermaster guards of both companies at Berthier. One officer, two non-commissioned officers, and 24 men remain behind to be embarked on *Liberty*. At nine-thirty everything was ready for the departure and the ship *Liberty* was still missing. At eleven o'clock we went to Lieutenant Colonel Carleton in order to suggest that both companies at Berthier march to the place where that ship lay to transport the Anhalt-Zerbsters to Trois Rivieres. - The answer - That is just what His Excellence had suggested, but he had made the change and ordered that the ship was to sail to Berthier. Nevertheless, that was the best solution and he would suggest it again to His Excellence.

We then went to the general. At the same time Captain Schenk came and reported that the wind had swung to the east and the ships could not sail toward Kamouraska without running aground and risking the lives of the troops. This was reported to His Excellence who was sick. Lieutenant Colonel Carleton was summoned and then the winter quarters were completely changed according to the following situation. Lieutenant Colonel Carleton came back from the general and told the brigadier that the von Ehrenkrook Battalion would enter winter quarters of their previous year and he would soon receive the orders therefore. Thereafter the brigadier went on his way and I remained until one o'clock in order to obtain the general order from Major [Richard Bernhard] Lernoult. He went home and told me that as soon as the order arrived, to send it to him at once. Next I was sent to Lieutenant Colonel Carleton by the brigadier to suggest to him that Parish Repentigny was the indispensible winter quarters location for the von Ehrenkrook Battalion. Answer - He had already given the same thought. The Parish LaValtrie should be left unoccupied and the von Ehrenkrook Battalion, instead of Repentigny, should only enter L'Assomption. Next I sent to Major Lernoult at three o'clock to ask if the order were ready, as both ships *Polly* and *Lark* were underway and still had no orders, and at the same time, if *Liberty* had arrived, and could embark both companies. Answer - He still had no orders, but awaited them at any moment.

Next to the castle. I asked Captain von Tunderfeldt if the general still had not directed the orders to be prepared. I told him about the embarrassment as we did not know if we should embark on *Liberty*.

He therefore asked His Excellence, who replied that everything was arranged as the colonel suggested and that von Schlagenteufel's Company could embark on *Liberty*. I then went to Lieutenant Colonel Carleton. He said the quarters for the von Ehrenkrook Battalion remained firm in the previously mentioned parish. The von Schlagenteufel Company should try to load at once and get under sail as quickly as possible. The quarters' location for Captain von Schoell's detachment began at Deschambeau and extended to and included Ste. Anne. A march order would be prepared for Captains von Schlagenteufel and von Schoell, that if the ships could not sail farther, they were to debark at once and march on land. Lieutenant Colonel von Creuzbourg would receive his orders tomorrow morning.

By the time of my arrival home the brigadier had already received the order and the winter quarters locations. I received the signed warrants sent to me for the senior field cashier and the contingent accounts from 24 June 1779 to 24 June 1780 from Captain Matheus. The order that Captain von Schlagenteufel's Company could embark immediately was taken by Lieutenant von Sommerlatte to the camp. In order to see it, I and the brigadier went to the lower city. The *Liberty* lay at Drummond's Wharf unloading some cargo and items so as to be able to take on the troops. There Lieutenant Sommerlatte met us and said the companies were already on the march to the ship when they were ordered to turn around and to load tomorrow morning. Upon our arrival home, we learned that this order had been issued due to a misunderstanding. Therefore Captain von Schlagenteufel received the written order to march at once in order to embark this evening at Drummond's Wharf, together with all the baggage, because the ship *Liberty* was to sail at two or three o'clock tomorrow morning.

Captain von Schlagenteufel was to report to the brigadier's quarters and Lieutenant Sommerlatte was to lead the troops to the embarkation. I prepared the clearest orders for Captain von Schlagenteufel, covering every possibility and read them to him so he would forget nothing. After that I prepared an order for Lieutenant Colonel von Ehrenkrook as to how he was to move both companies into cantonment quarters at Berthier and that he was not to unload all the baggage from the ships until the quarters were determined. He commented however, that His Excellence could send nothing sooner than with the ordinary mail. I had my reasons for describing this situation so completely, because I had been blamed for a good many things, so that I wished from the bottom of my heart to see an end soon to all this pile of trouble.

A general order concerning the change of winter quarters. For the von Ehrenkrook Battalion and the von Schoell detachment it remained as already mentioned. Lieutenant Colonel von Creuzbourg's Corps was assigned at St. Vallee, Berthier, and St. Thomas, St. Francois, and St. Pierre, and the Artillery under Colonel [Forbes] MacBean was to go to Quebec tomorrow. A company of Lieutenant Colonel von Creuzbourg was also to enter the barracks at Quebec, and was not to make that move prior to the sixteenth. It is to be the company of Captain von Castendyck.

12 November - The Artillery under Lieutenant Colonel MacBean marched into Quebec.. Those destined for Sorel returned into camp and are to be embarked aboard ship for Sorel. At the levee Lieutenant Colonel Carleton was asked to approach His Excellence on behalf of the Prince Friedrich Regiment entering winter quarters also. Carleton promised to do this at an appropriate time tomorrow morning, so that His Excellence's decision can be sent to the regiment with tomorrow's post. We dined at Dr. McBean's. Present were myself, the brigadier, von Loos, and several ladies, among whom was an intimate friend, Madame Schendler.

13 November - Lieutenant Colonel Carleton had suggested the parishes of Lachine, Terrebonne, and the Island of Jesus to His Excellence as quarters for the Prince Friedrich Regiment, so that this regiment would border close to us and the corps would finally be together. His Excellence agreed with this, but when he discussed the provisioning with Commissary General Day, it was not a workable solution. Thereafter the order was issued that the Prince Friedrich Regiment should immediately march into the quarters where they were originally assigned. They were to march in four divisions, leaving the excess baggage in the fort at Chambly, about which Lieutenant Colonel Carleton would be given written instructions.

22 November - Our departure from Berthier. Captain von Tunderfeldt wrote that His Excellence ordered that our detachment at Trois Rivieres, consisting of one officer, one non-commissioned officer, and nine privates, be withdrawn and replaced with immigrants. We dined with Mons. Lavaltrie and arrived at L'Assomption at one o'clock. The brigadier was well satisfied with his quarters; mine were not as nice as they had been made out to be.

23 November - Captain von Plessen's Company moved in here. Several visits to English families. The order to Lieutenant Bielstein according to which he was to be assigned two non-commissioned officers and twelve men - one non-commissioned officer and six men from each battalion. The senior field cashier arrived here this evening. Haeberlin and Tausch quartered with Cashier Wolff. Mine is the best one, after the brigadier's, that I have had in Canada. I was lodged with a rich merchant named le Rouse, whose daughter is about eighteen years old, the most beautiful person that I have seen in Canada. She is said to be engaged to the son of a rich merchant.

December

14 December - Except for a few letters to Quebec, nothing new. The brigadier and I took a stroll today to a concession area of L'Assomption called Stohigan, where Lieutenant Hertel was situated. We found this region to be so beautiful that it is certain that no other parish in Canada is so thoroughly developed as this one. L'Assomption has seven militia companies and is said to have 3,000 adult inhabitants, of whom most are well-off. It is of special interest that there are fewer mosquitoes and swamps here. This evening my host told me about the upper country, where he had been at the time of the French, primarily about the Mississippi River and Louisiana. According to his description that is the most blessed land of the world. It is a shame that no one but savages, who have only hatred for most Europeans, live there.

Journal of Lieutenant Friedrich Julius von Papet

January 1781

1 January - With the most sincere wish that this might be the last year that I must spend in Canada, I also made the wish for the well-being of my family and friends in Germany. - Many orders and letter -- Lieutenant Colonel von Ehrenkrook and all the officers of the battalion were at dinner with the brigadier today. The richly endowed Jew French passed from Montreal to Quebec today and also dined with us. His tale of Madame Campbell with [a series of dashes]. At six o'clock the entire group disbanded. French took our letters to Quebec. During the previous night Drummer Ahlruth injured his left hand when accidently struck by a shot when his weapon misfired, and during the afternoon half of his thumb was cut off.

2 January - During the evening to supper with the merchant Carree, where the discussion dealt with our future get-togethers and balls. For this purpose a subscription will be circulated and persons responsible for various committees were designated. The day of the get-togethers, or club as the English call them, was settled and is to be on Mondays. The days for dances however were not settled in order to reduce the all-too-frequent objections.

3 January - Ensign Haeberlin paid a visit to Major Grey. The brigadier and I took some medicine and thereafter I did not feel well, and as a result did not give strict attention to my host's family.

6 January - According to letters from Captain von Tunderfeldt an express has arrived at Quebec from New York with dispatches for His Excellency. However the contents are still unknown and are assumed to be nothing good. No one will be able to speak to the messenger and he took lodgings outside the city with Major Holland. This messenger had told how toward the end of October, a German general, who had been a prisoner, died at New York and been buried in the Lutheran Church at that place,[43] attended by six cannons and all the officers. He did not know the general's name, but by all indications it can be none other than Major General von Riedesel. This report so disturbed the brigadier that he nearly lost his self-control. His Excellency is supposedly very busy, from which several observations can be made from our point of view. That means His Excellency will soon travel to Montreal.

Journal of Lieutenant Friedrich Julius von Papet

10 January - It snowed heavily. Many letters from Quebec and the Prince Friedrich Regiment. Captain von Tunderfeldt confirmed the order from His Excellency that the reward money for eight deserters, who deserted from the camp at Berthier, was to be paid to Colonel MacBean, and the cost was to be carried in the half-yearly accounts. At the same time the announcement that His Excellency intends to issue 25 pairs of snowshoes to each company so that the troops can practice and therefore only strong, young men are to be chosen. During the afternoon a visit from Captain von Gleissenberg. In the back of the monthly reports each time are to be listed how many officers, non-commissioned officers, surgeon's mates, drummers, privates, and servants are in each parish and on command.

13 January - The brigadier was not feeling well, but was better toward noon. I and Haeberlin took a drive to Captain von Zielberg's in the brigadier's carriage. Absolutely nothing new in today's letters from Quebec. Still no one knows what the two couriers have brought from New York. Nevertheless everyone believes despite this that what they brought can not be good.

16 January - I was invited to a grand dinner in Varennes by my host. I rode there with him, his daughter, a Madame Loyhel, and the merchant La Rock in three carriages. The dinner was hosted by my host's nephew, a rich merchant named Massier. We found a gathering of thirty persons, among whom were many minor nobility, all very proper people. Initially card games were played, then dinner, and then dancing to the music of a small organ until four o'clock. Varennes is one of the richest parishes; the houses, all rather well-built, lie close to one another. I found the host at the billiard table and closely watched most men playing the game.

17 January - We departed from that place in three carriages and ate at the new house of the merchant La Rock, concerning whom I noticed he had an interest in my host's daughter. She was driven by a merchant named Boutellier, from Montreal, and twice was thrown about on the road. After dining we departed and arrived at L'Assomption at six o'clock. I reported to the brigadier and found nothing new in the works. Boutellier took lodgings with my host and I again had to dine with him, and we danced again until twelve o'clock.

20 January - I arranged for janizary music for the brigadier, for which the lieutenant colonel had borrowed all the instruments.

Journal of Lieutenant Friedrich Julius von Papet

Today's letters from Quebec contained much that is new and hinted that we here in Canada are to be attacked at two places. The Light Infantry Company of the 44th Regiment has already marched and the 31st Infantry has also received orders to march, and still more are to follow. The Prince Friedrich Regiment received 100 pairs of snowshoes with which the troops are to exercise. From all of these movements, nothing definite can be surmised.

25 January - The brigadier and Haeberlin drove to St. Sulpice and brought Ensign Reinerding back with them. Certain letters from Quebec mention that many rebels are gathering at Albany and supposedly the couriers from New York saw them there. The Hesse-[Cassel] Jaeger Corps von Wurmb at New York supposedly has been almost completely destroyed. In case the rebels should actually pay a visit here, General Haldimand appears determined to attack them with a part of the army. The council of the province, which had been called together, has now adjourned, and Mons. Cuthbert has offered 400 men for the defense of the province. A courier is awaited daily from Halifax. During the last expedition by Lieutenant Colonel Carleton it was discovered that the rebels had begun to make a new road to come from Connecticut, and were far advanced therewith. I sent the contingent accounts for the von Ehrenkrook and von Barner Battalions to Captain von Tunderfeldt today.

26 January - Today we dined by the Englander Carterret and Madam Robinson. Everyone says for certain the 31st and 44th Regiments are already on the march to St. Jean and that in a few days the general is to go to Montreal. At Stillwater 15,000 rebels, including 6,000 French are said to have assembled. The events which follow will make clear if this report is true.

27 January - An order to Lieutenant Colonel von Ehrenkrook's Battalion, all siegneurs and justices of the peace, when they request shelter or help, are to be granted such at once. The merchant Franks came from Quebec today and dined with the brigadier. The 31st and 44th Regiments had not yet marched on the 22nd. He brought some Argenterie for me from Quebec.

30 January - Yesterday at a grand assemblage which took place in the Recollet Cloister at Montreal, the proclamation and order of His Excellency was delivered. The entire city followed with an address to His Excellency of their trust and appreciation for his defense of the

Journal of Lieutenant Friedrich Julius von Papet

province, and that they would support the government against every attack with their goods and their blood. Captain von Zielberg dined with the brigadier. During the afternoon the brigadier received a letter from Lieutenant Colonel von Barner, in which he promised to make a visit to the brigadier with Brigadier MacBean.

31 January - Exercises are to be conducted with cannons on the ice, and actually on sleds. News is expected soon from Carillon. We dined today at Mons. Macheath's.

4 February - Most people believe that the rebels will undertake nothing against us, but it is believed in Quebec that the general is contemplating an expedition against them. His Excellence has given command over the English in Trois Rivieres to Lieutenant Bielstein. Lieutenant von Sommerlotte dined with us today. His Excellence is pleased that we have a supply of weapons at Trois Rivieres and desires to borrow them from the brigadier.

17 February - Letters from Quebec hint at an expedition coming from Connecticut, but nothing is confirmed concerning this report. A letter to Mons. Jordan concerning the warrants for the forage money for 166 days in 1780 and for our pay. Ensign Haeberlin returned from Montreal today.

20 February - His Excellence's address, to which they promised to defend and support the province with goods and blood, is in the local Montreal and Quebec newspapers. We dined at Mons. MacBeth's. During the evening I was invited to attend a ball at Achigan by Madame Loysell. I attended and had already returned home with my host's family at one o'clock.

28 February - We were notified from Quebec that Commissary of Muster Major Holland would conduct a review of all the troops in the coming days and to that end would depart Quebec on 2 March, first going to Lieutenant Colonel von Creuzbourg's Corps, then to Ste. Anne, L'Assomption, Montreal, and then on the south side of the St. Lawrence River to the Prince Friedrich Regiment. From here the corps and the brigade was notified on

1 March - It was announced that winter clothing is available and to be issued for those troops which came with Captain von Schlagenteufel, Jr., and for the von Ehrenkrook Battalion at Sorel and the von Barner Battalion at Montreal. There is now much talk that the province of Virginia has been taken from the rebels. Williams Fort

Journal of Lieutenant Friedrich Julius von Papet

surrendered without a shot being fired and the private soldiers captured there have all joined the royal army, and are marching on Maryland. During the afternoon a stroll to visit Lieutenant Colonel von Ehrenkrook, who is rather ill. The reports and paroles were sent out.

3 March - In Quebec it is still said that the general will go to Montreal. Major Gray and Mr. Macheath were to dinner with the brigadier and during the evening to tea at Mr. Macheath's, from which I left early.

4 March - In the afternoon we were informed by an orderly from St. Sulpice that His Excellency passed here at eleven o'clock this morning in three carriages. The brigadier immediately decided to go to Montreal tomorrow. First, during the afternoon, we drove to St. Sulpice in order to inquire more precisely, and there we learned that it had been the judges, who now, as usual, were traveling about in the country to hold court. Therefore it was believed the general had gone to Sorel. The trip planned for tomorrow was then cancelled.

5 March - A repeated order to Lieutenant Bielstein concerning sending off weapons. Three savages arrived at Montreal from Detroit with letters for His Excellence and Montreal is now full of savages. Today we held our last club meeting. Ensign Haeberlin was so sick with stomach cramps that he had to go to bed and appeared to be in great danger.

9 March - Major Holland arrived in St. Sulpice yesterday evening at eleven o'clock and took lodgings in the rectory St. Germain. At eleven o'clock the company of Lieutenant Colonel von Ehrenkrook was mustered and because of the brigadier's indisposition, I alone was present. After dinner at the lieutenant colonel's, I and the major and his son Harry went to L'Assomption. They dined with the brigadier and took quarters with the English merchant Carree.

10 March - Here in the village the general staff and the companies of von Plessen and Zielberg were mustered. Dinner was served at the brigadier's and consisted of fourteen covers, at which we enjoyed Turkish music. Most of the officers returned home after dinner and we drank tea at Madam Robinson's.

11 March - Major Holland remained with the brigadier and all the local English officers were invited to dinner. A Canadian insulted the brigadier several times. He was placed in arrest and is to be escorted

Journal of Lieutenant Friedrich Julius von Papet

to Montreal tomorrow by the militia captain. We drank tea this evening at Carree's house, where there were many lovely ladies. We young gentlemen played several games of forfeit with them until ten o'clock. The brigadier and I did not remain to supper, but returned home. Several questions from the Prince Friedrich Regiment concerning the uniforms.

12 March - Major Holland went to the von Barner Battalion at six o'clock in the morning in order to muster it and in so doing will begin at Pointe au Tremble. The inhabitant who was arrested yesterday was pardoned at his request, to the extent that he will not be sent to Montreal. However, he will be held in arrest here until the eighteenth and then at the intercession of his father, he will be publicly punished by his father with some flogging. This has been ordered by Militia Captain Belair in order to make an example of him.

13 March - Major Holland returned from Montreal at six o'clock in the evening and then took supper with the brigadier. It is his intention, very early tomorrow, to go to the Anhalt-Zerbst Regiment. It has been learned that an express messenger has arrived from Halifax.

14 March - According to a letter from Quebec this information has not been confirmed. Major Holland departed this morning at eight o'clock.

21 March - His Excellence has finally received the news from New York that the fleet awaited since last fall was already in the Gulf, but contrary winds drove it back to Ireland again, where it was necessary to spend the winter. General [William] Phillips has supposedly been exchanged and now commands the royal troops in Virginia. Concerning our Major General von Riedesel, nothing was mentioned. This afternoon I took a walk with the brigadier to Pointe du Jour to visit Captain von Zielberg. When we returned home at six o'clock we were notified by Mons. Macbeth that many women had arrived from Montreal, and because of this a ball had been arranged for this evening, and we were invited to attend the party. The brigadier assented thereto and as a result, I had no choice. We went there at eight o'clock. The brigadier wished to straighten out a misunderstanding by Carree, but unfortunately [a series of dashes] I did not dance at all and was already home before eleven o'clock.

22 March - Lieutenant Colonel von Ehrenkrook had both of his companies paraded so that their uniforms could be checked. During this opportunity Captain von Plessen invited the brigadier and me to lunch. We went there at eleven o'clock and remained until ten o'clock in the evening. When we returned home during the evening we again discovered that a ball had been arranged. We had also been invited to attend. However, because it was so late, the brigadier had no more desire to attend than I.

23 March - The Englanders, Flemming, McCord, Lock, Captain Loed, Carree, Dr. Selby, and MacBean, dined with the brigadier and most remained for supper, followed by much visiting.

6 April - As many inhabitants had a poor harvest due to the drought and gathered very little straw, everything is so expensive that at Montreal 100 buns [bales ?] already cost thirty piasters -- an enormous price. Previously it could have been purchased for three or four piasters. Because of a shortage of straw, much livestock must die. Therefore the straw from many barn roofs and even house roofs are stolen in order to feed the horned animals and the sheep. Supposedly an express has passed through here from New York with dispatches for His Excellency at Quebec.

6 May - The river ice at Quebec broke on 1 May and floated away. Today I received the land distribution for the Prince Friedrich Regiment. There is much talk about a camp at Crown Point. The English Captain [Paul] Minchin of the 29th Regiment dined with the brigadier.

7 May - An order to the Prince Friedrich Regiment to send four men to Quebec to cut boards; the von Ehrenkrook Battalion to provide an additional eight men, and all are to be sent to Quebec as soon as possible.

8 May - The river is presently so high that it has entered most houses. This is the result in part from much rain, in part from the spring flood which is always strongest here in the month of May. Nevertheless I have never seen the water so high previously. Dinner with the brigadier at noon, together with Captain Minchin, Carree, and Selby.

9 May - The water continues to rise. Still, the brigadier and I have nothing to fear because our quarters sit high. Commissary MacBean dined today with the brigadier and then took his farewell, as he goes to Carleton Island this summer and will be assigned there.

Journal of Lieutenant Friedrich Julius von Papet

12 May - We learned the following news today. Quebec, 9 May 1781 - Yesterday the first ship with rum-wine and other merchandise for a merchant in Montreal arrived. It had sailed from Sunen on 18 March and saw only a Dutch ship and an English privateer during its voyage. This ship brought the report that a fleet from Cork was to follow in a few days. All goes well in England and there is much activity and no shortage of sailors. A large fleet consisting of 38 ships-of-the-line sailed for Gibralter as a reinforcement, under the command of Admiral [Sir Francis] Geery. They are raising twenty new regiments in England and sixty new ships-of-the-line already lie at the ship wharves. No one in England is disturbed by the declaration of war in Holland on 1 December. Admiral Rodney has captured the islands of St. Eustatia and St. Martin from the Dutch, which resulted in a loss to the Dutch of 200 ships and three million pounds sterling in coins. The loss of ships in Europe is also reported as not small. Nevertheless, an expedition has reportedly sailed against Cape Bonne Esprance and it is thought that it may have already been captured. The French have made an attack against Guernsey, which was beaten back. The following officers of Burgoyne's army have been exchanged: Major General von Riedesel, Brigadier Specht, Major Maibom, Major de Luecke, Captains Fricke, von Schlagenteufel, Poellnitz, Gerlach, Baertling, Soemmers, Scholtelius, Geyso, Morgenstern, Cleve, Luetzow, Lieutenants Ungar, Fricke, Bottmer, Breva, Gebhardt, Meyer, Burghoff, Reichrodt, Burgdorf, Schoenewald, Andre, Reinicke, Specht, Rothe, Maibom, Stutze, Surgeons Pralle, Vorbrod, Heidelbach. Brigadier von Gall as well as several Hesse-Hanau officers have reportedly also been exchanged.

A large fleet, but no troops, is expected here, escorted from England, in a convoy under Admiral Edward, in fourteen days. The widowed queen has died. As a result of all of these wartime events, it has been reported in a private letter that modest prospects for peace have been proposed and there may soon be reason to hope for such. The fleet which returned from here during the previous fall arrived safely in England, except for a single ship which sank near Anticosti. When Admiral Rodney captured the island of Eustatia, the Dutch admiral had departed for Europe a short time previously, with thirty large merchant ships. Therefore Rodney sent Captain Harvey with two ships-of-the-line to overtake that fleet. The convoy under the

Journal of Lieutenant Friedrich Julius von Papet

count was defeated and the entire [merchant] fleet was brought back. The Dutch admiral, Count Bulan was killed during the engagement.

19 May - The brigadier returned from Montreal during the evening and brought much good news with him. An officer from Niagara who had passed through Montreal had said that it was well-known among the rebels that a French fleet of four ships-of-the-line and numerous transport ships, which sailed from Rhode Island with the mission of surprising the general and recapturing Baltimore, was itself captured. General Clinton received timely reports about this and sent Admiral [Marriot] Arbuthnot in pursuit at once. He met up with the French just as they began an engagement with the English warships lying in the bay at Baltimore. The result of this affair was that the English captured all the French.

General [Augustine] Prevost has again thoroughly defeated the rebels in the southern [provinces] and driven them into the mountains.

21 May - From an express sent to the merchants in Montreal from Quebec, the news was confirmed that two ships have again arrived from London with merchandise for the merchants in Montreal.

Captains von Schlagenteufel and von Zielberg, Lieutenant Sommerlatte, and Ensign Reinerding dined and ate supper with the brigadier.

23 May - From our mail from Quebec today we were informed of the news of the arrival on the 29th of ships from London and from Porto. Captain Matt [rest of the name is missing in the manuscript] received a letter from London, dated 18 March, from Captain Willoe, in which was written that General von Riedesel and thirty other officers had been exchanged and must be on their way to Canada. Supposedly the Dutch have already lost more than 700 ships. The Parliament has voted more than 2,080,000 pounds sterling for the present war, as requested by the King. The Emperor is allied with England and had offered to serve as a mediator among the warring powers and the ministers could gather at Vienna. From the English side it would be the Duke of York. France is strongly fortifying the borders at Brabant and Alsace and gives the appearance as if the Emperor plans something there. A personal meeting between the Emperor and the Russian Czarina has taken place. The fleet from England for Canada sailed in March and it is thought that it should arrive here in June. There are also reports that a ship from New York is in the river and much hope that our general will soon arrive. Of all the news, that which I most wish for is an early peace. No one wishes more sincerely for that than I. ----------

26 May - The brigadier inspected both the von Plessen and von Zielberg Companies. He was extremely well-pleased with the first and its officers dined with the brigadier. A report from Lieutenant Colonel von Barner's Battalion of two deserters from Captain Thomae and something about Lieutenant von Wallmoden. A special list was requested from the von Ehrenkrook Battalion as to how the last new uniforms had been issued and what was still available.

29 May - The brigadier inspected the von Schlagenteufel Company at ten o'clock this morning and was quite satisfied. At dinner there was talk of [a series of dashes in the manuscript]. Afterward the brigadier and I visited our landlord of the previous winter's quarters. It was decided at that time that because of the great heat, we would depart for St. Sulpice in the cool of the evening and spend the night in the post house at that place. That did not please Captain von Schlagenteufel, Jr. He offered us his quarters and arrived there himself at eleven o'clock at night.

30 May - At ten o'clock the brigadier inspected the von Ehrenkrook Company. The brigadier made the inspection to insure that everything was in the best order, and that it was now the best and best appearing in the entire corps. We dined then with Captain von Plessen at Lieutenant Colonel von Ehrenkrook's. The brigadier and Ensign Haeberlin departed already at four o'clock. However Captain von Plessen and I only at eleven o'clock. According to letters received today from Quebec, two more ships have arrived at Quebec from London and one from Madeira, which bring confirmation not only of the first news, but also of the following. There are nine ships with provisions in the fleet coming from Halifax, where they had to spend the previous winter. The ship *British Lion*, with 36 cannons, is not far from Quebec, with dispatches from the general, many items for the Engineer Department, and money on board. The Hereditary Stadtholder marched from Amsterdam with 25,000 men as the city is primarily responsible for the break with England. All the individual letters speak of peace this year. The Kaiser is of the opinion that if England were left alone to deal with her colonies, and if the other powers do not want to make peace, then he could declare himself against their actions. Gibralter fortunately has been relieved and this important place has once again been provided with provisions and troops. Reports from Niagara again speak of Admiral Arbuthnot's victory over the French. It is said that Generals von Riedesel and Philipps have been assigned to the army of General Clinton and will apparently not be returning here.

1 June - Nothing new.

2 June - According to letters from Quebec, the ship *British Lion*, of 32 cannons [sic], and the *Hussar* [34 cannons], a ship with a beak-like bow, have arrived at Quebec. The first carried dispatches for His Excellence, but not a single letter for us. We are thoroughly convinced that peace is very near. The ministers of the warring powers probably have already gathered in Vienna. So little is heard from the other ships of the fleet as is heard from New York. Six rebels have again escaped from Trois Rivieres, for which Lieutenant Bielstein was declared innocent [of neglect].

6 June - His Excellence sent the brigadier a copy of the list of recruits embarked at Stade on 28 May 1780. They consist of two non-commissioned officers, two drummers, 132 privates, and two drivers for our corps. Two captains and two non-commissioned officers escorted them here on two ships *Success* and *Ranger*. His Excellence desires an investigation as to how six rebels could escape from Trois Rivieres. Therefore I had to write to Lieutenant Bielstein that he should submit a *Species facti* and he should send five complete jaeger and two musketeer uniforms to the von Barner Battalion, and deliver all the musket flints there to the von Ehrenkrook Battalion. Lieutenant Colonel Praetorius reports that the uniforms of the Prince Friedrich Regiment are now in tatters and that now assembling the companies for the purpose of carrying out drill is awaiting orders from the brigadier. A stroll to St. Sulpice.

7 June - A question from the brigadier to His Excellence, to allow the companies to draw closer together within their cantons for the purpose of conducting drill. Lieutenant Colonel Praetorius will await the answer here. The list of awaited recruits was given to him. I wrote to Captain von Tunderfeldt about the brigade's missing equipment [traverse scheine]. Today a hearing was conducted here concerning Ensign Reinerding's arrest of Count von Rittberg and afterward the first one dined with the brigadier and was then taken to

St. Sulpice in the brigadier's coach. This afternoon Captain-at-arms Rosenthal reported in from Trois Rivieres as ordered.

10 June - From a ship which arrived from Cork it was learned that the awaited fleet had not yet sailed at the time this ship departed, because the escort was not yet complete. Also, our recruits will be very late or are possibly not to be expected. The above noted ship made the crossing in eight weeks and had not seen a single enemy ship.

Among the recently escaped rebels from Trois Rivieres, was a French spy, concerning whose escape His Excellence was seriously disturbed.

13 June - His Excellence has not yet given his permission for assembling the companies. Instead he has ordered the troops to be advised that they were to camp during the first days, but the time and place have not yet been decided. Lieutenant Colonel von Ehrenkrook, Captain von Schlagenteufel, and Ensign Reinerding dined with the brigadier and during the afternoon we took a walk to Captain von Plessen's.

23 June - The brigadier traveled to Montreal with Ensign Haeberlin and will go from there to St. Jean. Letters from Quebec do not mention the arriving ships. His Excellence has news that the frigate *Pandora*, on which is General [Thomas] Clarke, departed from Cork on 2 May in order to join the provisions fleet for Quebec. His Excellence is satisfied with Lieutenant Bielstein's report concerning the escaped prisoners. During the afternoon a stroll to St. Sulpice.

30 June - A newspaper from New York supposedly contains a proclamation by General von Riedesel in which all deserters from the corps have been offered a pardon if they return. Musketeer Hellmann of General von Riedesel's Regiment has ransomed himself, and said he had been told by Captain von Baertling that Major von Mengen had died and that Ensign Haeberlin's servant, Schulze, had married in Albany. In Montreal a serious plot had been discovered in Sir Johnson's Corps to kill him and several of his officers. The plan was discovered and the plotters arrested. Among them was a deserter from our corps by the name of Steckhan, who had deserted at Carillon in 1777 and since then had taken service in Sir Johnson's Corps under the name of Wagner. Because of this misconduct he had been tried by an English court-martial and sentenced to 300 lashes. However, during his visit to Montreal the brigadier had stopped this sentence, reclaimed the deserter, and sought to punish him under our regulations for his crime. Therefore a letter was sent to His Excellence from Montreal. Today I received the contingency accounts from the von Barner Battalion. Reliable information indicates that General MacLean has died at Halifax.[44] A letter to Lieutenant Colonel von Ehrenkrook that Musketeer Hellmann of Major von Mengen's Company of General von Riedesel's Regiment had ransomed himself, had arrived at St. Jean on 28 May 1781, and drawn rations for himself until 30 June. He was to be sent to Captain von Schlagenteufel's Company and there issued a new uniform from the supplies on hand.

English Artillery Lieutenant Doebernet dined today with the brigadier [a series of dots]. Of the six prisoners who recently escaped from Trois Rivieres, four have been recaptured at St. Francois by the Indians and turned over to Militia Captain Schmidt at Yamaska.

Reportedly the other two have been arrested at St. Jean.

10 July - The complaints of the inhabitants from here to Quebec about the locusts and a kind of small caterpillar, which have devoured everything during a prolonged dry spell, are exceptionally numerous. Many believe they have lost this year's harvest. And if the Heavens do not send rain soon, a period of food shortages can be anticipated. A stroll to Lieutenant Colonel von Ehrenkrook's, where I alone remained for supper.

11 July - A two-masted ship arrived at Quebec on 9 July from Antiqua, with a cargo of sugar and rum. It brought the news that Surinam was captured from Holland and that Curacao also experienced the same fate from an expedition which had been sent there. The French made a landing on St. Lucia and remained there three days, but in the end were forced to withdraw with heavy losses. This brig made the voyage from Antiqua in five weeks and had met no enemy ships underway, nor seen anything of an English fleet.

12 July - The drought continues. For some days the wind has been favorable for the awaited fleet. If it does not arrive soon, our situation regarding provisions will become critical.

13 July - In a private letter I have seen the news that nor far from Detroit a battle occurred between the rebel Colonel [George Rogers] Clark and the well-known Captain Brant, who is the chief of the six Indian nations. In the battle the first was thoroughly defeated and his entire corps, consisting of 800 men, was scattered.

Journal of Lieutenant Friedrich Julius von Papet

Early this morning the brigadier and Ensign Haeberlin went to St. Sulpice and then returned during the afternoon.

18 July - According to a letter from Quebec today, nothing has been heard of the fleet. A newspaper from the rebels at Philadelphia of 3 April 1781 reports the following from Charleston as of 6 March 1781. Several days ago the Brunswick recruits under Captains Ruff and Weiss, the Hanauers under Captain Thomae, and the Anhalt-Zerbst recruits under Lieutenant Starckhof arrived at Charleston. Pending further orders they are to serve with the Bose, Huyn, and Ditfurth Regiments. His Excellence believes these recruits must now be at New York, because he had received a letter of 9 May, from Major General von Riedesel, brought by the last express from there, in which he wrote that he will soon arrive in Canada with 900 Brunswickers, Hanauers, and Anhalt-Zerbsters. The Brunswickers with them consist of the general, five staff officers, sixteen captains, 24 subalterns, 53 sergeants, and about 400 men. Not all of the privateers from St. Eustatia seem to have been captured yet, because they are making the Gulf very dangerous. Two of them, *America* and *Brutus*, each of 28 cannons, have already taken four West Indian and one English ship. The local frigate *Hind* chased one but because of having put on too much sail, lost both masts. Captain Twiss had eight royalist workers desert. The announcement was sent to the brigade. Two merchant ships from last year's fleet, which spent the winter in Newfoundland, are expected in the coming days.

25 July - According to letters from Quebec today, the von Lossberg, von Knyphausen, and von Creuzbourg Regiments, and the 31st and 44th Regiments, have moved into camp near Quebec. A detachment of 150 men from the Prince Friedrich Regiment has been sent to the Chaudiere River in order to cut wood. For each cord of wood the men are paid fifteen pence. Brigadier von Rauschenplat sent a detachment of workers to Quebec without asking His Excellence if another relief was desired, but His Excellence sent it back. A ship from last fall's fleet, which had spent the winter in Newfoundland, arrived at Quebec. En route it had spoken with the frigate *Oiseau*, by which it was informed that Admiral Arbuthnot had defeated the French fleet in Chesapeake Bay and supposedly captured two ships-of-the-line and burned five others.

Journal of Lieutenant Friedrich Julius von Papet

28 July - Still nothing from the fleet. A rebel ship, *Brutus*, of 28 cannons, 9-pounders, captured three ships in the Passage Gulf in the latitude of Canzo. Another ship from Antiqua has arrived at Quebec, bringing the news that the French had captured the Island of Tabago. The report from Lieutenant Colonel Praetorius that the 150-man detachment for wood-cutting on the Chaudiere River was commanded by Captain Sander, Lieutenant Wolgast, and Ensign Langerjahn. This detachment had to cut 61 cords of wood every day. The Hessian Jaegers perform the duty in Quebec and the other regiments in the camp do the work.

8 August - The three companies of the von Ehrenkrook Battalion were mustered again. Ten persons dined with the brigadier. Afterward the brigadier rode with Major Holland to Montreal, where the von Barner Battalion is to be mustered. The letters from Quebec indicate a ship, which lies at anchor at Bic, and which sailed from Portsmouth with the fleet the end of May, had separated from the fleet on 6 June. This fleet is said to consist of 150 sail, of which fifty are bound for Canada. They were escorted by a 50-gun ship and four frigates. Reportedly a Dutch fleet of four ships-of-the-line and four frigates burned a small English village. The death of General Phillips has been reported from Halifax but nothing is heard from New York.[45]

9 August - The von Barner Battalion was mustered this morning. Major Holland ate only a little breakfast and immediately departed so as to be able to muster the Anhalt-Zerbsters and the Prince Friedrich Regiment.

10 August - The brigadier returned from Montreal at ten-thirty in the evening. For my part, I visited at St. Sulpice. In Montreal the news is frequently repeated that General von Riedesel and all his troops were embarked at New York on 3 June.

11 August - Two ships, which were sent to New York last year, have reportedly foundered. It is reported that forty transport ships arrived at Boston with French troops, and at the same time, a reinforcement of 1,000 men arrived in the West Indies.

15 August - Finally, on 11 August, six ships of the English fleet and one from Eustatia to Quebec, arrived. Among the first there are three provisions and the latter is loaded with salt and wine. The entire English fleet consists of 150 sail, of which 63 are bound for Canada, having sailed from Portsmouth on 24 May. The 50-gun ship *Portland*, commanded by Captain Pringle, and four frigates are the escort. A strong wind near Newfoundland scattered the fleet, and it is believed those bound for Canada have rendezvoused at St. Johns. There has also been a provisions fleet for Quebec, from Halifax, in the Gulf, which was attacked by three French ships, so that they had to change course. Meanwhile the brave effort of the escort held off the frigates and all the transports were saved. The captain of the *Jack* was captured. Captain Young of the *Hind* was forced to leave his station by two French frigates, and is now blockaded at St. Johns by those ships. The English frigate *Veslate* recaptured the frigate *Torm*,[16] which had been sent from New York and which had 24 cannons and a copper bottom, from the rebels near Newfoundland. Many of the ships loaded with booty, which were sent from Eustatia to England, were recaptured by the French and Spanish. Admiral Rodney's fleet in the West Indies now consists of 22 ships-of-the-line, and the combined enemy fleet of 27, with a preponderance of frigates. It is believed therefore that ours are blockaded. Captain [Thomas] Graves, who escorted the fleet returning from here last year, has, because of his negligence, due to always wanting to take prizes, been cashiered. The ship from Eustatia reported that on 16 June, General Riedesel was at New York with nearly 2,000 men and was awaiting an escort to Canada. A secret expedition had embarked 5,000 men at New York. Cornwallis had conducted another successful battle with the rebels, during which Colonel Tarleton again distinguished himself, and had advanced into Virginia. The death of General Phillips was confirmed. The Cork provisions fleet sailed back to England three weeks ago. No one, however, knows where it is now. The main French and Spanish fleet is supposedly at Cadiz. The Gulf [of St. Lawrence] is supposedly full of ships. Still, no letters have arrived for us Germans.

I had to report all this information to Lieutenant Colonel von Ehrenkrook, and also note that the battalion was to provide six men to the Royal Cavalry at Quebec, although none were to be taken from the Dragoon Company. For this service, each man was to receive fifteen pence and three pence for rum. ---- [In French - What an embarrassment.] ---- Toward evening I took a stroll with the brigadier to visit Captain von Plessen, who invited the brigadier and Lieutenant Sommerlatte to dinner tomorrow.

Journal of Lieutenant Friedrich Julius von Papet

18 August - An announcement to the brigadier concerning four Hesse-Hanau jaegers and a member of the 44th Regiment who deserted at Quebec on the fifteenth. The *Pearl*, [*la Perle*], a ship of [18 or] 28 cannons, which was formerly a French frigate, arrived at Quebec from Bristol, bringing the following news. The Spanish, prior to the arrival of the English relief fleet, bombarded Gibralter, causing considerable damage to the city, but retiring as soon as the English fleet arrived. The cashiering of Captain Graves was rescinded. The Kaiser had a seven hour meeting with the Duke of Gloucester at Ostend. A report about two English and two Dutch frigates, which alternately captured one another, and which finally were all taken by two French warships. It has been reported that General von Riedesel left New York on 3 June. However, many doubt that report because of a dispute between General Clinton and Admiral Arbuthnot.

22 August - Letters from Quebec report with certainty that finally the fleet from England and the Cork provisions fleet have arrived in the Gulf without the loss of a single ship, and that they are under the escort of a 50-gun ship and six frigates. His Excellency, who had sent his aide-de-camp, Cullons, to Bic so that he could make inquiries, had himself discovered the frigate *Pandora*, on which was General [Thomas] Clarke, lying at anchor and personally spoken with the general. The *Pandora* had separated from the fleet in the Gulf and the fleet is now awaited anyday at Quebec. The provisions fleet had provisions for two years on board and the entire fleet contains 65 sails. Concerning Admiral Arbuthnot, it is reported that he has been blockaded by a vastly superior French fleet. Clinton reportedly has defeated General Washington, and Brigadier Arnold has done the same to a strong French corps. All this certainly needs confirmation.

As little as there appeared to be good prospects for us, now everything has changed to our advantage, if only misfortune does not overtake us, as no letters and no news have been received from Germany. Major Grey came to dinner with the brigadier. A secret account of the royal confirmation about Musketeer Nehrengard to Lieutenant Colonel von Barner.

25 August - His Excellency's answer to the brigadier's letter of the twentieth. On the 21st General Clarke and his staff arrived at Quebec on the frigate *Pandora*. This frigate had seen the fleet in the Gulf, coming this way. However, no ship of that fleet has arrived in

Quebec, and therefore no letters for the Germans. His Excellence sent a list, which is different than the first one, of our recruits to the brigadier.

In the list are noted: Captain Weiss, one corporal, one drummer, seven chasseurs, 31 fusileers, three women, and one child. Three are sick, who were embarked on the ship *Success-Moncton* on 17 September 1780. That means that Captains Willoe and O'Connell should be in this year's fleet. Concerning uniforms, His Excellence has not the least information. This morning we were invited to dine with Captain Plessen on the 27th. During the afternoon a visit from Lieutenant Colonel von Ehrenkrook, during which he claimed he would improve his conduct.

29 August - An order to the von Ehrenkrook Battalion and the von Schoell Detachment to send all possible miners and stone blasters to Quebec. Captain O'Connell is now in Quebec and initially will remain in the suite of the brigadier. Of all the news from the letters received from Germany, for the military the old system prevailed. Several had died ---- the government of our present glorious prince was greatly praised.

30 August - The reports and many letters were sent to Quebec. This morning two dragoons, Kempel and Hosang, reported they had been exchanged at Connecticut and then escorted to St. Jean with three men from our Grenadier Battalion, 30 English, and seven Canadians. How their exchange had been brought about, they did not know. Supposedly at Rutland some of our prisoners are still being held in the barracks, including Lieutenant Gebhardt. The independence of the Green Mountains from the Congress was confirmed by these men. To dinner with the brigadier, Captain Zielberg, the Englishman Carteret, and Captain [Daniel] Robinson. The latter arrived with the fleet from England and remains here with his family. An order to the regiment to submit a list of all the prisoners who have arrived here, whether exchanged or having ransomed themselves.

5 September - On 1 September the Prince Friedrich Regiment received the order, including the detachment at Chaudiere, to move into the camp at Quebec so as to be able to work on the defenses at that place. Lieutenant Colonel Praetorius reported at the same time that because of a shortage of tents and tent bottles, he found it necessary to requisition such from the [English] government. General Clarke is sick and from all indications will remain at Quebec. Captain Willoe supposedly assured Captain von Tunderfeldt that Colonel Specht is to come here this fall. His Excellence has been informed that a small fleet has arrived here. The savages at St. Francois encountered one of our deserters in the woods at Kennebic River and because they saw that he sustained himself on human flesh, they scalped him. He had a German Heperbach with him and according to all indications, that is the famous Dragoon Petersdorf of the von Ehrenkrook Battalion.

10 September - The brigadier sent his two horses to the general at Quebec, because they were unneeded. I was reprimanded in a letter I received from General von Riedesel because I opened a mail pouch for the chaplain, although we had ourselves sent the courier there. I had to do that on the brigadier's orders. Captain Cleve arrived during the afternoon. On the ninth General Haldimand, accompanied by General Riedesel traveled from Quebec to St. Jean. The plan to submit [copies] of all the dispatches to Germany will create so much work that Cleve and I will be forced to work day and night. Today I tried to determine the logic of the end purpose of this.

11 October - This morning the brigadier departed for Berthier to pay his compliments to the general. Incorrect uniform lists from the von Ehrenkrook Battalion were returned today. During the evening the brigadier returned from Berthier and this evening he still sent a strict order to the von Ehrenkrook Battalion. We are now working day and night on the copies of the dispatches and have put five copyists to work. It is now certain that Major General Riedesel will be assigned to Sorel and the brigadier to Montreal. Because the list of uniforms, weapons, and field items for the von Barner Battalion are at Trois Rivieres, I had to send an express to get them.

13 October - An order to the brigadier this morning from His Excellence for the brigadier to proceed to Montreal at once to assume command of the MacLean Brigade, as that officer is returning to England with his family, and the brigadier set out for Montreal today. The departure of the invalids to Quebec. Instructions for the departing Free Corporal Sohlemann; letters concerning this to Lieutenant Bodemeyer. Completion of the conduct lists. Not much progress with the lists to be sent to Germany. At eleven o'clock the brigadier and

Ensign Haeberlin departed for Montreal. Cleve and I remained here working together. An order to Lieutenant Colonel von Ehrenkrook to support us here in everything and to send two copyists here.

23 October - The general inspected the companies of Rosenberg, Hambach, and Thomae of the von Barner Battalion. During the afternoon he and his suite and the brigadier returned to Sorel. On the way there, they will inspect the companies of the Combined Battalion before the regiment is reformed, which will be explained to the battalion. An order to the regimental commanders, that everything concerning the organization of the regiment is to sent to Captain Cleve at Sorel, as soon as possible. From which they will be provided with all the news concerning such, so that each regiment will be able to complete their strength lists in fourteen days.

24 October - During their tour the generals inspected the von Ehrenkrook Battalion. Because of the bad weather little could be done. Reportedly Lieutenant Colonel von Ehrenkrook is very sick. [A different, very difficult to read, handwriting change takes place at this point.] More than twenty officers have dined with him and all supposedly are already on the march. The brigadier returned here at one o'clock in the night.

28 October - At eight-thirty this morning the von Barner Battalion marched out of Montreal. During the march the troops for the Rhetz and Specht Regiments will be given up at St. Sulpice. The von Riedesel Regiment replaced the garrison.

1 November - A report from Major Grey that during the past night, of the twenty captive officers from the rebels who had been held on Perault Island, fifteen deserted. A detachment of light infantry from Lanoagen was immediately sent in pursuit and the posts at St. Jean were notified. Everything was reported to His Excellency today.

28 November - Eleven rebel officers, one woman, and two children, were escorted here from Niagara. Twenty privates had been left in Couteau du Lac. All these captives had been taken on the Ohio River by the famous Brant.

1 December - Major General von Riedesel went to St. Jean a few days ago, and after that trip will go to Quebec.

29 December - The brigadier and I traveled to Sorel at nine o'clock and arrived there during a steady storm at seven o'clock in the evening. We met with the general and his entire suite in the best manner. The general had occupied his former house, which considering the comforts between Montreal and Quebec, is certainly one of the best houses. We also met with Major Luecke.

30 December - We returned to L'Assomption.

Journal of Lieutenant Friedrich Julius von Papet

March 1782

4 March - Letters from Quebec contain information that General Haldimand left Quebec yesterday. He traveled to Sorel first and to St. Jean yesterday, and then will come here. [Montreal ?]

15 March - At five o'clock His Excellence and General von Riedesel, as well as their suites, arrived here. All of them have forbidden honors being rendered and had previously dined with Lieutenant Colonel von Creuzbourg.

16 April - During recent days three expresses have arrived from New York, but we can learn nothing as to the news they delivered.

As His Excellence is not in a very good mood these days, we do not expect much good.

30 April - His Excellence, the brigadier, and suites dined with the seminarians, to which the entire island of Montreal apparently belongs, and the cloister of which lies a half-hour from the city. The dinner consisted of forty covers and we dined magnificently. Madeira, Rhine wine, Champagne, Burgundy, and Bordeaux were in an overabundance. Significantly, this cloister is one of the richest in America. It is built in the Gothic style and surrounded by a wall.

? May - Yesterday the first division of batteaux with provisions for the Indian Department (with the exception of Colonel Johnson) was loaded and departed for Carleton Island.

? May - This evening the long awaited express arrived from Niagara. He brought many letters for the local merchants, and also the news that in the upper country of this province everything is quiet and peaceful. At the same time the report was circulated, which previously was considered very secret, namely that from our side, posts as far as Oswego are to be constructed, like posts previously in use and which were burned down by Colonel St. Leger in the previous year, during the retreat of his expedition. Before the war His Excellence was in command there. Now two strong blockhouses must once again be constructed there.

7 May - It was learned at headquarters that two companies of the 84th Regiment received orders with today's date, to move out immediately and to march to Carleton Island.

13 May - Lieutenant von Burgdorf, with two non-commissioned officers and eighteen men marched out toward Carillon, and if it has been lost, they are to return here.

30 May - Sir John Johnson has been awarded a payment of 1,000 pounds sterling as inspector general of all the Indian Departments and has come here again with all of his family, as has Brigadier MacLean.

10 June - The general [Riedesel] departed [from Sorel] this morning at nine o'clock, and will spend the night in La Nonroit, and will not need to be present at the executions tomorrow, when two delinquents are to be shot. For that purpose each regiment is to provide a detachment of one officer, two non-commissioned officers, and 24 men.

11 June - After the four who are in arrest, Scott, Schulze, Mueller, and Wehr had played for their lives [rolled dice], Schulze and Wehr (both of General von Riedesel's Regiment) were the losers and were to be shot. The other two were sent aboard a ship, as slaves, for life.

29 June - Captain von Zielberg received orders to march with his company to Pointe du Lac.

30 June - Yesterday Captain Robinson of the 84th Regiment from Oswegoschie returned from an armed reconnaissance along the Mohawk River. This reconnaissance did the rebels much injury by burning a mill (the only one on this river), and took fifteen prisoners. Today General von Riedesel is to travel from Quebec to Sorel. The 44th Regiment is to commence its march to Quebec, in order to commence work there, as soon as the 53rd Regiment arrives from Ile aux Noix.

3 July - Colonel von Creuzbourg is to go to Quebec day after tomorrow to form Captain von Schoell's Detachment at that place into a battalion, following which the promoted Major [Georg] Pausch is to assume command. Captain Hugget received his release and his [jaeger] company is to be given to Captain [Philipp Jacob] Hildebrand.

5 July - At [illegible], fifty miles above Detroit an engagement occurred in which the rebels were defeated with heavy casualties and many captives.

17 July - The Light Infantry Company of the 84th Regiment, under Captain Hoescher, marched through here on its way to Carleton Island.

Journal of Lieutenant Friedrich Julius von Papet

13 August - Today I saw two Indian chiefs, one of whom is the famous Joseph Brant, who commands the Six Nations and who had come from Oswego. He speaks very good English and has done the rebels a great amount of harm. Generally he is called Captain Brant, even by the government, which gives him the pay of a captain and holds him in high esteem. The second one is a young man, who in the year 1778 was made chief of a nation by His Excellence during the assembly of nearly 5,000 Indians at Montreal. At that time the following was told as a true story. After being presented as chief of that nation of Indians, a chief of another nation said it was not permitted for such a young man, who still had not adequately demonstrated his bravery, to represent a nation. He, against whom this was said, then entered the camp of that nation and with his tomahawk, a kind of battle ax through which the Indians also smoke their tobacco, struck the old chief dead. He then entered the house of [illegible], where many savages were assembled, said to one of them that he should poke a hole through the flesh of both his arms, which was done. They then gave him a red ribbon, put it through both holes, and then tied his arms behind him therewith. In this condition he appeared before the nation whose chief he had just killed, and said this, that he was the one who had committed the murder, explained the reason he had done that, and placed himself in a position where they could take revenge. As angry as the nation was, it was dumb-founded by the young man's daring, and in the end he was forgiven for the murder. Still it is said that the insulted nation will get revenge for the murder, because in such a situation, the savages are unforgiving.

17 August 1782 - An invitation from Colonel Claus to attend church service in the morning at the new establishment for the displaced savages on the Mohawk River at La Chine. We went there on

18 August - at eight o'clock in the morning in five carriages. This establishment is still quite new and since 1779 has been covered with [illegible] wood. The savages originally had only miserable huts with laid on tree bark, but now have adequate, clean, and very efficient quarters. Most had to leave the most beautiful houses and best farms on the Mohawk River. These savages make a better impression on me than any others which I have seen. In part they are more intelligent and better disciplined. They were in a large house, which was apparently only for their council, (as entrance therein is forbidden to women and children), in the middle of an establishment. From the chiefs of both nations, one is elected to be king, and he is accepted as such by the chiefs of each family. The eldest of them spoke to the brigadier, the gist of which was to offer their thanks for the honor of our visit, with the further comment, which is common with all of their speeches, that [The next few lines could not be transcribed sufficiently to provide a certain translation, but have an apparent meaning – they had been loyal to the King of England, and the brigadier assured them of his friendship.]

26 August - The von Riedesel and Specht Regiments received orders to march to Ile aux Noix. For defensive garrison duty, 200 men of the 29th Regiment, and Major Campbell, two captains, and six non-commissioned officers will be ordered here.

27 August - The Riedesel and Specht Regiments were embarked here and transferred to Longueuil, and entered camp. On

28 August - they entered camp near Chambly. On

29 August - to St. Jean and Ile aux Noix.

31 August - An order from Quebec that the rest of the 29th Regiment was to go to Ile aux Noix, also, and the garrison was to be provided by the rest of the 84th Regiment and Sir John Johnson's 1st Battalion. The brigadier was dissatisfied with the unclear orders affecting the present situation.

5 September - The 29th Regiment marched away from here. The Grenadiers and the Light Infantry of Sir Johnson's 1st Battalion entered the local garrison today.

6 September - The rest of the 84th Regiment, 150 men under Major [John Adolphus] Harris, came here and were assigned permanent quarters in the local suburbs.

7 September - An order from Quebec that Sir Johnson's Regiment was to send fifty men from here to Ile aux Noix. They will have to work very hard. Each day 600 men are assigned to work details. Everyone is still healthy. We have vegetables in an over abundance.

8 September - Captain Maurer received a letter from Quebec in which it was reported that in the last letters from Halifax, the preliminary peace treaty has been signed in Paris and confirmation is awaited on the first ship from England. God grant that finally my most desired wish be fulfilled!

12 September - In a certain letter to the local English Doctor Black, there was information that during the month of July the combined French and Spanish fleet, with a strength of 32 ships-of-the-line, had been in the English Channel and had captured 23 ships of an English merchant fleet sailing to Canada. On one of the captured ships the doctor had lost all his most valuable medicines (worth 1,000 guineas).

14 September - The frigate *Hussar* which came from New York and Halifax, brought the report that Captain [Urban] Clage and his 218 recruits [coming from Brunswick] are at Halifax.

17 September - Letters from Sorel contain information that Captain Clage and the recruits have been ordered to Penobscot. The garrison at Oswegatchie is to be reinforced by one officer and twenty men from Johnson's 1st Battalion, and all the local savages sent to Decouoerten.

12 October - Brigadier MacLean, accompanied by Lieutenant Colonel von Barner, came here from Quebec. The first is going to Niagara, to take command there. All the officers who arrived from New York departed for Quebec yesterday in order to be quartered at Sorel and in the surrounding area.

15 October - All the officers and troops of our corps, who came from New York, are marching from Quebec under Major Maibom and are to be supported at Sorel until winter quarters assignments are made.

19 October - The brigadier was informed in letters from Quebec that winter quarters had been determined and that according to those orders he would not remain in Montreal, but that both the Grenadier and Barner Battalions would be under his command; the first at Berthier, LeNaseroit, and La Valtrie; and the latter at L'Assomption, Repentigny, and St. Sulpice. The brigadier was to choose his quarters within these parishes. Also contained therein was notice that General von Riedesel desired his quarters at Berthier.

22 October - The general will arrive at Sorel today and on the 24th and 25th assign the recruits to St. Omar and St. Denis.

23 October - We received the winter quarters assignments by today's mail and accordingly, the brigadier will have command in the district from Maeschiete to Repentigny. Also, according to the order, the 84th Regiment is to march to Carleton Island on the 29th. It is to be relieved by the 34th Regiment. The new brigadier, St. Leger, will take over command at Montreal, for the time being, from a brigadier. [Note at the bottom of the page - That one has been in command at Montreal; St. Leger at St. Jean.]

(On 1 November General von Riedesel's wife gave birth to a daughter, one hour after the [illegible].[47] Immediately following, she wrote a prayer of a few lines to her husband. The baptism was on the 15th. Haldimand was the godparent. Frau von Riedesel was present and laid a cloth on the altar.)

Journal of Lieutenant Friedrich Julius von Papet

February 1783

14 February - I went with the brigadier to Sorel. An order for the Brunswick Corps that one captain, three officers, nine non-commissioned officers, three drummers, 1 surgeon's mate, and 91 men were to march to St. Jean to join the savages at that place and build huts in the forest. Colonel Creuzbourg is to send a company of jaegers to Ile aux Noix. The Dragoons are to assemble closer to Chambly. The Light Infantry Company of the 31st Regiment and Schlagenteufel's Company of the Rhetz Regiment are to march to St. Jean. The detachment is to be well protected from the cold and each man is to carry forty cartridges and his snowshoes with him. The Grenadiers are to provide one non-commissioned officer and sixteen men to this detachment and are to march upon receipt of this order.

7 March - General von Riedesel wrote to the brigadier that he had received information that more than 1,000 rebels with six cannons were at Ticonderoga with the intention to make an attempt against Point au Fer, but had been prevented by the onset of warm weather causing a thaw.

8 March - The news arrived with an express that the rebel Colonel [Marinus] Willet, with 700 men, planned to attack Oswego. However, while still some miles away, a deserter from those troops warned Major Ross of their plan. When Colonel Willet saw that his plan was exposed, he retreated so quickly, head over heels, that the force sent in pursuit could make only a few prisoners.

11 March - We were informed that the Specht Regiment has already entered its former quarters at St. Denis from St. Jean, and that all the other troops have moved forward during the march to the south from their former quarters assignments.

16 March - This afternoon a merchant arrived here (Berthier) from Montreal with the news which was most pleasant for me, to the effect that the rebels had arrived at St. Jean with news from England of a general peace having been made. According to the report New England was given up [to the rebels] and England retained possession of Canada, Newfoundland, and Nova Scotia.

17 April - There are many who no longer wish to hear about peace, and instead speak of expeditions to the West Indies and across Lake Champlain.

Journal of Lieutenant Friedrich Julius von Papet

19 April - During the past night the general received an express from His Excellency, to the effect that a cease fire existed, and, thank God! the confirmation that the peace treaty had been signed.

21 May - Letters arrived from Urban Clage at Penobscot, confirming peace and accompanied by the following news. The English regiments are to be reduced by fifty men and most of them are to be sent to the West Indies. It is believed that all the German troops will be sent to Canada, then to embark for Europe. The Frau General [Riedesel] arrived in Quebec on the 19th and will remain there for the time being.

4 June - All the regiments paraded (to Sorel) in a line, and at twelve o'clock fired a *feu de joie*, after which 21 cannon shots were fired.

21 June - We received news from Berthier that the ship for our baggage had already arrived at Sorel. On

22 June - At four o'clock in the morning all our baggage was sent to Sorel. (At this time the letters being sent from Canada by the regiments were picked up.)

1 July - General von Riedesel issued an order thanking all the troops in his district and turning over command to the brigadier. The general dined today with his regiment and thereafter departed in a batteau for Quebec with Captain Clage.

(On 2 July, meanwhile, the general's wife remained with the regiment.)

8 July - Captain von Poellnitz, the war chest, and the entire general staff, departed (from Sorel) for Quebec at five o'clock in the morning.

16 July The so-long wished-for march order arrived. All the regiments at this place marched in two divisions; the first, consisting of the Dragoons, Grenadiers, and Rhetz Regiments, under Lieutenant Colonel von Mengen, departs on the 18th and will arrive in Quebec on the 27th. The second division, consisting of the Riedesel and Specht Regiments, under Lieutenant Colonel von Hille, depart on the 19th and are to arrive at Quebec on the 28th. Lieutenant Colonel von Barner is to depart from Montreal with his battalion on the 18th. Our Convention prisoners, 448 in number, departed from New York, under Lieutenant Reinerking, already in June, so only Lieutenant Gerbhardt, with some prisoners of war, who are supposedly now in New York, remains behind.

28 July - The first division, Dragoons, Grenadiers, and Rhetz, were mustered at Quebec, and immediately embarked. Prior to the embarkation, His Excellency inspected the regiments.

29 July - The Riedesel and Specht Regiments were embarked.

30 July - I had the opportunity to see the waterfall of Montmorency, and I would have always regretted not having seen it, because it is the thing most worthwhile to see in all of Canada. General Haldimand had the height of these falls, which drop perpendicular on the rocks below, measured recently and found them to be 241 feet, which is 39 feet more than those at Niagara. The falls are the most beautiful in the winter. The Barner Battalion embarked today, after being mustered.

31 July - Colonel von Creuzbourg embarked today.

1 August - Prince Friedrich and the Hesse-Hanau Regiment embarked today.

2 August - We took our farewell from His Excellency and all our acquaintances, and embarked at noon, the brigadier and Haeberlin on the ship *Wehr*, and I on the ship *Providence*. With this embarkation another chapter of my life begins, and just as my ship is called *Providence*, I recommend myself again to the mercy of God, who has watched over me so well. Those assigned to our ship are Major von Luecke, Captain von Schlagenteufel, Sr., Captain Ahrend, me, Lieutenants von Dobeneck and Mayer, Ensign Ehrich, Regimental Surgeon Schrader, the auditors, and 200 men, [all of the Rhetz Regiment]. The ship is three-masted and 327 tons. We have provisions for three months.

3 August - We went under sail at ten o'clock, but had to stop again at Beauport Bay because the ship's captain, Heppley, who did not appear to me to be the best one, had forgotten something. He returned in an hour and we continued on to Orleans Island.

4 August - The anchor was raised at eleven o'clock, but because the ship had lain at anchor so close to land, during the ebb tide it could not turn, and it could have been driven on land by a strong wind. Therefore the anchor was lowered again to wait for the flood tide. During this time the wind was so strong that the ship made violent movement as if it were on the ocean. Some of our companions became seasick, however it did not effect Ahrend or me. At eight o'clock, despite the strong wind, the anchor was raised. We reached the center of the river and lay at anchor there. Our fine captain was drunk most of this time and our pilot managed the whole ship.

5 August - We went under sail with a good west wind at eight o'clock. We passed the dangerous Traveste at St. Roc, where during my time in Canada so many ships had wrecked, on the sea side. Fortunately by five-thirty in the afternoon we had passed it and the pilot had directed us very masterfully.

6 August - Because of foggy weather the pilot had anchored not far from Ile Verde at one o'clock during the night. The anchor was raised at four o'clock and we went under sail at seven o'clock. At one o'clock in the afternoon we had reached Bic, where we joined seventeen ships lying at anchor, including the frigate *Pandora*.

7 August - Still at anchor, where we will remain until the rest of the transport ships from Quebec join us. Today we took fresh water on board and the pilot left us. Spruce beer was brewed for the German troops.

9 August - Six ships from New York passed us on their way to Quebec.

12 August - Captain Poellnitz came aboard our ship with orders from the general. He explained to us that he had left Quebec on 6 August with the last transport ships and had arrived here only yesterday with the [illegible]. General [Friedrich Wilhelm Augustus, Baron von] Steuben of the Provincials had arrived with the ships from New York, to inspect the places included in the peace treaty, but not yet surrendered, on the lakes and at Point au Fer, and to take possession of them. General Haldimand did not wish to speak to him in Quebec, but had sent him to Sorel to find his own way.

13, 14, and 15 August - Still at anchor to await the remaining eleven ships, which carried an agent.

17 August - At nine o'clock the frigate fired two cannon shots, whereupon the anchor was raised. At eleven o'clock seventeen ships set sail.

18 August - Under sail at night. We passed the Lady Mountains toward evening.

19 August - At one o'clock the wind swung to the northeast and was contrary to us. A turn was made to the north after a cannon shot,

Journal of Lieutenant Friedrich Julius von Papet

and we sailed cautiously for two hours until we turned again and sailed ahead of the wind, directly toward Anticosti, which we saw at about one o'clock. Many of us were again seasick due to the motion of the ship. Our ship was the last one and only fourteen ships could be counted.

20 August - During the night the wind swung to the southeast and was contrary. We tacked until twelve o'clock at night. Strong wind and on

21 August - with the same wind, a half storm. Toward four o'clock in the morning there was such a heavy fog that if we had not had daylight shortly thereafter, we would have wrecked on the outer end of Anticosti. The ship was turned away from there with the greatest haste and we tacked on Gaspe Bay. It rained hard. At nine o'clock we turned again. The wind changed somewhat so that we could travel our course, directly out of the Gulf. The movement of the ship was so strong that most of us remained in bed. At six o'clock in the evening we were again with the fleet and moved steadily ahead.

22 August - At four o'clock in the morning, fortunately we passed Magdalena Island and the many rocks lying in this region. At eleven o'clock we passed through the M----- of --------and St.Paul Island and left the Gulf.

23 August - A very restless night. During the afternoon the wind abated, and became calm toward evening.

25 August - Toward evening there was a half storm and a contrary wind. The course was toward the West Indies. A restless night. We turned during the morning and with a strong wind our course was directly toward England. Our ship was alone and far to the right we could see three ships. In passing the Grand Bank of Newfoundland the entire mast was lowered in order to allow time for fishing.

26 August - The wind was so strong that nothing could be cooked and most men remained in bed.

27 August - High seas, strong wind, and good progress.

28 August - Still a favorable wind from the west. At twelve o'clock in the night Grand and False Banks were passed and no bottom was found at ninety fathoms.

30 August - During the night one storm after the other and the most restless night I have ever experienced.

Journal of Lieutenant Friedrich Julius von Papet

31 August - According to our reckoning we have passed the halfway mark. Note - The English figure the trip from Quebec to England from St. Paul to the English Channel.

1, 2, and 3 September - The wind very strong; restless nights.

6 September - During the night, the strongest wind that we have had.

7 September - Beautiful weather and favorable wind.

9 September - During the morning dark weather with much rain so that we could not see nor know where we were in the Channel, with our ship. Our mate was therefore very upset. Fortunately we met a small ship with which we spoke. It gave us the news that we were twelve miles beyond Portsmouth. At noon the weather cleared and we could very clearly see the coast of England and the province of Dorshire.

10 September - At twelve o'clock at night there was a total eclipse of the moon. We anchored near Deal. The entrance to Dover is between numerous sandbanks and requires a knowledgeable helmsman such as ours. This entrance was indicated by three bull horns at night. Our captain, who otherwise was always drunk, wanted to give other orders, but our major removed the captain from the deck and gave full control of the ship to the first mate. As the ship was fortunately brought to anchor, it became apparent that almost all the sailors were drunk.

13 September - The order came from Colonel von Speth this morning to go to Deal. News of the entire fleet from Canada. General von Riedesel is still in London and is expected this evening at Deal.

17 September - Finally the order to proceed under sail to Stade with the first favorable wind. The wind is contrary.

19 September - Under sail at ten o'clock, initially with a weak wind. The ship for the general and the brigadier remained behind.

20 September - Toward three o'clock in the afternoon we saw [illegible].

21 September - During the night a strong gust of wind. Our Captain, from Schwerin, and the first mate tried a second time to [words appear to be missing] out and the ship. We passed Helgoland about eight o'clock, where the Hessians sailed to the right toward Bremerlehe and we went to the left toward Stade. We received

Journal of Lieutenant Friedrich Julius von Papet

several pilots at twelve o'clock noon. Toward three o'clock we passed Cuxhaven and if the wind had remained steady, we could have reached Stade. However, as it became dark and the ebb set in, we anchored.

23 September - We reached Stade with the flood tide at noon and anchored. The corps, including Captain Ahlers and his company, had arrived at Stade already on 17 September. Ensign Bode died at Stade on the 19th. Toward evening Colonel von Speth sent me an express boat and I had to travel to Stade at once, in order to draw up orders to debark the troops, because General von Riedesel had not yet arrived.

24 September - The Dragoon, Prince Friedrich, and Rhetz Regiments, landed.

25 September - General von Riedesel arrived during the night. He had come with the post [mail coach] from Cuxhaven. With the orders for the entire corps completed by me, the three regiments which debarked yesterday passed the muster by the captain from the east.[48]

26 September - The general's wife arrived with her children during the night. The departure march for the three regiments, Dragoons, Prince Friedrich, and Rhetz, the first division, was in two columns, under the command of General von Riedesel. The debarkation of the Grenadier Battalion and the von Riedesel, Specht, and von Barner Regiments and their mustering. Toward evening the arrival of the Quebec order to the regiments concerning discipline on the march, and concerning the warehousing of the baggage left behind, which would be sent to the regiments by water after our departure to Lueneburg, and from there to Bruanschweig on the Axe River. Although, after our arrival in Stade, we were given the strongest and best French brandy (16 groschen per bottle), it was too cold for us [?], and had the effect of a laxative, and the rye bread was not well received by us. The general's wife and children departed.

27 September - The general departed, following the first division over Harburg. Today the orders were issued for the regiments of the second division, for the entrance of the wagons for the baggage, the riding horses for the officers, and for the orderly march of the regiments, in two columns, taking different routes. All march routes for the four columns of the two divisions had been dispatched to Bruanschweig already two days ago with Ensign Haeberlin, who was sent as a courier.

Journal of Lieutenant Friedrich Julius von Papet

28 September - The Grenadiers, Specht, Riedesel, and Barner Regiments marched out of Stade at seven o'clock, the two last by way of Herenburg. I will remain with these last ones with the colonel. (Everything in Stade is very expensive, but cheaper in Herenburg. Colonel von Speth set the pace in a purchased coach pulled by five regimental horses.)

30 September - A day of rest. Ensign Haeberlin came back from Braunschwieg by way of Harburg, where he reported to our general. Our early arrival in Stade was so completely unexpected by the people in Braunschwieg, that all were surprised. Lieutenant Rhenius of the von Barner Battalion died this evening and is to be buried tomorrow without a cannon salute.

1 October - We arrived in the village of Schneverdingen.

2 October - At seven o'clock both regiments that are here were ready to march to Soltau.

4 October - At six o'clock the regiments marched toward Bergen.

6 October - At seven o'clock the regiments assembled at the village of Offen and marched to Celle, where we arrived at eleven o'clock. Prince von Mecklenburg commanded there. Colonel von Speth, his wife, Lieutenant Colonels von Hille, von Barner, and I, and all the captains of the corps were invited to dinner tomorrow, in the moat around the city, by His Highness.

7 October - At ten o'clock a meeting with His Highness, who spoke pleasantly with almost everyone. At one o'clock we proceeded to the dinner in the moat, which like all the rooms [in the castle] was very magnificent.

8 October - At seven o'clock we marched out of Celle, to Brockel, and then to Eichlingen.[49]

9 October - We marched to Eltze, the last [illegible] in Hannover. Because of several desertions at this place, I had to prepare some arrest warrants during the night.

10 October - Both the Riedesel and Barner Regiments are to remain in Oelzen, Watenbuettel, and Lehndorf. During the afternoon we had many visitors from Braunschwieg. On the way to that place and during our entrance into Braunschwieg, we first met Commissary von Bellmore and later our serene Hereditary Prince, who received us graciously.

Journal of Lieutenant Friedrich Julius von Papet

11 October - At six-thirty we marched out of Oelzen. Near the Weisen Ross [White Stallion, probably an inn] both regiments assembled and then the march continued with dressed ranks through Braunschwieg, close to the high tower, and on to Wolfenbuettel. There was no shortage of on-lookers. The joy of our arrival could be seen clearly in every face.

End of the journal of the trip to North America

/s/ v. Papet

Journal of Lieutenant Friedrich Julius von Papet
Notes
To Introductory Remarks

1. British Museum (BM) Additional Manuscript 21813, "Copies of Letters to Officers of the German Legion, with Returns, Etc., 1776-1783", f. 4, 9 January 1776, of the *Haldimand Papers*.
2. *Journal of Du Roi the Elder*, Americana Germanica No. 15, trans. by Charlotte S. J. Epping, (New York, 1911), pp. 7-8. It should be noted at this point that William L. Stone in his translation of *Memoirs, Letters, and Journals of Major General Riedesel*, (Albany, 1868) translated Feldscher as chaplain instead of surgeon.
3. BM Additional Manuscript 21813, f. 21, 28 May 1776; f. 29, 29 May 1776.
4. *Du Roi*, p. 52.
5. *Memoirs ... Riedesel*, p. 269.

To Text

6. (p. 2) - Von Papet, as a member of the Rhetz Regiment, was in the 2nd Division of Brunswick troops.
7. (p. 3) - The brother was Lieutenant August Wilhelm von Papet, of the Specht Regiment.
8. (p. 3) - The mentioned *Anne Catherine* was listed by Du Roi as the *Jungfer Anne Catherine*, a ship chartered at Hamburg. *Du Roi*, p. 52. As with names of individuals, Papet often makes changes apparently based on how he heard the name or possibly to record them in a shortened form.
9. (p. 3) - This is probably a reference to officers' wives who were not sailing with the troops.
10. (p. 4) - Lieutenant Colonel Johann Gustavus von Ehrenkrook.
11. (p. 5) - The German mile was generally considered as equal to six English miles. Von Papet did not always make clear whether he meant English or German miles.
12. (p. 7) - The captain of the *Garland*, escorting the fleet, was Richard Pearson. Von Papet referred to fleet commanders as admiral as they were the senior officers present.
13. (p. 10) - Concerning the *Vriesland*, Captain Georg Pausch of the Hesse-Hanau Artillery Company made the following diary entry on

Journal of Lieutenant Friedrich Julius von Papet

18 June 1776. "On one of the Brunswick ships ... called *Friesland* - there were 450 men, not counting women and children. In three shifts it is impossible for all of them to enjoy fresh air on deck. The colonel himself, with sixteen officers and the ship's captain, all live in one cabin." Georg Pausch, *Journal and Reports of the Campaign in America*, Trans. by Bruce E. Burgoyne, (Bowie, MD, 1996), p. 18.

14. (p. 11) - This may be an incorrect name for the ship as von Papet used another spelling, which I have changed to *Liable*, later in his account.

15. (p. 13) - As noted earlier, Richard Pearson commanded the *Garland*. Von Papet's spelling is apparently phonetic.

16. (p. 25) - Unless a new ship had joined the fleet, this probably should be the Dutch ship *De gude Sacke*, as listed by Du Roi. *Du Roi*, p. 52.

17. (p. 35) - A German hour, when used as a measure of distance is equal to four kilometers or two and one-half English miles.

18. (p. 55) - Despite frequent references to disaffected parishes, the inhabitants never mounted a serious insurrection.

19. (p. 56) - Although the Battle of Valcour Island was an English victory, Benedict Arnold was not captured. The battle delayed the English further advance toward Albany until 1777 when the English under General John Burgoyne were finally defeated in the Battles of Freeman's Farm and forced to capitulate.

20. (p. 60) - This and much of the following information was false and only rumors.

21. (p. 64) - I do not know with any certainty which Du Roi this might have been, but think it was probably Anton Adolph Heinrich, the younger Du Roi, assigned to the Specht Regiment.

22. (p. 69) - The other German troops were assigned either to Burgoyne's command, or to Lieutenant Colonel Barry St. Leger's command, which was to proceed along the Mohawk Valley.

23. (p. 70) - The Scheiter recruits were recruited in Germany to fill the ranks of the English regiments.

24 (p. 70) - Frau von Riedesel had been pregnant in Germany when her husband sailed to America in 1776. She followed him to Canada the next year and even accompanied him during Burgoyne's advance toward Albany. After Burgoyne capitulated, she accompanied her husband into eventual captivity.

Journal of Lieutenant Friedrich Julius von Papet

25. (p. 71) - That Hesse-Hanau Jaeger Company was commanded by Captain Caspar Heinrich Kornrumpf.

26. (p. 71) - Lieutenant Ruff was escort officer for several Brunswick recruit shipments. It is possible that a diary which he maintained and which exists in Germany will be translated in the near future.

27. (p. 72) - Creuzbourg was the commander of the Hesse-Hanau Jaeger Corps which was sent to Canada in 1777.

28. (p. 72) - When the Hesse-Hanau Jaeger Corps was mustered at Nijmegen, Holland, each company was seventeen men over strength to allow for losses en route to America, and each company reported a corporal or quartermaster sergeant already in America. This is a rather conclusive indication that "advance party" personnel were sent to America by the Hessian units, much as such personnel are used today by the United States military. BM Additional Manuscript 23651, "Papers Relating to the Hanau and Anspach Troops, 1776-1778", f.89, 15 March 1777; ff. 125 and 126, 26 March 1777; ff. 162 and 163, 11 and 12 April 1777, of the *Rainsford Papers*.

29. (p. 74) - The Battle of Bennington was fought on 16 August 1777. The Americans under General John Stark completely defeated the Brunswick Dragoons and the Brunswick Grenadiers sent as a reinforcement. The Germans suffered heavy losses in killed and captured.

30. (p. 75) - The losses indicate that the Battle of Bennington may have been a much more important engagement than it is usually considered to have been.

31. (p. 76) - Although my friend Robert Cowan believes the *Niger* is incorrect and that it should have been in the West Indies at that time, I find it difficult to believe von Papet did not know which ship he had been on. One possibility is that his diary is based on notes, written up at a later date, and that the handwriting change in the manuscript was the result of different portions being copied by different copyists.

32. (p. 92) - Lieutenant Kaempfer was originally assigned to Lieutenant Colonel Lentz Company of the Hesse-Hanau Regiment.

33. (p. 95) - The Rauschenplat brothers were initially the commander and second in command of the Anhalt-Zerbst contingent. The unit chaplain, Johann Gottlieb Siegismund Braunsdorf gave both the title of count, although neither was such. Heinicke, Brigitte and

Journal of Lieutenant Friedrich Julius von Papet

Jahn, Georg. "Ein anhaltisches Militaerkirchbuch in Jever", *Norddeutsche Familienkunde*, Vol. 13, Nr. 1, (January-March 1986), p. 457.

34. (p. 96) - Reorganization of the Brunswick contingent, on orders from Germany, was necessary due to the losses during Burgoyne's invasion and the subsequent imprisonment of the Convention captives.

35. (p. 97) - I do not know which Lieutenant Wolgast was arrested.

36. (p. 97) - "Your Serene Highness, also to let you most graciously know the reason why the promotions of His Highness the Prince of Anhalt-Zerbst, which received its commissions already in 1779, were not announced to the army earlier than my major's patent, most graciously granted to me by Your Serene Highness, which I had the greatest pleasure to receive here only on 3 July 1782, with a duplicate thereof at the same time. The primary reason can probably be that something in the drawing up of the subsidy treaty with Anhalt-Zerbst was somehow overlooked, because the regiment had only one colonel, who became a brigadier general, and with one major, namely Rauschenplat's brother, who took over the regiment. By this promotion the regiment found itself with one colonel, one lieutenant colonel, and a Major Wietersheim, and an additional captain, so that it was augmented with one lieutenant colonel and one captain. For that reason and for the sake of economy at the royal treasury, they were not recognized by the governor, His Excellence, Haldimand, and even less so announced to the army, but each one remained in his former rank, duty, and pay. ... In 1781 the colonel and brigadier [one man] returned home, but nothing changed because he was still considered as colonel and commandant of the regiment. As finally, with my advancement, which the governor, after thinking it over, also granted and congratulated me, these were suddenly announced all together about ten days later in an order from the army headquarters. About eight days after the announcement, Lieutenant Colonel von Rauschenplat however, ordered his brother, the colonel and brigadier, to be completely removed from future and pending orders on all appointment lists, and for himself alone to be listed as commander." *Georg Pausch's Journal and Reports of the Campaign in America*, (Bowie, Md, 1996), p. 141.

Journal of Lieutenant Friedrich Julius von Papet

37. (p. 100) - There are several indications that the entries for November 1778 should be for November 1780. Among others, the description of Major Carleton's raid into New York and Colonel von Specht's exchange from prisoner status, both events which took place in 1780. Information for this note supplied by Robert Cowan of Kiowa, Texas.

38. (p. 102) - It appears that the December entries are for 1778 as Dominica was taken in 1778.

39. (p. 105) - Fuegerer may have been a surgeon as William L. Stone mistakenly translated Feldscher as chaplain in most instances.

40. (p. 106) - The severe weather of 18 January 1779 felled more Germans than many of the minor battles of the war. In addition to those who died, Barner Battalion reported 47 men suffered from frostbite. Of that number fourteen were hospitalized at Trois Rivieres. Johann Otto and Christian Bobeleben both lost fingers and thumbs of both hands. Joseph Zimmermann lost fingers and thumbs on both hands and the toes of his right foot and two toes on his left foot were mortified. Hermann Scharfemann lost fingers and thumb on his left hand and three fingers of his right hand. Valentine Mueller had the first joint of the right hand fingers and two fingers and the thumb of his left hand mortified. Joseph Zigelhofer lost two fingers on each hand and his left thumb. Corporal Wilhelm Kaufmann lost the little finger on his right hand and his left thumb. Heinrich Ziermann lost the first joint of three fingers of his right hand. Anton Raue had the first joint of three fingers of his right hand and his wrist mortified. The doctor's report was that Raue might lose his arm. Edmund Roth had the first joint of all toes on his right foot and two toes of his left foot mortified. Carl Carlmann (or Earl Ertmann - each name appears on only one list) lost the little finger of his right hand, and Friedrich Warnecke and Ludwig Basch suffered slight frostbite. BM Additional Manuscript 21857, "Correspondence with Officers of the General Hospital at Trois Rivieres, 1778-1788", Vols. I and II, f. 40, 1 February 1779; and ff. 42 and 44, 2 February 1779; and BM Additional Manuscript 21811, "Letters from Officers of the German Legion, 1778-1784", Vols. I and II, f. 79, 9 February 1779, of the *Haldimand Papers*.

41. (p. 128) - This would appear to have been Captain Hugget's Company, mustered at Dort, Holland, on 29 March 1779. BM Additional Manuscript 21813, f. 54, 29 March 1779.

Journal of Lieutenant Friedrich Julius von Papet

42. (p. 169) - Captain Schenk built the *Inflexible* in 1776 for use on Lake Champlain, and a pontoon bridge used by Burgoyne in September 1777. Information from Robert Cowan.

43.(p. 174) - Possibly the deceased was Hesse-Cassel Major General Johann Christoph von Huyn, who died in July 1780 and was buried at New York.

44. (p. 180) - MacLean died at Halifax on 4 May 1781.

45. (p. 188) - Phillips died 15 May 1781 at Petersburg, Virginia.

46. (p. 189) - The *Torm* previously had been an English sloop of sixteen cannons, captured by the American ships *Boston* and *Deane* in 1779.

47. (p. 200) - Another daughter named Canada had died in 1782.

48. (p. 207) - This is an apparent reference to an English officer.

49. (p. 208) - Eichlingen is actually northwest of Broekel and would have been reached first. Both are on the present highway 214.

FULLNAME INDEX

----, A 6 Abraham 8 Harry 178
   Petriman 113
A, Capt 8
ACKERMANN, Nick 13
AHLER, Capt 15 61
AHLERS, Capt 3 4 11 207
AHLRUTH, Drummer 174
AHREND, 19 52 55 58 78 204 Capt 4
   18 59 61 64 67 90 203
ANDRE, Lt 181
APITAIL, Dr 122
APLAIN, Capt 165
ARBUTHNOT, Adm 184 187 190
   Marriot 182
ARNOLD, Benedict 55 Brigadier 190
   Monsieur 164 165
AUGE, Capt 116
BAERTLING, Capt 181
BARNER, Lt Col 127
BARNES, Capt 160 161 163 Lt 119
   120 140 141 142 153 Monsieur 142
   146 157
BAUM, Lt Col 44 75
BECKMANN, Cpl 109 110 123
BELAIR, Capt 179
BERNT, Surgeon 87 108
BEYERSEN, Capt 13
BIELSTEIN, Lt 113 163 166 173 177
   178 184 185
BISHOP, of Quebec 81
BLACK, Dr 199
BODE, Ensign 207 Jacob Wilhelm 143
BODEMEYER, Lt 80 85 115 133 134
   146 147 149 150 156 161 166 170
   192
BOHEMEYER, Lt 69
BOTTMER, Lt 181
BOUTELLIER, 175
BOUTLER, 25
BRANT, 193 Capt 186 197 Joseph 197
BRENDIS, 89
BREVA, Lt 181

BREYMANN, Lt Col 78
BULAN, Count 182
BURGDORF, Lt 181
BURGHOFF, Lt 181
BURGOYNE, 91 100 116 148 181
   Gen 76 78 79 John 74
BUSCH, 123
BUTLER, Col 128 136 John 128
CAMPBELL, John 144 Madame 174
   Maj 198
CARLETON, Col 119 121 122 163
   164 167 Gen 57 60 62 65 66 67 68
   70 71 72 75 76 78 79 81 82 83 85
   88 89 90 92 93 99 Gen Sir Guy 44
   57 Lt Col 142 147 148 149 152 164
   165 167 168 170 171 172 176 Maj
   89 100 101 165 Mr 135 Mrs 89
   Quartermaster Gen 102 Sir Guy 88
   Thomas 119
CARLTON, Gen 89
CARREE, 174 178 179 180
CARTERET, 191
CARTERRET, 176
CERHERAN, Monsieur 150
CHARLES, Duke of Brunswick 25
CLAGE, Capt 199 202 Urban 199 202
CLARK, George Rogers 186
CLARKE, Gen 190 192 Thomas 185
   190
CLAUS, Col 197
CLEVE, 65 192 193 Capt 4 181 192
   193 Lt 65 154
CLINTON, Gen 102 116 150 163 182
   184 190 Henry 79 149
COLBERT, Monsieur 138
COLLIER, Adm Sir George 143
   George 143 Monsieur 134
CONFES, Lt 95
COOK, James 144
CORNES, Engineer 114
CORNWALLIS, 167 189 Gen 165
CRAMACHE, Lt Gov 77

CRAMAHE, Lt Gov 90 112 147
CREUZBOURG, Col 201 Lt Col 72 80
CULLONS, 190
CUTHBERT, Monsieur 146 152 176
CZARINA, of Russia 182
D'ANNIERES, Lt 74 Lt Jr 75
D'ESTAING, 141 Charles Hector 95
    Comte 120 125 143
DAY, Commissary 150 Commissary
    General 119 141 172
DELUECKE, Maj 181
DESPUIS, 127 128
DETONNECOUR, Chevalier 135
    Col 93
DETRIFF, 123
DIETRICH, Capt 129
DOEBERNET, Lt 186
DOMMES, Capt 75
DOUGLAS, Charles 44
    Commodore 51 89
DOVE, Lt 70 71 80 154
DRUMONT, Miss 114 Paymaster 114
DUKE, De Chartres 167 of Brunswick
    97 of Cumberland and Gloucester
    164 of Gloucester 190
    of York 182
DUNDAS, Alexander 163
DUPRE, Maj 80
DUROI, Lt 62 159
DYON, Privy Councillor 141
EDGE, Fane 141
EDWARD, Adm 181
EHRENKROOK, Lt Col 138
EHRICH, Ensign 203
EMPEROR, Holy Roman 110 116
ESTIMONVILLE, Monsieur 152
FAUCITT, Col 3 William 3
FERONCE, Privy Councillor 88
FISCHER, Col 153
FLEMMING, 180
FONGLES, 26
FOY, Capt 67 80 98 99 116 120 125
    Edward 67
FRANKS, 176
FRASER, 122 Capt 125
FRASIER, Malcolm 125
FRAZER, Alexander 78

FRENCH, 169 174
FRICKE, Capt 181 Lt 181
FROMME, Ensign 144
FUEGERER, Chaplain 105
GATES, 167 Gen 165 Horatio 81
GEBHARDT, Lt 75 181 191 202
GEERY, Sir Francis 181
GELBKE, 162
GERLACH, Capt 77 181 Gen 44 Lt 60
GEYSO, Capt 181
GLEISENBERG, Capt 165
GOEDECKE, 56 84 85 104 Ensign
    114 115 Senior Cashier 55 65
GORDON, Brigadier 126
GRAEFE, Cornet 140 141 144 145
    146 152 155 156 157 158 161
    Count 127 Ensign 134
GRANT, David 125
GRAVES, Capt 190 Thomas 189
GRAY, Maj 178
GREEFES, Monsieur 161
GREY, Maj 174 190 193
GRUBE, Cpl 94
GUICHI, Monsieur 111 114 121 122
    137 151 Mr 115 Seigneur 93 101
GUNTERMANN, Craftsman 115
HAEBERLIN, 141 149 173 175 176
    203 Cornet Count Foender 100
    Ensign 127 137 141 144 146 147
    152 153 154 157 160 161 168 174
    177 178 183 185 187 193 207 208
HAHNE, 120
HALDIMAND, 129 200 Gen 89 90 92
    93 95 97 99 154 176 192 195 203
    204 Lt Gen 88
HAMBACH, 193 Capt 129
HAMILTON, Commander 118 Henry
    114
HANNEMANN, Lt 82
HARD, 155
HARDY, Adm 167
HARRIS, John Adolphus 198
HARVEY, Capt 181
HARZ, Lt 77
HEIDELBACH, Surgeon 181
HEINEMANN, Musketeer 135
HEINRICH, Prince 116

HELLMANN, Musketeer 185 186
HENCKE, Musketeer 127
HEPPLEY, Capt 203
HERLET, Lt 103
HERTEL, 161 Lt 73 137 159 163 173
HILDEBRAND, Philipp Jacob 196
HILDEL, Monsieur 142
HOESCHER, Capt 196
HOHENFELD, Lt 75
HOLLAND, 158 Maj 129 146 147 148 157 158 159 174 177 178 179 188 Samuel 125
HOSANG, 191
HOWE, Gen 57 60 76 79 82 Richard 95 William 31 60
HUGGET, Capt 130 149 196
HUTTINGER, 162
INDIAN, Brant 193 Capt Brant 197 Captain Brant 186 Joseph Brant 197
ISERHOF, Surgeon 110 Surgeon's Mate 116
JACOBS, 140 Capt 44 Maxim 13
JENSEN, 111 Monsieur 110
JERUSALEM, Col 66
JOHN, Friedrich 121
JOHNSON, 199 Chevalier 167 Col 195 Col Sir 153 John 87 196 198 Sir 95 100 108 135 141 152 153 165 185 198
JORDAN, Monsieur 177 Mr 158
K----, Secretary 96
KAEMPFER, Friedrich Ludwig 92
KAISER, The 183 190
KATHERINE, The Great 139
KEMPEL, 191
KENNEDY, Dr 85 Dr Gen 150
KEPPEL, Augustus 120
KINADAY, Dr 85
KING, of England 3 198 Of Prussia 110 116
KNESEBECK, Lt 136
KOLTE, Ensign 106 107 112
LAMAISTRE, Mr 125
LAMAITRE, Monsieur 151
LAMOTTE, Capt 82
LANANDIERE, 117

LANDON, Field Marshal 116
LANGARA, Y Huarte Don Juan De 149
LANGE, 136
LANGERJAHN, Ensign 188
LAROCK, 175
LAROS, Capt 145
LATTERIERE, 112 114 Monsieur 110 113
LAVALTRIE, Monsieur 144 152 153 172
LEMAITRE, 150 Capt 94 Francis 97 Monsieur 96 97
LENANDIERE, Seigneur 122
LERNOULT, Maj 170 Richard Bernhard 170
LEROUSE, 173 Miss 173
LOCK, 180
LOED, Capt 180
LOOS, Brigadier 156 168 Col 143 154 Johann August 138
LOYHEL, Madame 175
LOYSELL, Madame 177
LUECKE, Maj 194
LUETZOW, Capt 181
LUTWIDGE, Skeffington 44
MACBEAN, 146 180 Brigadier 177 Col 175 Commissary 180 Dr 148 149 Forbes 172 Lt Col 172
MACBETH, Monsieur 177 179
MACHEATH, Monsieur 177 Mr 178
MACKBEY, Maj 87
MACLEAN, 134 Allen 147 Brigadier 137 138 196 199 Francis 77 130 Gen 143 144 186 Lt Col 147 Neil 125
MAIBOM, Lt 181 Maj 181 199
MASSIER, 175
MATEUS, Capt 150
MATHEUS, Capt 171
MATHEW, Capt 149
MATHEWS, Capt 125 Robert 124
MATT----, Capt 182
MAURER, Capt 198 Mr 119
MAYER, Lt 203
MCBEAN, Dr 172
MCCORD, 180

METZDORF, Gottlieb 168
MEYER, Lt 181
MINCHIN, Capt 180 Paul 180
MODRACHE, Lt 66
MORGENSTERN, Capt 181
MUELLER, 196 Cpl 166
MURRAY, Barracks Master 149 168
NEHRENGARD, Musketeer 190
NOERDEN, Maj 123
NOSS, Capt 19
O'CONNELL, Capt 59 65 191
OGS, John 111
OLIVER, Capt 142
OLIVIER, Capt 145 160
PABY, Magistrate 111
PARKER, Peter 148
PAUSCH, Georg 196
PERI, Father 107
PETERSDORF, 192
PETRIMAN, 113
PFEIFER, Cpl 127
PHILIPPS, Gen 184
PHILLIPS, Gen 188 189 William 179
PICQUET, Brigade Maj 149 Carl Friedrich 105
PIQUET, Carl Friedrich 105
PLESSEN, Capt 53 72 160 191
POELLNITZ, Capt 181 204
PORTIERS, Miss 134 Mr 134 Mrs 134
POWELL, Brigadier 147 148 150 Henry Watson 101
PRAETORIUS, 129 Col 125 126 Lt Col 80 81 82 91 103 104 115 119 122 126 132 137 140 142 148 150 152 154 156 163 168 184 188 191
PRALLE, Surgeon 181
PREVOST, Augustine 182
PRINCE, Hereditary 208 of Mecklenberg 144
PRINGLE, Capt 189
RAABE, Capt 132 134
RAUTENBERG, Herr 2 Pastor 2
RECKIN, 27 Agent 31 Mr 26
REICHRODT, Lt 181
REINEKING, Capt 75
REINERDING, Ensign 112 119 137 138 139 153 176 182 184 185

REINERKING, Lt 202
REINICKE, Lt 181
RETZER, Henry 124
 Mrs 124
RHENIUS, Lt 208
RIEDESEL, Frau 202 Gen 70 189 192 196 Maj Gen 192
ROBINSON, Capt 196 Daniel 191 Madam 176 178
RODNEY, Adm 149 181 189 George Brydes 148
ROSENBERG, 112 193 Capt 104 106 113 121 122 138 165
ROSENTHAL, Capt 185
ROSS, Adm 149 Maj 201
ROTHE, Lt 181
RUFF, Capt 95 96 187 Johann Conrad 71 Lt 71 72
SAINTLEGER, 200 Barry 94 Col 142 195 Lt Col 125 130 152 160 162 166
SANDER, Capt 103 104 142 188
SCHENDLER, Madame 172
SCHENK, Capt 169 170
SCHEPPELMANN, Capt At Arms 116 117
SCHICK, Capt 74
SCHLAGENTEUFEL, 201 Capt 3
SCHMIDT, Capt 103 106 163 186
SCHOELL, Capt 146 147
SCHOENEWALD, Lt 181
SCHOLTELIUS, Capt 181
SCHRADER, Surgeon 203
SCHULZE, 185 196
SCOTT, 196 Alexander 144 Capt 145
SELBY, 180 Dr 180
SENF, Vice-corporal 98
SENFF, 151
SIEFERT, Lt 87
SILL, Commissary 146
SILLS, Commissary 118 119 137
SINCLAIR, Patrick 125
SOEMMERS, Capt 181
SOHLEMANN, Cpl 192
SOMMERLATTE, Lt 110 112 152 171 182 189

SPECHT, Brigadier 64 66 181 Col 10
    24 51 52 53 55 58 59 192
    Johann Friedrich 2 Lt 181
SPETH, Brigadier 129 Col 59
STARCKHOF, Lt 187
STECKHAN, 185
STEEL, Capt 140
STERNBERG, Ensign 91
STOETER, Capt 95 96 98
STUTZE, Lt 181
TARLETON, Col 189
TAUSCH, 173
TESSIER, 3
THEODOR, Father 93
THOMAE, 193
    Capt 32 70 71 73 77 78 81
    97 104 105 106 112 119 120
    121 122 129 132 134 138 142
    183 187
THOMAS, Lt 162
TOHNEEBOROUGH, 145
TONNECOUR, Col 93 110
    Monsieur 115
TONNENCOUR, Col 71 78
TONNIES, Drummer 165
TUNDERFELDT, Capt 114
TWISS, Capt 141 148 149 158 161
    187 William 109
UHLIG, Lt 75
UNGAR, Lt 181
VON, Castendyck Capt 172
    Creuzbourg Lt Col 144
VONBAERTLING, Capt 185
VONBARNER, Col 127
    Lt Col 93 94 96 98 100 101 102
    103 104 106 108 111 112 113 114
    115 116 117 118 119 120 121 122
    123 124 127 129 132 133 137 138
    139 142 150 177 183 190 199 202
    208
    Maj 5 8 9 11 14 32 71 75 82 83 84
    85
VONBELLMORE, Commissary 208
VONBRAUN, Privy Councillor 134
VONBUELOW, 2
VONBURGDORF, Lt 196
VONCASTENDYCK, Capt 129

VONCREUZBOURG, Carl 72 Col 119
    196 203 Lt 135 Lt Col 72 84 86 91
    102 103 128 129 130 132 135 136
    137 139 140 141 151 152 153 154
    167 171 172 177 195
VONDOBENECK, Lt 203
VONEHRENKROOK, 137 153
    Brigadier 97 129 Col 55 69 79 Lt
    Col 129 132 137 138 139 142 143
    144 151 152 154 157 158 159 160
    161 165 166 168 171 174 176 178
    179 183 185 186 189 191 193
VONFERONEC, Privy Councillor 163
VONFRANCKEN, Maj 129
VONFRANKEN, Herman Albrecht
    141
VONFROHENHAUSEN, Col 156 157
VONGALL, Brigadier 181
VONGLEISENBERG, Capt 100
VONGLEISSENBERG, Capt 127 175
VONHAMBACH, Capt 83 87 92 96
    97 102 103 104 105 106 107 108
    127 130
VONHANSTEIN, Ludwig August 154
VONHILLE, Lt Col 130 140 142 149
    202 208
VONKNYPHAUSEN, Wilhelm 158
VONLOOS, 172
VONLUECKE, Maj 4 9 10 11 12 41
    61 68 203
VONLUETZOW, Capt 61
VONMAIBOM, Maj 77
VONMECKLENBURG, Prince 208
VONMENGEN, Lt Col 202 Maj 185
    186
VONPAPET, Miss 97 98 134 166
VONPINCIER, Lt 87 114
VONPLESSEN, 119 138 178 Capt 51
    86 89 96 97 98 99 104 109 110 112
    117 129 132 137 141 154 173 180
    183 185 189
VONPOELLNITZ, Capt 202
VONPRAUN, Privy Councillor 134
VONRAUSCHENPLAT, Brigadier
    109 130 149 166 187 Col 97 105
    Friedrich 95
VONREITZENSTEIN, Lt 97

VONRHETZ, Maj Gen 131
VONRIEDESEL, Frau 200 Gen 64 66
   70 71 73 74 182 184 185 186 188
   190 192 195 196 199 200 201 202
   206 207
   Maj Gen 70 154 155 157 163 164
   174 179 181 187 193
   Miss 200
   Mrs 70 71 73
   Mrs (?) 207
   Wilhelm 157
VONRITTBERG, Count 184
VONROSENBERG, Capt 129
VONSCHICK, Capt 75
VONSCHLAGENTEUFEL, 129 171
   Capt 11 61 69 75 85 97 104 107
   124 127 138 144 146 151 152 153
   157 160 169 171 181 182 185 186
   Capt Jr 156 160 177 183 Capt Sr
   203
VONSCHOELL, Capt 87 92 102 128
   129 135 136 147 149 150 151 156
   169 171 196 Friedrich Ludwig 78
VONSOMMERLATTE, Lt 124 152
   171
VONSOMMERLOTTE, Lt 177
VONSPECHT, Lt Col 100 101
VONSPETH, Brigadier 133 137 149
   Col 125 127 206 207 208 Lt Col
   128 129
VONSTEUBEN, Friedrich Wilhelm
   Augustus Baron 204
VONSTOETER, Capt 95
VONTONNECOUR, Col 109 112 122
   123 125
VONTUNDEFELDT, Capt 147
VONTUNDERFELDT, Capt 76 77 78
   79 80 84 85 87 91 93 94 95 96 97
   98 99 101 107 117 118 119 121
   125 132 134 136 138 140 143 146
   147 148 149 150 156 157 158 159
   160 161 164 165 166 167 170 172
   174 175 176 184 192
VONTUNDERFELT, Capt 71 74 75
VONWALLMODEN, Lt 183
VONZIELBERG, 119 129 138 Capt
   76 77 80 97 99 106 118 121 124
   132 133 137 145 146 152 161 169
   175 177 179 182 196
VORBROD, Surgeon 181
W----, Lt 96
WAGNER, 185
WALKER, Richard 108
WALLMODEN, Lt 122
WASHINGTON, 120 Gen 74 79 82
   190 George 60
WECHSEL, Capt 132
WEHR, 196
WEISS, Capt 95 133 134 187 191
WIEDMANN, Cpl 87
WILLET, Col 201 Marinus 201
WILLOE, Capt 73 87 182 191 192
WILSON, Capt 40
WITCOUR, 126
WITTGENSTEIN, Count 129
WOLFF, Cashier 173
WOLGAST, Lt 97 104 115 132 188
WOLPERS, Auditor 121
WOLTE, 134
WUELNER, 144
YOUNG, Capt 162 189
ZIELBERG, 178 Capt 78 104 157 191

Other Heritage Books by Bruce E. Burgoyne:

Aboard a Dutch Troop Transport: A Diary Written by Captain Ludwig Alberti of the Waldeck 5th Battalion

A Hessian Officer's Diary of the American Revolution Translated from an Anonymous Ansbach-Bayreuth Diary and the Prechtel Diary

Canada During the American Revolutionary War: Lieutenant Friedrich Julius von Papet's Journal of the Sea Voyage to North America and the Campaign Conducted There

CD: A Hessian Diary of the American Revolution

CD: A Hessian Officer's Diary of The American Revolution

CD: A Hessian Report on the People, the Land, the War of Eighteenth Century America, as Noted in the Diary of Chaplain Philipp Waldeck, 1776-1780

CD: Ansbach-Bayreuth Diaries from the Revolutionary War

CD: Canada During the America Revolutionary War

CD: Diaries of Two Ansbach Jaegers

CD: The Hessian Collection, Volume 1: Revolutionary War Era

CD: They Also Served. Women with the Hessian Auxiliaries

CD: Waldeck Soldiers of the American Revolutionary War

Defeat, Disaster, and Dedication

Diaries of Two Ansbach Jaegers

Eighteenth Century America (A Hessian Report on the People, the Land, the War) as Noted in the Diary of Chaplain Philipp Waldeck (1776-1780)

Enemy Views: The American Revolutionary War as Recorded by the Hessian Participants

English Army and Navy Lists Compiled During the American Revolutionary War by Ansbach-Bayreuth Lieutenant Johann Ernst Prechtel

Georg Pausch's Journal and Reports of the Campaign in America, as Translated from the German Manuscript in the Lidgerwood Collection in the Morristown Historical Park Archives, Morristown, New Jersey

Hesse-Hanau Order Books, a Diary and Roster: A Collection of Items Concerning the Hesse-Hanau Contingent of "Hessians" Fighting Against the American Colonists in the Revolutionary War

Hessian Chaplains: Their Diaries and Duties

Hessian Letters and Journals and a Memoir

Journal of a Hessian Grenadier Battalion

Journal of the Hesse-Cassel Jaeger Corps

Journal of the Prince Charles Regiment
Translated by Bruce E. Burgoyne; Edited by Dr. Marie E. Burgoyne

Most Illustrious Hereditary Prince: Letters to Their Prince from Members of Hesse-Hanau Military Contingent in the Service of England During the American Revolution

Notes from a British Museum

Order Book of the Hesse-Cassel von Mirbach Regiment

Revolutionary War Letters Written by Hessian Officers: Generals Wilhelm von Knyphausen,
Carl Wilhelm Von Hachenberg, Friedrich Wilhelm von Lossberg, Johann Friedrich Cochenhausen, Friedrich Von Riedesel and Major Carl Leopold von Baurmeister
Bruce E. Burgoyne and Dr. Marie E. Burgoyne

The Diary of Lieutenant von Bardeleben and Other von Donop Regiment

The Hesse-Cassel Mirbach Regiment in the American Revolution

These Were the Hessians

The Third English-Waldeck Regiment in the American Revolutionary War

The Trenton Commanders: Johann Gottlieb Rall and
George Washington, as Noted in Hessian Diaries

Waldeck Soldiers of the American Revolutionary War